Handle with Care

ASAO Monograph Series

Andrew Strathern, *General Editor*

Pamela J. Stewart, *Associate Editor*

HANDLE
with CARE

Ownership

and Control of

Ethnographic

Materials

EDITED BY

Sjoerd R. Jaarsma

University of Pittsburgh Press

Published by the University of Pittsburgh Press, Pittsburgh, Pa., 15260
Manufactured in the United States of America
Printed on acid-free paper
10 9 8 7 6 5 4 3 2 1

Library of Congress Cataloging-in-Publication Data

Handle with care : ownership and control of ethnographic materials /
edited by Sjoerd R. Jaarsma.
     p. cm. — (ASAO monograph series)
Includes bibliographical references and index.
   ISBN 0-8229-5777-9 (pbk. : alk. paper)
   1. Ethnology—Research. 2. Ethnology—Field work. 3. Cultural
property—Protection. 4. Cultural property—Repatriation. 5.
Intellectual property—Moral and ethical aspects. 6. Anthropological
ethics. I. Jaarsma, S. R. II. ASAO monograph.
GN345 .H38   2002
305.8'007'2—dc21

                                                                    2002000264

Contents

Acknowledgments

A conversation I had with David Akin at the 1997 conference of the Association for Social Anthropology in Oceania (ASAO) at San Diego provided me with the first idea for this volume. He was preparing to work on the academic estate of Roger Keesing, who had died a few years earlier. Keesing's family had donated his field materials to the Melanesian Archive and had been exploring with David, Kathryn Creely, and the Kwaio people the possibility of making copies of some of the materials available to the Kwaio through an institution in the Solomon Islands. Briefly David sketched out for me the work involved and the problems he faced (now set out in detail in chapter 5). Talking about this at some length we both agreed that these problems were not unique to the Kwaio case, and that they deserved to be explored in a more general framework.

Back home in the Netherlands I searched for the available literature on the subject of repatriating ethnographic materials and turned up very little of any use to me. The main literature in existence involved the ongoing discussion on ethnographic museum collections being reclaimed by Third and Fourth World peoples. Little, if anything, substantial had been written on anthropological knowledge and ethnographic description in this context.

All this prompted me to place a message on ASAOnet, ASAO's Internet list, calling for people interested in participating in a session series entitled "The Repatriation of Field Material: Possibilities, Prospects, and Problems" starting at the next annual meeting. The call was repeated in the April 1997 newsletter and on the ASAO website. The response was encouraging, and we met for an informal session in Pensacola (Florida), where seven abstracts were presented and two people explained their ideas on the spot. The Pensacola meetings provided an ideal setting to begin our work on this volume, as they allowed us well over six hours to talk about what repatriating field material could and should involve.

The volume has evolved considerably from the initial ideas presented in Pensacola. What remained, though, is the practical focus on the possible impact of the return of field materials, as well as the stress on ethical behavior found throughout all the contributions. The volume provides a useful, broad exploration of a wide array of problems and pitfalls inherent in the process of returning information to where it originally came from, which face not only anthropologists but other disciplines that deal with ethnographic data routinely. Questions such as "what, when, and how to return materials," as well as "whom to return to" and "who should have or control access" are more easily asked then answered. The composition of the group—a mixture of anthropologists, ethnomusicologists, archivists, and librarians—has perhaps forced us away from the depth of analysis that might have been provided by looking at, for instance, the historical development of the exchange of information in anthropology, or that of comparison to the role of repatriation in museum anthropology. Whether this is a loss I leave to the individual reader to judge. Given the lack of available literature, I wonder whether such analyses would not have been premature anyway. The cases presented in the volume are not intended to provide clear-cut answers, but to engender awareness of the effects of something that is very much part of this time, the "age of information." This consideration, too, is why the volume ends not with an analytical conclusion, but with a set of open recommendations.

Editing this volume by myself would not have been possible without the ready and professional cooperation of all the contributors involved. They came together as a team at the three conferences where we worked on this project. Thanks are also due to the people who sat in on the various sessions and provided comments and suggestions that often proved very useful. I owe a special debt of gratitude, though, to David Akin, who helped me set up this project; to Alan Howard and Geoff White, who invested time and effort to serve as discussants during the working session in Hilo; and, last but not least, to Keith and Anne Chambers, who came up with the idea of ending the volume on a set of recommendations (and were subsequently saddled with the ungrateful task of making sense of the hours we spent discussing this idea).

I also wish to thank the ASAO Monograph Series editors, Andrew Strathern and Pamela Stewart, for their early recognition of this volume as a potential addition to the Monograph Series and for their support throughout the process of getting it published. Thanks are, of course, also due to the anonymous readers who not only approved of the manuscript but also provided valuable comments.

ASAO Editors' Note

Andrew Strathern and Pamela J. Stewart

This volume is the last in the series of Association for Social Anthropology in Oceania monographs published through the University of Pittsburgh Press since 1990, when editorship of the Monograph Series passed from Margaret Rodman to Andrew Strathern, and a new arrangement for publication was negotiated with the University of Pittsburgh Press. With the addition of the present volume, the overall number of monographs published becomes twenty, eight of them with the University of Pittsburgh Press and five of them with Andrew Strathern and Pamela J. Stewart working together as series editor (Strathern) and associate editor (Stewart) on behalf of the Association. Monograph number ten, originally published with University Press of America (1985), was republished in 1992 by the University of Pittsburgh Press. We want to thank the editors at the Press for their unfailing efficiency and professionalism in working with us to produce these volumes and for their initial friendly cooperation in agreeing to take on the series with financial terms enabling it to flourish and to return royalties to the ASAO Monograph Series fund, giving it a sound footing for the future. As well, we want to take the opportunity to thank all the contributors, especially the volume editors, who have put their labor and creativity into the series. Bringing a volume into being by sustaining interest in it over an ASAO cycle of meetings and nurturing and nudging it into a published product is not an easy task, as we know ourselves, and we are proud that we have been able to work with so many people over the years to keep the series moving forward.

The present volume addresses a topic of agreed and growing significance in our discipline, one that reflects the impetus to reflexivity and the pressures of globalization that have become historically evident in professional practice for more than a decade. The question of how to make returns to the people we work with and, in broader terms, how to maintain patterns of communicative reciprocity with them is here taken up in depth and in complexity by the various contributors whom Sjoerd Jaarsma has assembled for this task. For complex questions no simple answers can work, but this collection can take its place among the emerging literature on the topic and the parallel debates regarding intellectual property rights and indigenous knowledge. It is important to recognize the agency of all those involved in these issues. Jaarsma has already coedited one volume on related topics with Marta Rohatynskyj (Jaarsma and Rohatynskyj 2000), and another recent volume explores the active agency of Pacific people themselves in contexts of collections of items of material culture (O'Hanlon and Welsch 2000). These works show anthropologists reflecting on their pasts, recognizing the peoples they study as collaborators and autonomous agents, and thereby moving toward recreating their discipline for the future.

Handle with Care

Thinking through Repatriation

*L*eslie was fidgeting. She knew she had been delaying the inevitable too long. Her thesis had been approved weeks ago. She should send it to Abraham and his daughter, Edie, who had done so much for her. It had been drummed into her over and over again, ever since the first-year courses, "You have to send copies of your publications back to the field. It is the ethical thing to do. Never neglect this; you owe your informants a debt of gratitude."

Finally, Leslie made up her mind. She took out some stiff packing paper, hunted through a drawer for a roll of sticky tape, and wrapped a copy of her newly finished thesis. She would make sure they received it in one piece, whatever happened. Minutes later she was looking for stamps. She knew she had enough of them to send the package, but could she simply drop it in the mailbox? She decided against it. Too many letters and packages became lost in the mail to the island. She would do the sensible thing and use a courier. She knew of one a few blocks down the road.

Leslie came out of the courier's office disgruntled. Never again! It had taken her thirty minutes to explain to the airhead behind the counter where *to find the island. She expected these people to have at least some basic knowledge of geography. She recalled parts of the conversation, inane as it was, "Where? Never heard of it. You worked there? Doing what? Ah, an anthropologist, that explains it! I'll phone the main office. Maybe they'll know whether this place exists." Anyway, the package was on its way. Now she hoped and prayed it arrived safely.*

Edie walked in on Abraham, who was smoking contentedly. She talked excitedly. "A package for you, father. Jonathan brought it down from the mainland." Abraham stood up and looked bemused at the battered package. Who would send him a package? Then he recognized the handwriting and he knew. Leslie! Carefully, he started unwrapping the package, noticing it had been sent well over two months ago. Having removed all the paper he admired the book. This was what Leslie had always been talking about, her book about them. He realized that this was not just meant for him. Leslie had talked to everybody in the village and then some. He would have to show it around.

Glad to be back on the island after years, Leslie walked up the final slope. As always, it had been a difficult climb; some things never changed. She waved to Jonathan from the distance and saw him running off to the village to announce her arrival. She wondered whether the village would look the same. She had finally been awarded a new grant to do further research and come back, as she had promised. She was surprised how much everything still looked the same; some houses had been repaired, others replaced, but still the village looked familiar. Then all of a sudden she noticed the new building. It looked utterly unlike the other buildings, more like buildings on the mainland or at the mission post. She knew she should be looking for Abraham, but curiosity won out. She walked in the open doorway and waited till her eyes had gotten used to the dimly lit interior. Looking around, she immediately noticed the book, her thesis, sitting by itself on a shelf. She chuckled softly and said to herself: "Well, well, that's one for the books: the first public library on the island."

❧

This entirely hypothetical tale raises many important questions. Why did Leslie think she "owed a debt of gratitude" that involved sending back her thesis? Why did she feel compelled to send back just the thesis? Had nothing else been "taken" from the field? Why did the community consider the thesis itself worth saving? A host of similar questions could also be asked. Efforts to repatriate field data, ethnographic knowledge, and other cultural materials express our current awareness of ethical behavior. They also express the gradual shift in relations between the researcher, the people being researched, and the various audiences that consume the knowledge and publications produced by academia (Rohatynskyj and Jaarsma 2000). One result is that the flow of information, knowledge, and ethnographic materials—usually going from the field to the researcher—can become reversed. Leslie's act of returning her thesis to her host community is a simple but increasingly common example. The effects of the return of ethnographic materials have so far received relatively little attention within the discipline.

We cannot address the issues posed by the return of ethnographic materials (repatriation for short) solely from a disciplinary perspective. Our acts as anthropologists are part of a larger pattern of reestablishing rights to self-determination by indigenous peoples. Yet while this focus highlights the "Other" side of the story, what we—as academics and anthropologists—can or should contribute must also be an important part of the discussion. The indigenous peoples we study are within their rights—morally and often legally—to ask us to be circumspect with the information we gather and the knowledge we produce, whether we obtain it as anthropologists doing research for an academic thesis or as ethnobiologists working for a pharmaceutical company.

Not surprisingly, the cases presented in this volume will deal with anthropologists and ethnographic writing in one form or another. Yet it would be a mistake to deem the repatriation of ethnographic materials as strictly an anthropological problem to be dealt with by anthropologists in line with "anthropological tradition" or as a sign of the changing place of the discipline in today's world. While such a narrow focus might perhaps provide for a clear analytical framework, it would ignore the interests of our research subjects—who are curious about what we have written on them—and the librarians and archivists caring for the field notes and audiovisual materials we leave behind, to mention the obvious. The focus used here will essentially be explorative, looking at the possible consequences of the return of ethnographic materials with an aim to develop further debate on the subject. With that particular aim in mind, the volume will not end with a set of conclusions, but with a series of recommendations.

State of the Art

Anthropology's public castigation for its colonial role by critics from inside and outside the discipline has related primarily to the nature of the images it engendered rather than to the commonly held attitudes regarding the disposition of field materials. Perhaps this is because the gathering and use of research data on Third and Fourth World peoples has been an inherently unequal process for the disciplines involved. Academics have generally approached indigenous knowledge as a resource that could be exploited at will. Like the material resources of these peoples, their cultural heritage has been easily appropriated and estranged for economic profits, political purposes, and personal benefits (compare Stanley 1998; Crocombe 1994b). Not until the end of the 1980s did a move to counter this kind of exploitation gradually gather momentum.

Discussion focused initially on the acknowledgment of indigenous economic interests, but subsequent statements went well beyond this, proclaiming indigenous culture and knowledge an indivisible whole, the rights to which can and should be reclaimed by indigenous people themselves. For example, the "Mataatua Declaration," which was written during the First International Conference on the Cultural and Intellectual Property Rights of Indigenous Peoples (1993), stated that "Indigenous Peoples . . . have the right to self determination and . . . must be recognized as the exclusive owners of their cultural and intellectual property . . . Indigenous Peoples are capable of managing their traditional knowledge themselves" (quoted in Posey and Dutfield 1996, appendix 7).[1]

Conferences organized by indigenous interest groups, nongovernmental organizations, and academic organizations established a common ground from which to limit the claims by Western commercial interests to indigenous knowledge and resources.[2] The countermeasures did not aim at putting a complete stop to this process, but rather at establishing a basic awareness that ongoing exploitation was occurring. Indigenous peoples were to be made aware of the economic potential of their knowledge (see Brown 1998, 195). "Native peoples must have the right to choose their own futures. Without economic independence, such a choice is not possible" (Posey 1990, 15). The key concepts foregrounded were self-determination, traditional resource rights, cultural property rights, and community intellectual property rights.[3] On the academic side of the equation, professional associations have revised their rules of conduct and their ethical codes to acknowledge the role of indigenous agency in research planning. In anthropology, these ethical revisions are regarded as an ongoing "work in progress" (for example, AAA 1998).[4]

Parallel developments related to museum holdings of indigenous arts, artifacts, and human remains have also affected anthropology's professional engagement with repatriation efforts. The audience for museum holdings has gradually grown and diversified since the 1970s, fostering increased awareness among indigenous peoples of the nature of museum collections.

The 1990s growth market for eco- and ethnotourism lent further impetus to these developments and has moved the issues beyond the immediate surroundings of Western museums into Third World villages (Stanley 1998, 86–87). The growing tide of indigenous nationalism in Fourth World nations also added further stimuli to this discourse.

A landmark was reached with the 1990 passage of the Native American Graves Protection and Repatriation Act (NAGPRA) in the United States. The negotiation process this law set in motion between museums and Native American and Hawaiian peoples was closely monitored by museum personnel and indigenous rights groups across the world. Discourse on NAGPRA has raised issues about accessibility of knowledge and information in regard to Native American peoples in particular: "Indigenous beliefs about knowledge of the sacred conflict directly with the majority's commitment to the sacredness of public values. This is a classic collision of irreconcilable values. To resolve it, both sides will have to reflect carefully on the global implications of their respective positions in order to achieve a suitable compromise" (Brown 1998, 198). These issues go well beyond a simple recognition of economic, political, or even aesthetic values of cultural resources. Indigenous peoples are becoming increasingly aware that aspects of their culture may need to be safeguarded from unwarranted access, because the value of public access conflicts with the values of privacy and sacredness. Academic use of research information has also come under increasing scrutiny, because "Publishing information, traditionally the hallmark of academic success, has become the means for conveying restricted (or even sacred) information into the unprotectable public domain" (Posey 1995, 1–2). Three main factors loom large in all these debates. First, the legacy of past and present exploitation of indigenous resources, both cultural and economic, is widely recognized. Second, indigenous peoples are asserting their rights to control their cultural identity and integrity, implicitly reasserting their ownership of cultural knowledge. Third, sincere efforts are being made to right past wrongs with respect to the first two issues.

What then is repatriation? Clearly, the term can refer to a whole spectrum of actions. At one extreme is our conscientious hypothetical anthropologist. Leslie's one-time donation is the "minimal thing" that most anthropologists feel responsible for doing nowadays—making the products of our research accessible to the people we study. But the other end of the spectrum contains a complex of more involved repatriation possibilities: the "return" not only of our published and unpublished ethnographic writings, but also of the notes we made,[5] the field diaries we kept, the audiovisual recordings we made, as well as any material items that may directly or indirectly be relevant to the work we did.[6] These days the physical return of materials is not necessarily the central issue.[7] Providing access to the materials we store may be more essential in some cases. In the long run, repatriation may require transferring the rights to control access to those who originally "owned" the information or to their descendants.

Two axioms seem basic in repatriation decision making: (1) we should not harm either the community we have studied or the individual informants we have consulted while in the field; (2) we should not harm the interests of continued academic research.

These axioms are both encapsulated in existing codes of anthropological ethics (see also chapter 3). While most national associations of anthropologists have defined their own ethical standards, these have mirrored in one way or another the spirit of the 1971 code formulated (subsequently reformulated) by the American Association of Anthropologists (AAA 1971; AAA 1998).[8] As Peter Pels (1999) has indicated, the ethics of anthropology are an evolving debate that actively mirrors the social conditions in which anthropology is practiced at any one time. Thus it is not surprising that the 1998 AAA "Code of Ethics" applies principles different from the 1971 "Principles of Professional Responsibility." Pels notes that ethical codes in present-day anthropology effect a self-control over anthropologists' actions "that may keep—by selective performances to sponsors, or semi-contractual deals with people studied—increasingly larger chunks of the workings of anthropological research out of the public eye" (31). Since repatriation requires taking into account the interests of both indigenous communities and academia, it is to be expected that by challenging and subscribing to this type of "closure," the practice of repatriation will eventually affect the ethical standards applied in anthropology.

From Access to Control

Access is fundamental to any repatriation process and thus forms the core issue in the first section of this volume. The variety of topics covered in "Issues of Access" illustrates the complexity of problems involved in repatriating materials. Providing physical access is only one part of the process. We can go to great lengths to make academic publications available, but as long as it takes a Western education to make sense of them, intellectual access will remain very limited. Chapter 1, by Dorothy and David Counts, draws attention to the increasingly esoteric nature of anthropological narratives and discourse. This stems both from the use of cryptic, often pedantic jargon and from the highlighting of theory at the expense of eth-nographic detail in publications. Since its enormous growth in the 1960s and 1970s, academic anthropology has increasingly engaged in conversation with itself. The Counts describe their efforts to publish the results of their research among the RV (recreational vehicle) community in an accessible manner. Motivated by repeated queries from their research subjects, and by promotional activities from relevant interest groups, the Counts had to participate in extensive media representation of their research and research population. Their chapter illustrates a variety of problems related to access and accessibility, as well as the responsibilities this access invokes.

The physical aspects of access are taken up in chapter 2, where Alan Howard describes his posting of various sources concerning the island of Rotuma on the Internet and considers the tricky question of what material should be made accessible. To this end he introduces James Clifford's dis-tinction (1990) between inscribed and transcribed texts to distinguish mate-rial that has been subjected to further analysis by the ethnographer from straightforwardly descriptive materials. He suggests that repatriating in-scribed material might, because of the nature of its construction, involve more complications. He ends his contribution by postulating some variables that should be considered in assessing the pros and cons of repatriating various kinds of materials under varying circumstances.

Briefly exploring at the outset of chapter 3 the historical development of the gathering and exchanging of information by anthropologists in the field, I go on to discuss how the issue of repatriation has brought the shifting relations between anthropology, its audiences, and indigenous communities to the fore. Stressing the need for an impact analysis prior to repatriation, this chapter furthermore draws attention to the ethical responsibilities the repatriation process will give rise to now and in the future.

Clearly, we must take responsibility for making our ethnographic mate-rials accessible. Characteristically, scholars do not consider what they need to do with their research materials until the end of careers (see for in-stance Jackson 1990, 8–10). Some have made prior arrangements, but most of us only leave some general and usually insufficient instructions, effec-tively dumping the responsibilities on an archivist or librarian. Mary Mc-Cutcheon's evocatively titled chapter, "You Can't Die till You Clean Up Your Mess," is drawn from her experience as an archivist. She describes a variety of measures—and in some cases lack of measures—taken by ethnographers to protect their materials and informants. She also gives us a good idea of how this affects (and is affected by) existing archival policies and current

United States' laws on privacy and related issues. The wealth of examples in McCutcheon's chapter is a prelude to the more detailed case studies of repatriation that comprise the remainder of this volume.

"Managing the Collected Past," the second part of this volume, provides us with cases that look at the problems of and possibilities for repatriating ethnographic materials stored in archives and museum libraries. In chapter 5 David Akin and Kathryn Creely describe the disposition of field materials and other ethnographic information produced by the late Roger Keesing during his long research career among the Kwaio of the Solomon Islands. The authors first describe the objectives of the Melanesian Archive, where his family deposited Keesing's materials. Subsequently, they analyze the problems that result from setting access limitations on the materials that will eventually be placed in the control of the Kwaio themselves.

Chapters by Suzanne Falgout and Karen Peacock focus on post–World War II archival material relating to the Trust Territory of the Pacific Islands. Falgout deals with the work of district anthropologist Jack Fischer, who gathered extensive ethnographic material on Chuuk and Pohnpei, material that he later deposited in the Bishop Museum Archives in Honolulu. She provides an overview of the way the material was gathered and of the types of archive materials he deposited. Of particular concern are the restrictions Fischer placed on access to this collection. Falgout provides an assessment of the implications these restrictions have for present and future use of this material.

In chapter 7 Peacock details the case of the Trust Territory Archives, placed in the care of the University of Hawai'i Library for indexing and preservation. While the administrative record of United States' control over the Micronesian area between 1947 and 1994 contains much ethnographic material, the focus in this chapter is not on the return of the ethnographic materials contained in this collection, but on the institutional role of the University of Hawai'i Library in providing access to and distributing the material across the respective national libraries and archives in the region. Peacock describes the work necessary to conserve these archival records, as well as some of the political (and academic) squabbling that accompanies a multinational effort that is still in progress.

The final contribution in this section, by Amy Stillman, evaluates the history of access to the hula collections in the Bishop Museum as set against the background of the Hawaiian cultural renaissance that started in the 1970s. The contents of these collections were organized and indexed, but remained inaccessible to local hula performers. The resurgence of interest in the hula repertoire fostered determined research into these collections, leading to a deinstitutionalization, which Stillman describes as a "reunification of performers and poetic repertoire" in the 1980s and 1990s. She also describes the consequences of reintroducing old, often sacred materials into a radically changed social situation. Stillman's analysis of the ambiguity of her role as native scholar highlights additional repatriation complexities.

The third part of the volume contains three cases where the repatriation of actual materials is at stake. As the title "Transformation, Interpretation, and Ownership" suggests, the focus of this section involves indigenous assessments of the materials returned. The contributions by Anne and Keith Chambers and Bryan Oles deal specifically with questions of access to genealogical material, looking at the interest in such material within the communities studied and among islanders living elsewhere. Distinct differences between the two cases are also apparent, however. These stem equally from the researchers themselves and the communities they studied. The Chambers discuss their repatriation of a variety of types of ethnographic materials, both on their own initiative and on request from the local community. Because they were engaged in long-term fieldwork, they could manage the process of repatriation to some extent. Oles, on the other hand, found his research threatened by local responses to ethnographic reports by previous researchers that were considered misrepresentations. His own efforts at conducting research were subsequently frustrated by a general distrust of ethnographers within the Mokilese community. While the Chambers and Oles draw different conclusions about the repatriation process, both chapters give useful insights into the interplay between academic and community views on the return of ethnographic materials.

The final contribution, by Nancy Guy, highlights some of the negative consequences of mismanaging access to field materials. Indigenous music has been used as a source of inspiration for Western musicians for some centuries now. Because the potential profits from successful music production are immense, its exploitation potential is also great and may result in considerable abuse of indigenous rights. Guy describes a case in which traditional singing by two aboriginal Taiwan performers found its way through the recordings of an ethnomusicologist to the introductory tracks of a megaselling hit single. Contrary to most such cases, this incident made it to court (and was eventually settled out of court), providing a challenge to the claims of copyright. Guy provides us with an interesting vista on the tortuous routes that our ethnographic materials may take. She points out that given current copyright law, we may inadvertently become the de facto copyright holders on some of the material we gather.

It is somehow indicative of the pitfalls surrounding repatriation that I end this overview on a few legal notes. As copyright is part of Western law, it becomes part of the researcher's responsibility to apply it properly. We can hardly expect our research subjects to have an understanding of the applicable laws. In that respect Darrell Posey's chance remark that anthropologists (among others) will be uncomfortable with a tighter regime on their research material, because they may become obliged to share the profits of their "lifestyles," may be more to the point than we think. "Incomes from published dissertations and other books, slides, magazine articles, gramophone records, films and videos—all will have to include a percentage of the profits to the native 'subjects.' It will probably be negotiated with native peoples prior to the undertaking of initial fieldwork" (Posey 1990, 15).

Several legal layers may apply to our research information, and we may be legally obliged to conceal or to display parts of our research data regardless of what agreements we may have made with our informants. Guy, as an expert witness to the court case she describes, is unable to detail the legal deliberations. While privy to most of testimony given prior to the court case, she also signed a declaration to keep these details confidential.[9] McCutcheon's consideration of the effects of the Freedom of Information Act and its subsequent amendments (chapter 4), as well as the response made by the American Anthropological Association to Circular A-110 of the Office of Management and Budget (OMB 1999a) are also worth taking into account here. Different laws may apply in different countries, and research data may be (or may become) subject to the laws of both the country where the research was done and the country where the researcher lived at the time of the research. While several of the contributions to this volume touch upon such issues, I do not pretend that we deal adequately with the legal minefield that surrounds repatriation.

Some "Home Truths"

Most of the cases in this volume derive from fieldwork in the Pacific Islands. Nevertheless, the issues they raise are relevant to all of anthropology, and what should be clear from the various contributions to this volume is that the demand for repatriating ethnographic materials, and for an indigenous role in the decision-making process, is certain to grow in the near future (see also Stanley 1998, 87). New Zealand Maori, Australian Aboriginals, and Native Hawaiians all have condemned Western appropriation of indigenous knowledge. While expressions of outrage may be less audible elsewhere in the Pacific, they are nonetheless growing (see Lindstrom and White 1994b). Libraries and archives in the region are taking the lead in making research materials in their collections accessible or repatriating them locally. Most of the small island nations in the Pacific have a considerable percentage of their population living abroad in major urban centers. They are part of a growing audience interested not only in published ethnographic knowledge on their home societies, but also in any information of this nature available on the Internet.

In sum, the changes that will eventually affect anthropological research and ethnographic writing boil down to the granting of partial or shared control over research to the people who are research subjects. Though we can talk in theory about self-determination of indigenous peoples, this goal can only be reached by giving the people we study the ability to assess the nature of the information we gather and the methods we have used to gather it. This may sometimes result in attempts to force research into "politically desirable" or "ideologically correct" directions (Keesing 1989; Keesing 1991; Trask 1991; van Meijl 2000), but if this an evil it is one we will have to learn to live with. However we proceed, researchers will inevitably have to yield some control over the research process. At the moment, we anthropologists—as members of an academic discipline—largely "police" ourselves and determine the fate of our research materials without much need to consider outside interests. We are subject to laws that vary from country to country, but the only real common denominator is the code of professional ethics drawn up by the discipline. It is doubtful that this will remain the case for long. I expect that a combination of laws protecting research subjects' rights and regulating the accountability of researchers will eventually make us more responsive to outside interests in the way we set up and conduct research. If we do not react responsibly, our hand will inevitably be forced in this respect. Repatriating our field materials, voluntarily or not, is only one aspect of the changes evolving in the relations between our research subjects and us.

Although most of the data we gather in the field, as distinct from its analysis, ought to remain available for future reference, it is not always necessary to expose personally authored materials to public scrutiny.[10] In repatriating ethnographic materials, the interests of the people studied, those of the discipline, and those of the individual researcher should be weighed against each other. In the final measure, as Howard indicates (chapter 2), there is nothing holy about field notes; we should not be afraid to destroy materials if allowing open access to them seems likely to do more harm than good.

We should never lose sight of the fact that what we return as field data (and implicitly its interpretation) may potentially be more incendiary than what we took out. Whether intentional or not, we often end up overriding indigenous limitations on access to sensitive information. As indicated earlier, our research becomes public domain if we start returning available information or (re-)establishing access and control over it.[11] This aspect of repatriation must be dealt with in regard to different cultures in different ways, in harmony with each setting's unique problems and needs. The various contributors to this volume provide a wide range of examples and choices in this respect. There is not one generally applicable, easy solution, however. Repatriation is not an add-on to research already done; it needs to be a part of research projects from the start.

If we take this challenge seriously it will profoundly change the way we work. Theoretical sophistication and exclusionary jargon will no longer be the primary measure of our work, but will be superseded by a demand for clarity and accessibility. Sophisticated analysis, however fruitful in its application, cannot serve any community's long-term purpose if it virtually encrypts the knowledge it produces. In the long run, the production of ethnographic knowledge defeats its own purpose if it does not become available and accessible to a wider audience, including the people we study.

It is not our role as anthropologists to be judgmental or paternalistically protective here. We should feel obliged to comply with expressed indigenous wishes for repatriation, regardless of our perceptions of the damage that may result. While we should avoid causing unnecessary damage, we should also be aware that cultures forever change, and that there is no constructive change without decay. We cannot hold the tide from coming in. Where a written record of land rights might permanently change the oral discourse on land rights and the way land rights are passed on from generation to generation, we should not think that we can stop the incursion of literacy and of written records (see also McCall 2000, 81–83). If our research populations express a wish to have access to the data we collected from them, we should comply for two related reasons: (1) an awareness of the existence of our written records may cause as much if not more damage than actual access to them; (2) a lack of compliance to such a request is not just judgmental, it can do damage itself.

We are basically entrusted with other people's knowledge to use and to work with, but our "ownership" remains limited to what we add as interpretation. The communities we study have equal—if not more legitimate—rights to the ethnographic materials we gather. These rights are only mitigated by our obligation to prevent damage deriving from any access we provide to this material. There is a basic truth here that we dare not neglect and cannot hide from. As academics we have earned the reputation of living in an ivory tower because we seem intent on impressing one another at the expense of excluding people outside of academia from our conversations. If we do not make ourselves accessible and accountable, we will eventually be forced to do so, if not by legal means, then by diminishing prospects for future research.

Part I *Issues of Access*

Dorothy A. Counts and David R. Counts

1

Talking to Ourselves, or Getting the Word Back

If one cannot state a matter clearly enough so that even an intelligent twelve-year-old can understand it, one should remain in the cloistered walls of the university and laboratory until one gets a better grasp of one's subject matter.

MARGARET MEAD,

Margaret Mead: Some Personal Views, ed. Rhoda Métraux

This volume addresses the problems and challenges of returning information to the people from which it came. The information involved is in at least two forms: publications (books and scholarly journal articles) and raw data (field notes, photographs and other visual images, and tape recordings). While the books and articles are the end result of the research process, they are also *interpretations* of the data gathered by the researchers. The "raw" data may seem more like archival truth (the *facts*), but these data, too, are the product of selection and interpretation. We are obligated to return these materials, but we are also obligated to consider how we do so and what the result of so doing might be.

For more than two decades we did research with and wrote about a community—the village of Kandoka—in Kaliai, West New Britain, Papua New Guinea. Nevertheless, we have little experience with returning our published data to this community. With one exception—a volume of myths and folktales in Tok Pisin and English—our work is only minimally accessible to the people who were our hosts. Although we sent our publications to the University of Papua New Guinea (UPNG) library and to the relevant provincial office, they were written in academic English and not easily understandable to most Kaliai.

In more than thirty years only one person from Kandoka village has read much of the material we have published, and Ursula Kolkolo is unique. As far as we know, she is the only Kaliai woman with a graduate degree and the only Kaliai who has a graduate degree earned abroad. Consequently, Ursula spent many years in school away from her village. When she visited our home while pursuing graduate study in Canada, we asked her to read our publications. She spent many hours doing this and, to our great relief, said that she learned from our writing things about her people's history and customs that she had never had the opportunity to learn. We also discussed with her the best strategy for returning our unpublished data to Papua New Guinea. We were particularly concerned about protecting those who were our informants. Ursula suggested that we deposit our field notes in the UPNG library (as well as the Melanesian Archives), but that we seal them until 2025. She also advised us to retain the real names of people in our notes because changing them would ruin their value as historical documents for later generations of Kaliai. Most Kaliai, including the more traditional people who figure most prominently in our notes, might not agree with this reasoning. We are aware of the irony of our asking *her* to comment on the accuracy of our writings and to help us find the best way to return information to her people.

For the purposes of this volume, it is important to note that most anthropologists agree on two general principles. First, we are obligated to foster knowledge. Second, in fostering knowledge, we must try to assure that no harm comes to "our people" as a result of our actions. These principles are the core of the ethical guidelines suggested by the American Anthropological Association, the Society for Applied Anthropology, the Canadian Anthropology Society, and other professional anthropological societies. Arguably, when injury comes to the people that anthropologists study, it comes as an unintended result of their reports and publications and not from their behavior in the field. Our writings are, then, potentially sources of both benefit and harm to the people who share their knowledge with us.

Harm may result when government and other officials use our data or information from our publications to control, tax, or punish the people we wrote about. More subtle is the problem of authority. When we write it down, and especially when we publish it, we give substance and authority—ipso facto—to an edited version of history, of reality, of truth. Multiple versions, interpretations, and experiences become one and multivocality is lost. As Keith and Anne Chambers note (chapter 9, page 153), the process and semantics of returning information is complex and "the repatriated materials (and even the repatriation process itself) alters the local culture and research context forever after."

For example, as we mentioned above, in 1982 Dorothy published *The Tales of Laupu*, a volume of oral history, legends, and folktales in Tok Pisin and English, through the Institute of Papua New Guinea Studies. The book was inexpensive and accessible in the language many villagers read. It was also widely distributed in the country, sold at the teacher's college, the police academy, and the airports.

The main storytellers, Jakob Mua and Benedict Solou, were two of the sons of Laupu, who had been a renowned raconteur. Like their father, Mua and Solou are among the most knowledgeable men in the village and popular storytellers. Maria Sapanga, who contributed a story of domestic violence often told by women and considered by villagers to be a comedy, is the wife of Jakob Mua. Although the book was just a collection of stories, it was also interpretive. Dorothy selected which versions to include, edited them, and provided background information. For example, she chose two stories of the early settlement of the area for inclusion. She selected those because they were the stories of the two largest kin groups and because the tales were complex and had both plot and character development. The book's publication disseminated these versions of the stories throughout the country and gave them authority over alternative ones. In the versions published some people's ancestors were lauded for their strength of character and bravery, while others' ancestors—principally those from the lesser kin groups—were portrayed as weak or, at best, ineffective. A few copies of the book reached Kandoka village. When we returned in 1985, Dorothy was scolded for not having collected (and published) stories from other kin groups or other "more authentic" versions of the published ones!

Returning analyses of disputes over land tenure, accounts of marriage arrangements, discussions of the symbolism of songs or ceremonies, or interpretations of inheritance rules or chieftainship would be even more problematic. The Chambers (chapter 9) examine the problems of repatriating these sorts of data.

How, then, do we balance our desire to share knowledge and to return it to those who provided it against the potential harm sharing that knowledge might do? Will our publications harm or embarrass our informants (or their descendants)? Will the people whom our field notes name as accused sorcerers, thieves, or adulterers receive more benefit than harm from this knowledge?

Until the last decade most of us have avoided the issue. We who worked in the "exotic" regions of the planet with populations not yet literate in any of the world's major languages assumed that few if any of our informants would ever read our work. We made the results of our research known, but few members of the public, other than a small group of scholars who shared our interests, read them. The time when we can enjoy the luxury of speaking only to ourselves is over. As communications technology shrinks the planet, and as developing countries bring their populations to a state of literacy, we can no longer assume that Pacific Islanders will be unable to read and critique what we have said about them. They *will* read what we write, and they will be critical.

Our contribution to this volume is not a discussion of our experience in returning knowledge to the people of Kaliai who shared it with us. Rather we wish to consider what we have learned as a result of shifting our research focus to a North American population. Since 1990 we have done research with a well-educated, literate, and opinionated population who expect to read what we say about them and to make judgments about both its authenticity and its accuracy. It will not be long before the people of Papua New Guinea will also expect to know how we have interpreted the information they gave us and to contest our interpretation. We must prepare to face their criticism.

Who Is Our Audience?

The audience we anthropologists have addressed over the past decades has primarily been our own academic community. While some of us have shared information with indigenous scholars from the Pacific Islands and included them in discussion of our ideas about Pacific cultures, this has not been a primary concern for most of us. They are aware of our failure to give back knowledge. One Pacific Islander, commenting on *Tales of Laupu* and our West New Britain website, expressed it this way: "Too often research about us in the Pacific is used for other purposes and our people are no better off. I am impressed with your efforts to share the information about your research."[1]

In the past decade or so, our ability to communicate our ideas even among ourselves has been handicapped by heavy reliance on jargon that makes much of what we write almost impossible to understand. In 1995 James Peacock tackled this problem in his plenary presidential address to the American Anthropological Association. He asked how many in the audience had read an anthropology book *for fun* in the past year. Looking around at the absence of raised hands he observed that we have a problem. "If we only talk to each other," he said, "we're dead." The response to Peacock's question underscores the validity of the argument that anthropological writing is usually boring and often unreadable. As one frustrated scholar put it: "These days the most revealing question to ask one's colleagues is not whether they have read *Kinship among the X*, but whether they have finished it. While there have been some recent attempts to modify the genre, the sad truth still seems to be that, if academic anthropologists were not paid to read these weighty tomes, most of them wouldn't" (MacClancy 1996b, 237).

If Jeremy MacClancy is right that we usually have to be paid to read each other's work, it is no surprise that we are not good at sharing our findings with the general public, at "popularizing" anthropology. William Mitchell defines "popularize" as " 'to cause to be liked or esteemed,' and 'to present in generally understandable or interesting form' " (1996, 123), while Mac-Clancy notes "there are as many different ways to 'popularize' anthropology as there are audiences for it" (1996a, 5). What we (and MacClancy) mean by "popularize" is the process of making our work—in all its complexity—available to the public. We must write so that our work is accessible to the public at large.

People who live in recreation vehicles (RVers), with whom we have been working with since 1990, *expect* to be able to read what we write and to criticize what they read. They also expect to be able to use what we write to promote their own ends, primarily to make friends and family understand who they are, what they are doing, and why they are doing it. If we are to meet their expectations, we must make our work interesting to the non-academic members of our culture. They must not wonder, as Mary Louise Pratt does, why our work is so boring: "For the lay person, such as myself, the main evidence of a problem is the simple fact that ethnographic writing tends to be surprisingly boring. How, one asks constantly, could such interesting people doing such interesting things produce such dull books? What did they have to do to themselves?" (1986, 33).

Writing a respectable scholarly work in a way that enables interested members of the general public to read it requires a lot of thought. When we were writing *Over the Next Hill*, our RVing book, we sent an early draft to Asterisk Productions, a Canadian film company that was making a documentary on RVing communities. Sherry Lepage, one of the editors, after reading the draft wrote us suggesting that we should consider our audience. Who were we trying to reach with this book? Only our colleagues? Or were we writing it for RVers? Her question changed our attitude toward the book.

We wanted to write something the community we studied, and North Americans in general, could—and might want to—read.

In the next draft we asked our daughter and son-in-law to be "jargon police," marking in red all examples of stuffy academic pontification. We used the voices of RVers as much as possible, relegated the heavy stuff to endnotes and appendices, and tried for the "light touch." We intended the book to have a serious message but, as with first-year classes, we must keep our readers awake first. The results have been good. RVers tell us they read the text and then turn to the back to read the questionnaire results and the other appendices. Even better, they have ordered copies to give to family and friends. As one RVer put it, "so they'll know why I'm doing this. That I'm not nuts."[2] This response from the people we studied is possibly the best review we could have.

We must, as members of an academic discipline, take seriously those who, like Pratt and our RVing audience, want to read what we write. If these native English speakers found our work boring and inaccessible in 1999, what will the people of Papua New Guinea, Raratonga, and the Marquesas think of it in 2018? If they cannot understand it, contest it, and use it for their own purposes, then we are not doing our job: we are not fostering knowledge.

Reaching Our Audience Today

Even if the children and grandchildren of the people who share knowledge with us are able to read our work in the future, what about those who shared? How do we make our interpretation of their lives and cultures available to them? Can we ensure that Pacific people are better off as a result of our research?

The government of Papua New Guinea insists that we who do research there meet a part of our obligation to share our findings with the communities we study by sending copies of our publications to the university library. We do this, but it is not enough. Only the intellectual and political elite has ready access to the university library. Materials disappear from provincial offices. Only a tiny proportion of the population can read much of what we write. By sending copies of our work to national libraries, we communicate our results to Pacific Islanders who have a postsecondary education, but most of the people who were helpful to us can never read any of our work.

We discussed with Ursula our concerns about what to do with our field notes, but Ursula is a highly educated woman whose experience and training has distanced her from the concerns of her fellow villagers. We do not suggest that her ideas were wrong or that we should ignore them. In part our discussion is about how to make our work accessible to the children and grandchildren of today's villagers. But what about the villagers from whom we collected most of our information and who will never attend university? They also are, or should be, part of our "public," and they should be able to read our publications. Certainly the academic voice will not reach them. How can we, then, share our findings with them?

One possible solution is the one discussed by Alan Howard in this volume. He has established a website for Rotuma, using the Internet as an interactive way of disseminating information and encouraging conversation about his work and the work done by other anthropologists. We have recently set up a West New Britain website,[3] which includes photographs of the area, a comprehensive bibliography in process, copies of several papers about West New Britain, myth texts in both English and Tok Pisin, and information about current events in the province from academics who were recently there. The possibilities for sharing knowledge in this way are exciting. However, and again, our website will reach only members of the educated, urban middle and upper class in Papua New Guinea. None of them live in West New Britain villages where, as far as we know, there is no Internet access.

Another solution, one that relates to part of the earlier discussion, would be to translate our own work into a language spoken by the people we study. In the volume *Popularizing Anthropology* Alan Campbell says, "If it was *demanded* of academics that, to be taken seriously, every one had to produce a piece of work for the popular market . . . or something in that idiom, the exercise would generally be found enormously challenging" (1996, 80). What if each of us who worked in Papua New Guinea translated at least some of our work into Tok Pisin and put it on a web page? Challenging? Indeed! What would we do about the jargon that too often obfuscates rather than clarifies? Many of us would likely have to do as Margaret Mead suggested and hole up in our university's cloistered halls until we understood our subject better. And perhaps we would have to stay even longer if we were to avoid the pitfall of poor translation—not only of our work into *their* languages, but of their words into *our* languages. If our friends from the villages read the careless and shoddy translations that we sometimes make of their words (often defended as maintaining the "authenticity of their voices") they would be horrified and greatly offended.

Another challenge to making our work accessible to our host communities is finding a way for publications to reach them. How could work written in a language they could understand be gotten to them? The Internet is one possibility. Another might be a special series of publications in various vernaculars made available at cost. Would such projects be appropriate enterprises for our professional organizations, such as the Association for Social Anthropology in Oceania (ASAO)?

The two of us have the advantage of being retired. Nobody can refuse to grant us tenure or promote us to anything. However, the system we are all a part of makes the approach we used in *Over the Next Hill* difficult for younger scholars. If *anybody* can read it, it is not legitimate. If it looks like fun, it must be a scam. Must we apologize?

When we first proposed our recreation vehicle research in 1990, nobody took us seriously. The folks in the research office at the University of Waterloo laughed at Dorothy. The dean of social science at McMaster was embarrassed to support David's proposal, and one of David's colleagues suggested that when he finished the RVing research, the two of them should write a grant proposal to study Club Med (nudge nudge, wink wink). A McMaster graduate student, who did her master's thesis on Outward Bound, gave a presentation on her research at a departmental brown-bag colloquium. By way of self-justification, she showed photos of herself in a snow shelter and rock climbing. Her explanation: she had been "accused of being like the Counts, doing research that's fun. I want you to know it wasn't *all* fun."

During the nearly thirty years of our academic careers, we played the game—we got grants, went to the field, slept on the ground, and published stuff with colons in the title that even David's father refused to read. We were promoted through the ranks and held administrative positions. Nevertheless in 1990 we had trouble being taken seriously because our work was perceived to be "popular." What does this mean for junior scholars and, implicitly, for those whom they study and write about?

The Future: Dealing with the Press

James Peacock was right: if we only talk to ourselves, our discipline is irrelevant and eventually will be either dead or kept as an odd curiosity by a few universities. The question is, *how* do we address a broader audience?

Among the opportunities for communication is use of the press—television and print media—the fourth estate. As MacClancy says: "Instead of turning away from the fourth estate, anthropologists should use it to inform the public of their work, and of its value, especially if, in a time of shrinking public funds, they wish their subject to survive" (1996b, 44–45).

Maria Lepowsky has written about her experience with the press after her ethnography, *Fruit of the Motherland*, came to the attention of the popular print and television media (1994a, 1994b, 1995). This happened after Lepowsky's book was reviewed favorably in the *New York Times*. In it she had described a society in which there was little distinction between gender roles and in which there seemed to be true gender egalitarianism. Her thesis, though drawn from an "exotic" society in Papua New Guinea, spoke to concerns currently under discussion in North American and other industrialized societies. Sixty years earlier, Mead's Samoan work had also been directed to the concerns of modern societies. Throughout her long career, Mead made astute use of the media. She was, and still is, criticized for this practice.

While our new "exotic" research society of RVers is found on the roads of the United States and Canada, we have had our own run with the fourth estate. We wish, in the rest of this chapter, to use our experience with the media to offer suggestions about the promise and the pitfalls of doing work that becomes "popular."

In over two decades of doing research with and writing about the people of Kaliai, until the 1990s the only interest expressed in our work by a representative of the press was in 1967 when Dorothy was invited to be a guest on an afternoon television talk show in San Antonio, her hometown. The interview was brief, and the only question she can remember the host asking was "Where is Old Guinea?" In the 1990s press interest in our research in Papua New Guinea has been a spin-off from the attention given our research with RVers. One of the first questions we were asked on television by the host of a TV program for senior Canadians illustrates this relationship: "Why would anthropologists who have worked in PNG want to do research with RVers? Where are the bones in *their* noses?"

Since 1990 we have spent about eighteen months on the road doing research with people who live full-time in recreation vehicles (RVs). The scholarly publications resulting from that research are one major journal article, "They're My Family Now" (Counts and Counts 1992) and an ethnography, *Over the Next Hill* (Counts and Counts 1996). In contrast with our work in Papua New Guinea, the public interest in this research has been intense. We have been on public and commercial radio and TV in the U.S. and Canada. Newspapers have published interviews with us across the U.S. and Canada. One interview done by a Reuters reporter was picked up and published on the CNN website for two weeks, leading to live on-air interviews with radio stations in Japan and South Africa. Our research was the topic of two TV broadcasts, one a seven-minute spot on commercial TV, the other a twenty-five-minute documentary on a national cable network in Canada.

In the spring of 1995 and again in the fall months of 1997 and 1998, we were asked by the Recreation Vehicle Industry Association (RVIA) to do "media tours" on its behalf, publicizing our research. A public relations firm managed these tours on behalf of the RVIA. During the 1997 and 1998 tours we combined media interviews with public lectures on university campuses. From our perspective the tours worked well. It was good to meet with colleagues who were interested in both our research and the idea of the tour. The lively discussions sometimes suggested ways of looking at our data that had not occurred to us. From the RVIA's perspective it was successful because we attracted media attention. Most of the reporters were intrigued by our research and by the fact that it had been done by *anthropologists*, and much of the coverage was sympathetic and good-humored.

We have encountered some perils in this process. First, having "advance publicity" done by a public relations firm makes us uncomfortable. We wince at some of the claims they make for the results of our research. Second, some of the reporters were skeptical about our research because we were working with an associated industry. One reporter frankly asked, "Are you being paid to tout RVs?" While we had a straightforward negative answer to this question, it was disconcerting to have to field it. Yet the growing cooperation between university researchers and industry will make such questions increasingly frequent.

Third, the agenda of the *media* is to get the public's attention. Sometimes reporters try to accomplish this by emphasizing the negative or bizarre, by ridicule, or by misrepresentation. As Lepowsky observes (1994b), this leaves the anthropologist protesting "But that's not what I said." This protest draws no audience and remedies no misunderstanding.

How Do We Meet the Challenge?

What does our discussion of our experience with the media resulting from our North American research have to do with the repatriation of our Pacific data and publications and the accessibility of this work to the people of our own culture?

If the media interest and the subsequent public interest in our research with RVers occur because audiences in our home countries are interested only in themselves, then we must make what we have learned in other cultures relevant to the people of our culture. We must operate as though our work will interest them only if we address an agenda that concerns them, as Lepowsky and Mead have done. Anthropologists have some credibility with the fourth estate because we do interesting things. If we think of ourselves as storytellers—which we ought to be—then we might have a better chance to get the word out to those who finance our research and to the Pacific people whose lives provide us with the material for our stories.

Good storytellers must find a variety of ways to tell their stories. Our audiences are varied: some are literate in English and are sophisticated users of the World Wide Web, others have fluent literacy only in their own vernacular, while others communicate primarily through an oral tradition. Our challenge is to find ways to communicate to our audiences in ways that are comprehensible and appropriate to them.

As storytellers we must remember the danger that the version of the story we tell may become the only widely known version, inappropriately imbued with legitimacy. We must also remember that we are accountable to those who "own" the stories and that we are ultimately accountable for how others use the stories we tell. If a story harms the people about whom the story is told—then as Howard and the Chambers suggest—it may be best to leave it untold.

Some of our goals may be contradictory. We may not be able simultaneously to provide members of our culture with access to our work, make our work available to members of the societies that have hosted us, and protect the interests of those who provided us with the information in the first place. As we learned from our RVers and with the publication of the *Tales of Laupu*, if we "get the word back," some people may think that we have returned the wrong word or argue that our word is not the last word. Others may be disturbed by the implications and consequences of what we write. Other chapters in this work, particularly those by the Chambers and Bryan Oles, focus on these concerns.

Repatriation has risks, as does any other form of sharing knowledge. Yet in our view anthropologists—being aware of the pitfalls—are obliged to try to return information to the people to whom it belongs. We also think that our discipline is at much greater risk if we continue to be irrelevant, becoming merely a curiosity of academia "wandering round the attics of anthropology wearing Malinowski's jodhpurs."[4]

Alan Howard

2

www.repatriating__ethnography.edu / rotuma

For many years I have been concerned with the fact that people from the island of Rotuma have so little access to materials implicating their history. My concern was amplified when, in 1990, I discovered that few Rotumans expressed an interest in their history as a people. In Rotuman schools European history and to a growing extent the history of Fiji were emphasized. In part, I believe, this is a consequence of the unavailability of archival and published sources on the island (although other, culturally rooted processes also play a role; see Howard 1994). To remedy the situation, several years ago I began to explore the possibility of establishing an archive on Rotuma. I was prepared to make copies of the extensive materials I had collected over the years, but only if an appropriate repository was available. With this in mind I contacted UNESCO and was assured that money was available (the figure of 8,000 dollars U.S. was mentioned) if a proposal was submitted.

The snag was that the proposal could not come from me; it had to come from Rotuma. The district officer at the time enthusiastically supported the idea and went so far as to commit some land at the government station for a suitable building. The director of the Fiji Museum offered assistance in the form of training and equipment. In collaboration with the district officer I wrote a proposal, which he submitted through bureaucratic channels, where it died an untimely death. Though disappointed, I was not completely dismayed. Indeed, even when my enthusiasm for the project peaked, I harbored doubts about its viability, having seen so many other idealistically conceived programs go awry. In truth, the likelihood of paper documents, photographs, and other materials surviving indefinitely on the island without professional care—something little Rotuma can ill afford—was slim in my estimation. So I dropped the project, but not the long-term commitment to making materials of historical import available to the Rotuman community. The development of the Internet afforded another, more practical opportunity.

This chapter explores the use of websites as vehicles for making available published and unpublished ethnographic texts pertaining to Pacific cultures. I present a description of a website for the island of Rotuma on which are posted complete texts of a number of classic nineteenth-century sources, as well as Gordon Macgregor's 1932 field notes. The website is frequented by Rotumans around the world who consult it for news (posted on a regular basis) and use other features, such as its bulletin board. I contrast the Rotuma case with my research among Hawaiian-Americans, where field notes consisting of personal data were destroyed to protect people's privacy. The comparison of the two cases highlights a variety of ethical, pragmatic, and methodological issues.

The Rotuma Website

Toward the end of 1996, enchanted by the possibilities of the Internet for anthropological, and particularly ethnographic, purposes, I began construction of a site for Rotuma.[1] My goals were modest at the time. I wanted to create an accessible space where Rotumans could find news and communicate with one another, as well as to provide basic information about the island's history, culture, and language for interested Rotumans and non-Rotumans alike. To these ends I incorporated an interactive message board, a news page that I continually update, maps, information about recent publications, and a set of essays on population, history, economics, politics, myths, and other cultural topics. I also scanned a number of photographs and created a digital photo album. The positive feedback I received from Rotumans via e-mail and personal encounters encouraged me to invest more of my energies in the website and to add new features. One such feature was a proverb of the week, reflecting a project Jan Rensel and I had been working on with Elizabeth Inia, a Rotuman sage, to publish a book of Rotuman proverbs (Inia 1998). Another addition was an interactive on-line dictionary whereby a visitor could enter an English word and find Rotuman equivalents or vice versa.[2] More important for the topic of this volume, I decided to scan and make available the most important nineteenth-century publications on Rotuma. Doing so at least makes available to the Rotuman community materials that are vital to their recorded (as opposed to oral) history. Publications now on-line include

• An account by René Lesson, naturalist aboard the French corvette *Coquille*, which visited Rotuma in 1824. Lesson's account is entitled "Observations on Rotuma and Its Inhabitants."

• Peter Dillon arrived at Rotuma in 1827 and wrote an account, *Narrative . . . of a Voyage in the South Seas.*

• George Bennett, a physician aboard the *Sophia*, visited Rotuma in 1830. His observations on "The Island of Rótuma" were published in 1831 in the *United Services Journal.*

• Robert Jarman visited Rotuma aboard the whaling ship *Japan* and wrote an account of his visit in *Journal of a Voyage to the South Seas* (1832).

• Edward Lucatt's report of a visit to Rotuma in 1841, from his book *Rovings in the Pacific* (covering the years 1837 to 1849), published in 1851.

• Litton Forbes's account of his visit to Rotuma in 1872, from his book *Two Years in Fiji*, published in 1875.

• J. W. Boddam-Whetham's account of a short visit to Rotuma in his book *Pearls of the Pacific*, published in 1876.

• W. L. Allardyce, who was acting resident commissioner on Rotuma for a short period during 1881, the year the island was ceded to Great Britain, provides a general account of Rotuman society entitled "Rotooma and the Rotoomans," published in 1885–1886.

• Reverend William Allen was a Methodist missionary on Rotuma from 1881 to 1886. This account, simply entitled "Rotuma," was a paper read at a meeting of the Australasian Association for the Advancement of Science at Brisbane, Australia, in January 1895.

• J. Stanley Gardiner's "The Natives of Rotuma" appeared in the *Journal of the Royal Anthropological Institute* in 1898. Gardiner was a naturalist who visited Rotuma in 1896. His account is the most extensive and valuable record of nineteenth-century Rotuma.

Gardiner's publication alone, comprising over one hundred pages of descriptions, drawings, and tables, is a most valuable source of data on the early contact culture. I regard these postings as a form of repatriation in the sense that virtually all these materials have been buried in publications that for all practical purposes made them inaccessible to the broader Rotuman community.

More germane to issues of concern here, however, was my decision to edit and post Gordon Macgregor's field notes from his 1932 field trip to Rotuma. Macgregor spent six months on the island and interviewed a number of Rotumans about a wide range of topics, but published only a few short papers as a result. Shortly before his death he deposited his field notes at the Bernice P. Bishop Museum in Honolulu. I, of course, was delighted to have the opportunity to consult his notes and was impressed with their coherence. It was apparent that he had organized them with an eye toward producing a standard issue 1930s Bishop Museum monograph, one oriented toward determining Polynesia's history of settlement. The idea was to record "cultural traits" that could be compared with other Polynesian societies so as to unravel prehistoric connections.

In exchange for copies of Macgregor's notes (borrowed and eventually returned), I entered into an agreement with the Bishop Museum to edit and publish the notes with the object of rendering them accessible to Rotumans and interested scholars. The Bishop Museum was to have first rights of refusal when they were ready for publication. That was more than ten years ago, but for a variety of practical and personal reasons I placed the project on hold until recently. The development of the Rotuman website reinvigorated my interest in pursuing the matter, however, since I felt it would provide a more appropriate medium for making these valuable materials available. As a website publication, the notes are likely to be accessible to a much broader audience, without cost. Anyone can now download the notes and print them out for their personal libraries. If the printed copies are borrowed by a friend or relative and not returned (a frequent fate of loaned materials), they can be easily reaccessed and reprinted. The Bishop Museum agreed to the arrangement, provided appropriate credits and guidelines for citation were posted. My task was made easier by the fact that Hans Schmidt, a linguist who has worked on Rotuman language, had typed Macgregor's notes onto a computer, so scanning was unnecessary. I completed editing the notes in August 1997 and posted them on the website.[3]

Macgregor's Notes: Some Considerations

The first ethical issues I had to confront involved Macgregor's own intentions. How would he have felt about having his field notes exposed to public view? Did I have the right to make them available to public scrutiny? Many anthropologists seem to regard their field notes as personal, confidential memos to themselves and would certainly not want them exposed to others, including colleagues and the people they studied. Jackson (1990) suggests that anthropologists on the whole do not seem to concern themselves with the disposition of their field notes after their deaths, since the notes are often regarded as mnemonic devices to prod their own memories and are expected to be indecipherable to others. She also notes that many anthropologists regard the quality of their field notes as an indicator of their ability to do good fieldwork.

Macgregor, however, by the act of donating his notes to the Bishop Museum, must have perceived them as having archival value. Indeed, they are well organized and have been "worked" (typed from original handwritten notes) with the likely purpose of incorporating them (virtually verbatim in many instances) into the Bishop Museum–style monograph he never completed. Having a clear template and theoretical framework benefited him in comparison with many contemporary anthropologists who are ambivalent about, or may even despise, their field notes. Data were apparently unproblematic to Macgregor because his theoretical goals were clear and dictated what constituted appropriate information. Thus, although many anthropologists are reluctant to share their field notes for what they might reveal about themselves, Macgregor evidently had no such anxiety. Indeed, his field notes reveal him to be thoroughly professional, meticulous, and thoughtful. My own assessment, therefore, was that posting his field notes does him no disservice, but rather retrospectively enhances his professional reputation.

Macgregor's notes are essentially "transcriptions" rather than "inscriptions," a distinction made by Clifford (1990). Transcriptions refer to recordings from indigenous consultants in the form of verbatim texts concerning cultural events, procedures, beliefs, and the like. At their best, they are devoid of interpretation, translation, or editing. Unedited photographs, films, and videos, or observations recorded in words also qualify. Transcriptions are like snapshots of a culture at a point in time; in that sense they are integral to a culture's history. By contrast, inscribed field notes include the fieldworkers' interpretations, guesses at meaning, theoretical speculations, and personal reactions to what they have seen and heard. Clifford eloquently spells out the advantages of transcribing:

> The photograph of an ethnographer doing extended textual work with an
> indigenous collaborator reveals a kind of writing in the field that is often

not a matter of catching "passing events" of social discourse as much as
it is a process of transcribing already formulated, fixed discourse or lore.
A ritual, for example, when its normal course is recounted by a knowledgeable authority, is not a "passing event." Nor is a genealogy. They are
already inscribed. The same is true of everything paradoxically called "oral
literature." A myth recited and taken down, a spell or song recorded in
writing or on tape—these involve processes of transcription and explicate
translation. I have suggested elsewhere the difference it makes when transcription and indigenous forms of writing are moved toward the center of
ethnography (Clifford 1983, 135–42). For example, if writing in the field is
not seen as beginning with inscription, then the ethnographic writer less
automatically appears as a privileged recorder, salvager, and interpreter of
cultural data. Greater prominence given to transcribed materials can produce a more polyphonic final ethnography. (Clifford 1990, 57)

Macgregor's field notes in fact are polyphonic insofar as he identifies a
number of different consultants, each of whom is a source of specified items
of information. This presented me with another dilemma. Should I identify
Macgregor's informants on the website, or should I follow the anthropological custom of keeping purveyors of information anonymous? The issue was
complicated somewhat by the fact that Macgregor not only identified consultants by name, he had in his files an assessment of each one, including, in
some instances, his opinion of their veracity. In addition, I was able to
identify most of his consultants in my demographic files, making it possible
to place them genealogically as well as spatially (which district they were
from). My decision to include the names of Macgregor's consultants, along
with his assessments and my registry information, was based on three
considerations. The first was that they were all now deceased and therefore
were beyond embarrassment. It is possible, of course, that some of their
descendants might be teased for what they are reported to have said, but
teasing is endemic to Rotuman society and, in my opinion, essentially harm-
less. Besides, the material is generally not of an embarrassing nature.

A second consideration was the fact that the information on consultants
allows knowledgeable Rotumans to place them not only in time and space,
but genealogically as well, and since such contextualization of information is central to Rotuman epistemology, it seemed appropriate to include
it. Finally, there is the issue of credit. In fact, the information contained
in the notes "belonged to" Macgregor's consultants, and I believe they
should be given proper recognition. The way the notes are structured, a
viewer can click on the name of a consultant (attached to each entry) and

find a brief biographical note composed of Macgregor's comments and my registry data.

What results from these decisions is a rather postmodern (decentered, heteroglossic) perspective on Rotuman "traditional" culture. It is rather ironic that notes that were originally oriented toward producing a standard, homogenized monograph should turn out this way. On virtually every topic multiple voices are in evidence, providing divergent, sometimes contradictory information.

I also feel compelled to comment on my decision to edit Macgregor's notes, since this means that my interpretations of them are part of the final mix. I tried to keep editing to a minimum, a goal made easier by the fact that Macgregor had typed most of the notes from his original handwritten versions (which were also included in the Bishop Museum Archives). Still, some of the notes were cryptic and required interpretation or, more frequently, grammatical correction. For example, in a section on beliefs, Macgregor included the following note:

> If a person fell off a tree, they would put a white mat under tree where person fell, and wait for something to fall on mat and this quickly gathered up and rushed to injured person and thus his soul is brought back. Nothing on mat meant man would die.
> 1. if he dies, his soul went / won't return to the spot.
> 2. if he lives never fall again.
> two reasons for using mat.

After editing this note appears on the website as

> If a person fell off a tree, they would put a white mat under the tree where the person fell, and would wait for something to fall on the mat and this would be quickly gathered up and rushed to the injured person and thus his soul is brought back.
> If nothing had fallen on the mat, it meant that the man would die.
> 1. If he dies, his soul went and won't return to the spot.
> 2. If he lives, he would never fall again.
> These are two reasons for using the mat.

In order to facilitate understanding of decontextualized information, I included a column adjacent to Macgregor's notes where I made interpretive comments, translated key Rotuman terms, or added information I thought relevant. Thus the above note is accompanied by a comment stating that this ritual is called *hapagsu* in Rotuman. It appears in the following format:

Category: Beliefs (2)
Topic: Accidents
Consultant: Undisclosed
Macgregor's Notes   *Comments*

If a person fell off a tree, they would put a white mat under the tree where the person fell, and would wait for something to fall on the mat and this would be quickly gathered up and rushed to the injured person and thus his soul is brought back.	This ritual is called *hapagsu*.

If nothing had fallen on the mat, it meant that the man would die.
1. If he dies, his soul went and won't return to the spot.
2. If he lives, he would never fall again.

These are two reasons for using the mat.

Macgregor's transcription of Rotuman words was somewhat erratic, and I took it upon myself to introduce uniformity, consistent with contemporary Rotuman orthography (although because of network browser limitations I was unable to use proper Rotuman diacritics). For instance, he began spelling Malhaha, the name of a district, in the orthodox way, but switched to Malha'a after interviewing a consultant named Tavai from the district. His notes read:

Malha'a is spelled thus and not Malhaha.
    It means sacred place, which is in accordance with the fact that the district is, if not the oldest, the one in which the earliest events took place, and where the earliest migrants landed and where the Hanlepherua made the island from the baskets of earth.

Macgregor's note appears on the web page as written, but is accompanied by the following comments:

Today most Rotumans spell the name of the district "Malhaha," so
we have used this spelling although Macgregor used "Malha'a" in his notes
after talking to Tavai.
Hanlepherua are mythical figures who played an important role in the
story of Rotuma's founding.

In only a few instances did I decide not to reproduce notes, mostly because
they were too cryptic to be interpretable. For example, one note, accompanied by a drawing, consisted of three apparently unrelated words: *Vau*,
armea, chiefly. I have no way of knowing what these referred to (*vau*, a type
of fish or bamboo; *armea*, a type of bird or tree; or '*armea*, a type of fish).

I did not include Macgregor's sketches because they were generally too
crude to scan, and reproducing them would be too time consuming. Texts
accompanying drawings were also omitted if they relied on the drawings for
comprehension.

Finally, Macgregor included some genealogical material in his notes,
although he did not take down genealogies systematically. Where his notes
were clear enough I incorporated them into the website, but in some instances, where they were too cryptic or confusing, I omitted them. Given
the importance of genealogies for Rotumans in litigation over land and
chiefly titles, I was particularly cautious in this regard. Although I believe
that placing genealogical information in context by identifying who provided it minimizes unrealistic claims to exclusive authenticity, I saw no good
reason to post information that required questionable doctoring to make it
intelligible.[4]

In a way, I am pleased that the notes are not reproduced in their complete, unaltered form, since I believe serious scholars making use of the
notes for publication should consult the originals at the Bishop Museum.

The page introducing Macgregor's notes includes an instruction that
states: "Any electronic replication or publication of significant portions of
this material must receive clearance from the Bishop Museum." At the same
time, the material is now available in a comprehensible form for Rotumans
interested in learning more about their ancestors' views about Rotuman
culture.

Other Repatriation Projects

Several other repatriation projects are underway. In October 2000 I
posted on the Rotuma website all the journal articles and book chapters
that Jan Rensel and I have published about Rotuma. To date, that amounts

to thirty-one texts, published between 1961 and 1998. This makes most of our writings about Rotuma available to the global Rotuman community in an accessible form.[5] We intend to post additional texts following their publication.

Another project is to post our registry data (births, deaths, marriages, and divorces, dating from 1903 to 1960) in a form that will allow Rotumans to construct their pedigrees back a number of generations. But perhaps more germane to this volume, I would like to post A. M. Hocart's field notes from his visit to Rotuma in 1913 and my own field notes from 1959 to 1961. Both pose problems of sorts. Hocart's notes are in the form of a continuous stream of transcriptions amounting to over 500 pages of text. Breaking them up into usable segments—a necessity for practical website accessibility—is a daunting prospect.

This problem draws attention to discrepancies between archival, published, and electronic material that is far from trivial. Archival materials retain the form of their original production, whether as cards, notepads, or scraps of paper with scribbles. They may range from a continuous stream of prose, unbroken into units of any kind, to cryptic notes on index cards. Books are printed on pages, divided into chapters, topics, and subtopics. They are also edited for spelling, grammar, and style. Protocol for websites is still evolving. Faster downloading via newer technology (such as cable modems) makes it possible to construct web pages equivalent to several hundred published pages, allowing one to mimic archival material. This is especially the case if the information is presented as pictures rather than as text (essentially as a photograph of the original document).[6] The assumptions one makes regarding how materials will be used is therefore relevant to the way they are presented. The great advantage of electronic publishing is the use of hypertext, which allows users to follow links to related materials and permits searching for specific words or phrases. This makes it tempting to produce documents of limited size or page length, relying on linkages to make connections. Thus a rather different set of contingencies is involved in "editing" materials for electronic media.

My own notes are of a different kind from Hocart's, more inscriptions than transcriptions. Also, I was more interested in the culture of the day than in customs past, so I feel compelled to examine my notes carefully for the possibility that some entries might be offensive or misleading. In this case my elder (hopefully more mature) self would be reinterpreting and monitoring my younger self. At present I am inclined to entertain the possibility of altering, correcting, and omitting some of the notes before posting them.

Who Has Access?

The issue of repatriation inevitably raises the question of who ultimately has access to repatriated materials. If they are put in national archives, they are accessible to a different range of people than if placed in schools—or on a website. So whom do I expect to reach by website postings? Can Rotumans on Rotuma access the Internet? As yet, no, although the technological capability does exist. Last year Rotuma was outfitted with a satellite dish, and a phone system was installed that can accept direct-dial international calls. The current limitations are the excessively high cost of a web service provider and the cost of computers. But it is only a matter of time before these limitations will be overcome. More to the point, however, is that approximately 80 percent of Rotumans now live in urban centers abroad—in Fiji, Australia, New Zealand, Canada, the United States, and Europe. A rapidly increasing number of these people has Internet access, and if reports I have been receiving are accurate, those with access often download materials from the Internet (especially postings on the Rotuman news page) and share them with others in their local communities. I therefore believe that repatriation of materials via the Internet, if not an optimal solution now, will be so in the near future.

In contrast to an archive of hard copies, the Internet allows for inter-activity, so that Rotumans, or other interested parties, can post their own responses, corrections, and opinions to repatriated materials. Their responses then become part of the total record; their voices can be heard. To facilitate this possibility I inaugurated a Rotuman forum—web pages on which individuals can post their own versions of Rotuman history, customs, and cultural dilemmas brought on by change, or address any issue on which they wish to state an opinion. And given the organic nature of information on the Internet (the fact that it can be added to, subtracted from, or changed), the possibility of correcting errors and adding caveats provides an attractive alternative to words cast in concrete (or, more accurately, inscribed on parchment). This is not to imply that one can be frivolous about posting doubtful information, or that webmasters can post information they think might be offensive with the understanding that they can remove or correct it if people respond negatively. As participants in the session leading up to this volume rightfully pointed out, once information is on the Internet, it can be downloaded, copied, and circulated, giving it a life of its own. It might not be possible to undo harm once done. My point, rather, is that factual errors and misspellings can be corrected, alternative views can be added in response to those already made available, and, if discovered, offensive information can be removed to minimize damage.

To Repatriate or Destroy? Notes on the Dilemma of Notes

The discussion at the ASAO session that gave birth to this chapter was the liveliest I have participated in during recent years. The multiplicity of viewpoints represented underscored the complexity of ethical issues surrounding the repatriation of intellectual property. The lesson I drew from this discussion was that no set of abstract principles can be drawn up that will prove satisfactory, and that all ethnographers will have to decide for themselves what, when, and how field notes should repatriated, if at all. Every case is different. In some instances the decision may seem relatively clear-cut. I am reminded here of my decision to destroy all the information my research team and I had collected during a three-year study of a Hawaiian-American community from 1965 to 1968. The nature of the information made this an easy decision at the time. Whereas Macgregor's notes on Rotuma are mostly transcriptions of Rotuman custom, and hence were regarded as public knowledge by the Rotuman people, field data from the Hawaiian-American community were garnered from individuals and families and were explicitly expected to be treated as confidential. They included a great deal of personal data, for instance, answers to personal questions, financial information, reports of conflicts, and questionable activities. There is no way this information could have been made public without causing a great deal of harm, whereas possible benefits would have been small. The only justification I could think of for preserving it was the possibility that another social scientist might be able to use it to test hypotheses I had not considered. But this was a feeble argument compared to the covenant I felt had guided the research: that the personal and familial information people provided would remain confidential.

Field notes of a more general kind were also recorded during the three years of research and were destroyed along with the personal data. I do not rue their loss, however, since I do not think they would have proved an asset to the community we studied. The mandate for the study came from a Hawaiian welfare organization, the Lilioukalani Trust, which was dismayed by a report showing persons of Hawaiian ancestry to be overrepresented on a myriad of negative social indicators, including a high incidence of people living in poverty, of school dropouts, of criminal indictments and incarceration, and of spouse and child abuse. The focus of our research, therefore, was on social problems, and much of the data we collected would have given a very skewed picture of the community were it made public. Instead, prior to any academic publications, we published a book of articles—free of jargon, addressing issues of concern to the community—and presented it to them at a public gathering, so that they would be the first to know our findings (Gallimore and Howard 1968). Our presentation acknowledged the problems while pointing out the many strengths present in the community. This may be regarded as a kind of repatriation, in the form of our general findings along with our interpretation of them. I seriously doubt that turning over our field notes in their raw form would have done anyone in the community comparable, or additional, good.

My own field notes from nearly forty years of fieldwork among the Rotuman people constitute a much more ambiguous array. From 1959 to 1961 I studied Rotumans on Rotuma and on Fiji. I returned with my wife, Jan Rensel, in 1987, 1989, 1990, 1991, 1994, and 1996. Jan did her doctoral research during these return visits while I focused on the changes that occurred since my initial visit. In the course of our fieldwork we have accumulated a significant body of field notes, survey and census data, journal entries, and miscellaneous bits of data. I would like to make much, if not most, of this information available to the broader Rotuman community. However, since our notes are a somewhat ad hoc mix of transcriptions and inscriptions, I do not think it would be appropriate to make the entire corpus available as is.

While, in a certain sense, the subjects of study are the true "owners" of transcriptions, their claims to ownership of inscribed field notes are more problematic. Inscribed field notes bear the stamp of ethnographers to a greater degree, and they may be thought of as having at least as much right over them as the study population. This is not to imply that there is a clear case for all transcribed data being repatriated and all inscribed data being left to the discretion of the ethnographer. Some transcribed data, like malicious gossip or secret knowledge, may be quite harmful if made public. On the other hand, some ethnographers' musings may yield valuable insights into their perspectives and cast light on their interpretations as they appear in publications. One could argue that the subjects of our studies deserve access to our attitudes and biases, and how these evolved over the period of study. In response, one could argue that ethnographers are as deserving of the right to minimize embarrassment as the people they study. Ideally, ethnographers would make repatriation decisions in collaboration with a range of informed consultants, but that is usually impractical.

The practical solution is to screen the material for information that would be of value to the community, leaving out ruminations and gossip that might prove embarrassing to anyone, including the ethnographers themselves. After all, fieldwork is a process of discovery in which one's early impressions are often erroneous and misleading. Such ruminations, like personal diaries, were never meant to be made public. Just because something is written down does not require it to be treated as precious archival material. Portions of our field notes are often nothing more than mnemonic devices to help us remember "headnotes" that guide our research.[7] Sifting through the mounds of material we have accumulated will require a major undertaking, one we likely will not get to for several years.

The Final Say: Who Should Decide?

I would like to conclude by addressing the issue of who ought to have the final say about the disposition of ethnographic field notes. In their eagerness to appear sensitive to the "native peoples" we study, some scholars have urged that ethnographers yield all decision-making powers concerning intellectual property over to the people themselves. While this is an admirable principle in theory, I believe that adhering to it mindlessly could do far more harm than good (a point also made by Bryan Oles, chapter 10).

First of all, judgments must be made as to whose intellectual property is whose when it comes to field notes. Does the mere fact that I wrote something down in a particular village make it the villagers' property? Suppose I included jottings about my family back home or idle reminiscences of my childhood. Who has rights to them? It is certainly not obvious to me that the villagers do. On the other hand, transcriptions of customs, rituals, and other aspects of local culture would surely seem to be the intellectual property of the people under investigation.

Second, anthropologists are prone at times to assume a uniformity of opinion among the people they study that is unwarranted. It is rare indeed that people anywhere agree about what should be done with intellectual property, who should have rights of access, and when and under what conditions it should be made available. My point is that no abstract principle, or set of principles, can substitute for a decision informed by thorough knowledge of a particular instance. I would argue that ethnographers themselves, assuming they make a sincere effort to gather and assess all relevant details and to consult with as many of the affected individuals as possible, are in the best position to judge which of their materials should be made public (or repatriated, as the case may be), when they should be turned over, and where and in what form they should be stored. This is a responsibility each ethnographer must bear, lest we leave the dilemmas to archivists and librarians much less familiar with the relevant cultures and contexts and lacking the necessary knowledge to make informed judgments (see chapter 4). The latter will be forced to make judgments on the basis of ad hoc rules or abstract principles. My hope is rather that judgments will be based on well-informed assessments of the consequences of alternative actions.

Having offered these caveats, I would like to come down clearly on the side of repatriating materials whenever possible, even though some risks may be involved. In part this is the result of a political bias toward egalitarianism. Restrictions on information tend to serve hierarchy and differential power relations, whereas free access tends to promote egalitarian relations. Restricted access serves the status quo, while free access serves to foster competition and render social systems dynamic and subject to change.

It may well be that indigenous voices are raised in opposition to making information public, as in the case of the Mokilese (Oles, chapter 10). But Karen Peacock (chapter 7) illustrates the importance of taking steps to preserve important historical documents, even in the face of active opposition. While present generations may have little concern for historical records apart from their current political or personal implications, future generations will likely praise our efforts. I believe cultures follow a developmental trajectory with regard to their sense of history. In parochial island settings history is generally a family, lineage, or village matter, with little concern for the history of the broader linguistic or cultural group (stage 1). As group consciousness emerges and culture gets objectified as a result of outside experience and formal education,[8] an awareness of history develops, but initial concerns often focus on improving the present and looking forward (stage 2). It is the separation of people from their cultural roots, either spatially or temporally, that gives real impetus to a concern for societal and cultural history (stage 3).

Repatriation of historical materials in the first stage is likely to be of minimal interest to the people whose forebears produced the history; in the second stage they may prove embarrassing and disturbing (as in the case of the Mokilese). At the very least responses during this stage are apt to be mixed. But in the third stage I believe people universally cherish such historical documentation, and we must keep in mind that all the peoples we study will get to this third stage, and quite soon.

In some instances we need to go beyond merely making information that has been hidden from public view in archives or obscure publications available. Amy Stillman (chapter 8) makes an important distinction between repatriation and deinstitutionalization. Repatriation refers to making information accessible, while deinstitutionalization involves reintegrating knowledge, often knowledge that had been "lost" or rendered inaccessible, back into the active stream of social, artistic, and political life. For such knowledge—and artistic knowledge comes readily to mind, but is not the only example—it is desirable to go beyond repatriation to deinstitutionalization. This requires advocacy and activism on someone's part, preferably by members of the communities affected. In addition to activism in institutionalized political arenas, the Internet may provide opportunities for reintegration of lost information into a community's mainstream.

I came away from our conference sessions thinking in terms of an equation that one might process in determining the fate of hitherto inaccessible information. The main consideration involves balancing probable benefits against probable harm that might result from repatriation. This is not quite so simple, of course, as soon as one adds the complexities of time and place. And, of course, there is the matter of good for whom and harm to whom. How much should consideration for others, beyond the immediate community, enter into the equation (humanity at large, overseas émigrés, part-ethnics, educated indigenes versus uneducated, researchers themselves)? There are no easy answers, but these are issues we must take into consideration.

For any given body of data one can identify a number of variables that will affect the equation:

1. Relevant units implicated by the field notes.	Individuals, families, lineages or villages, societies or nations. In general, the broader the social unit implicated the less likely information is to be harmful to individuals.
2. The extent to which accounts are monolithic (suggesting a singular coherent social reality) or heteroglossic (projecting a contested, multifaceted, social reality).	In general, heteroglossic accounts permit people a more active role in interpreting the material and a better possibility for defending their interests.
3. The degree to which the information is inscriptive or transcriptive.	Transcriptive information, especially in the form of verbatim texts from identifiable consultants, is prime material for repatriation, since it amounts to a transcription of knowledge already available (to at least some individuals). Inscriptive notes may include initial impressions, offhand value judgments, or other commentary not meant

	for public viewing and needs to be evaluated accordingly. However, each type of information needs to be assessed for potential harm or benefit.
4. The expressed wishes of the community (including the original providers of information and their descendants).	Here it is important to keep in mind that views are likely to be mixed. We should do the best we can to assess the full range of opinions, past and present, before we arrive at an assessment.
5. The original disposition of the information: whether it is regarded as secret, belonging to specific individuals or groups, or as public knowledge.	In general, secret knowledge needs to be hedged with more safeguards and requires a continuous process of negotiation with its owners (if possible) regarding its disposition.
6. Applicable laws.	These include copyright and repatriation laws that might have a bearing, as documented by Nancy Guy and Mary McCutcheon (chapters 11 and 4 respectively).
7. The stage of a people's historical consciousness.	For some people (Mokilese, as described by Oles) the written word is authoritative; for others (Hawaiians) historical consciousness has developed to the point where outsider accounts are contested with accounts of their own, drawn from a broader array of sources than used by outsiders. In general, the more developed a people's historical consciousness the stronger the case for repatriating materials.
8. Our own independent assessment of the consequences of repatriating our ethnographic materials to specific individuals, institutions, or the public.	Who, in our view, is likely to benefit. Who might it harm?

I expect that as we plug into our equations the above variables, and more depending on particular contexts, we will find that in some instances the decision is fairly straightforward to repatriate or to withhold; in other instances (which likely will turn out to be the majority) there will be good deal of ambiguity—offsetting pros and cons—requiring us to make difficult decisions and to take responsibility for them.

Overall, I want to argue for anthropologists, archivists, and other scholars taking an active role in preservation and repatriation, while remaining sensitive to resistance and objections from the people they study. Indigenous responses to repatriation must be taken into account as part of the equation, but they should not necessarily be decisive. It may well be the case that this view amounts to the imposition of Western values on peoples who may not share them (at present). However, I have no problem with that if it will result in the preservation of materials that will allow future generations of Pacific Islanders to reflect on their pasts, employing a greater depth of information than they might otherwise contemplate. Let us trust them to sort things out for themselves, but make sure they have the materials to do a thorough job of it (but compare Oles, chapter 10, page 192).

At the same time, we should have the confidence to destroy records that are clearly likely to cause distress if disclosed with little likelihood of doing good. We should not treat everything written down, taped, or filmed as sacred. Some records were meant to be ephemeral, others have the potential to do much harm. Let us take the time to sift through our ethnographic records and sort the wheat from the chaff before leaving our legacies to archives, museums, or other repositories.

Sjoerd R. Jaarsma

3

Wish, Need, and Dilemma

Cultural research by First Worlders in a Third World region like the Pacific is always susceptible to accusations of exploitation or paternalism, and likely to be regarded as parasitic on the oral tradition which supplies so much of its data. Its reputation is not improved by publications which pursue academic agenda more or less unintelligible to most ordinary Islanders, sold at prices they cannot afford to pay, and these are poor defence against charges of profiting from their culture by rural people, or of academic imperialism by their educated compatriots.

BEN BURT

"Writing Local History in Solomon Islands"

Anthropology is in origin a creature of colonial times, which explains in part the accusations by Burt. Yet, it has changed considerably as a result of decolonization and subsequent globalization. This is true not only of anthropology narrowly defined as the academic discourse dealing with the analysis of ethnographic data, but also of the entire process of gathering data, "translating" these into formats we expect our audience to appreciate and disseminating the results for further consumption. The concept of ethnography invokes academic discourse. It invokes the relations between the researchers and the people they study, between audiences interested in the documents and knowledge produced, and even between settings of research and cultural policies defining what is to be researched and where.

Anthropological research no longer takes place with clearly defined power relations. The situation in which the people studied were a silent third party, denied responsibility for their own role, is history. Studying other cultures is no longer routine. It involves negotiation either with the people we want to study themselves or with persons and institutions acting for them, ranging from local authorities to advocates. In the past the people we studied lacked the ability to read, and even if our ethnographic statements found their way back to the field, these could at most be a piece of (possibly revered) junk. Literacy adds a new dimension, as the content of the ethnography becomes available. Information now flows back from us as the ethnographers to the people we study, either directly as a courtesy to the informants we worked with, or indirectly as a potential audience. Yet full comprehension of what we say by the people studied will depend on whom we write for, on the perceived level of sophistication of our intended audience.[1]

The people we study these days are more likely than not emancipated enough to require a say in why and how they are being studied. Increasingly, we are asked to bring back our books upon our return. Anthropologists may have heard similar remarks in the past, but the question might increasingly face us with ethical problems as the people studied may want to read the books written. This development is mirrored on an academic level. We, academic anthropologists,[2] as ethnographers are becoming aware that we cannot freeze the people we study in time, arbitrarily isolating them from the larger societal context. We cannot deny them voice and at the same time describe them as breathing, acting, thinking human beings (Jaarsma 1998; Rohatynskyj and Jaarsma 2000). The combination of emancipation of the people we study and our own reflexive tendencies creates a new situation, both in the field itself and in mediating the results of fieldwork. It is in this field of tensions that the question of the return of field materials, and the ethical considerations of access to this material, should be located.

This question has several dimensions, not only because it relates to considerations on very different levels—ranging from academic ethics to cultural politics—but also because it is in some respects firmly rooted in the past. First, we need to consider why we are sitting atop a heap of possibly sensitive information we now, all of a sudden, think should be returned. These are questions relating to past practices and present attitudes. Second, different audiences address or make use of the ethnographic product. The increasing rise of cultural politics and policies in the Pacific should be taken into consideration here. Third, a set of questions relates "simply" to the what, who, and when of repatriation. Here, we need to keep in mind that the return of ethnographic data and knowledge provides opportunity for more investigation, giving rise to further ethical considerations. Also, we need to consider the wisdom of acting ourselves. Should we take the initiative in these matters, or comply when a demand for repatriation arises, similar to the call for control over indigenous material culture presently residing in Western ethnographic museums? I will end with a discussion of the main ethical issues involved in which I will bring together what I have said on the wish, the need, and the dilemma that frame the repatriation of ethnography.

The Ethics of Access

In returning knowledge and data to their original locations,[3] we may be dealing with sensitive or "secret" issues.[4] Any culture consists of publicly available materials and resources that are privately "owned." We can speak of these cultural resources in terms of secrets, as they are often wholly or partially hidden from certain categories of people (women, children, the uninitiated, and so forth), but following Lamont Lindstrom (1994, 68–69), it is better to consider them copyrighted: "In many Melanesian communities strong systems of copyrights, or patents, protect a person's, or a family's, ownership of these sorts of cultural resources. The members of different lineages, for example, typically control the right to recount their own genealogies in public. Productive and artifactual technologies are also commonly copyrighted. . . . Only those people who possess a copyright can talk publicly with legitimacy about the knowledge in question. Copyrights, as property, are inheritable. . . . In many Melanesian societies, these rights can also be exchanged or sold."[5] As Lindstrom indicates, the knowledge involved can be known to everyone and as such is not a secret in the narrow sense of the word. But people "may not use, augment, reveal, or discuss publicly this patented knowledge without encountering reaction and opposition" (1994, 69).

The transfer of rights may depend on context, but the copyrighting of cultural resources is a very real issue in present-day postcolonial society, so much so that it may almost resemble the Western—legal—concept instead of the moral concept used here. The use of mud masks by the Asaro of Papua New Guinea provide them with a distinct identity, not only on a local level (Komunive), but also on a national one. The original "invention" dates back to the Eastern Highlands Agricultural Show in Goroka (1957) and led to a gradually developing success story with an increasing demand for "mud men performances." Ton Otto and Robert Verloop show that we are dealing with a fairly recent innovation that owes much to the trade of intellectual property in the area (1996, 356–60). They point out that the development of these performances was "the unplanned result of numerous interactions," and in that light the performances should be considered "an intercultural phenomenon" (1996, 359–60). Nevertheless, Ruipo Okoroho, the big man of Komunive and the "chairman" of the Asaro Mudmen, has initiated and won his fair share of court cases to establish the exclusive rights for the mud mask performance and its related ritual (1996, 361–62). While Otto and Verloop only evaluate a process that has run its course largely on its own steam, they end their article on a pensive and self-reflexive note (377, note 30), drawing on an increasing (and globalized) access to ethnographic information: "It is not unthinkable that our article will play a role in local conflicts about cultural property rights. Of course we do not hope this will happen. We have tried to avoid including information that may be sensitive and have restricted ourselves to those data we consider to be general knowledge in the area."

In the same sense they refer to Michael O'Hanlon's book *Reading the Skin* (1989) that was interpreted by the Wahgi as establishing their cultural copyrights, probably without O'Hanlon intending to do so. There are two issues acknowledged here that are of ethical importance, not only for ethnographic statements at large but also for efforts at repatriation. First, anything can these days become part of indigenous discourses on culture when it becomes accessible. Such discourses will not necessarily take what we write to be of the same relative value as we have meant it to be in the context of an academic anthropological discourse. They may very well be taken as data for a discourse on cultural politics. Second, there is the basic dilemma of whether we should provide access to knowledge that is not publicly available already.

The latter dilemma exists because we have been given access ourselves to such knowledge. In fact, we might be said to have a surfeit of such information, as we habitually access knowledge across different age groups and, these days, genders. Much information is actually publicly available, but may not be freely used or distributed. While we may be restricted in its use locally, nothing stands in our way when we wish to include indigenous knowledge in our ethnographies.[6] Beyond that there is a gray area where we as researchers need permission and cooperation to gather information. There are different ways to achieve results here. We can use different factions within the one group or compare closely related groups. Alternatively, the issue can be forced. Reo Fortune, for instance, on occasion put pressure on his Dobuan informants to elicit information:[7]

> I had a long and wearisome wait amongst openly glaring and hostile
> mourners in a long match of patience against patience before the secret
> emerged. It took the better part of a day and the early evening. I may add

> that this is not my preferred method, but I had only a month to spend in
> Basima, a time insufficient to create confidence in myself from everyone.
> (1932, 282)

> I got the family of the sick man alone, used cajolery, and I mingled with
> the cajolery some vague threats of Government and Mission getting *them*
> for sorcery if they would disclose nothing. My time was short in their
> place and I had to resort to rough and ready methods. (1932, 160; em-
> phasis in original)

In colonial days this was a relatively easy practice and probably a fairly
common one. These days the power balance in the field is more equal, and,
more and more, information is gained as the result of slowly gained trust.
For instance, it is not unusual anymore for anthropologists (both male and
female) to go through (parts of) the local initiation ritual to gain access to
(and implicitly ownership of) its knowledge.

This shift in relations developing as the result of fieldwork indicates that
the dilemma goes beyond gaining access. Frequently, the nature of our
access is subject to (local) scrutiny and consideration. Long-term fieldwork
or repeated short-term visits will be more likely to engender the level of
"trust" where copyrighted information is shared between researcher and
researched. Rapport is not only essential for the nature of the data found in
the field, but also for the receipt of repatriated knowledge and data. When
rapport between the ethnographers and the people they study is lacking
during fieldwork, the data that will eventually be repatriated may very well
be distrusted (see Bryan Oles, chapter 10).[8]

One of the first limitations on ethnographic description to be overcome
is the inability of the people studied to comprehend the process of being
studied, analyzed, and described (Jaarsma 2001). The community the ethnographer studied increasingly appreciates the nature of questioning and
the aim—if not necessarily the purpose—of ethnographic description. The
ethnographer participating in rituals, going through initiation, and entering
into a pupil-teacher relationship with a knowledgeable informant accesses
information in a depth and detail previously deemed impossible. Accompanying this increase in rapport and trust, ethnographers are increasingly
aware of their responsibilities to make their information part of publicly
accessible knowledge, as Mary MacDonald's case shows:

> In my research among the Kewa my informants were always people I had
> known since I first went to the area in 1973 or people who were related to

them. . . . One of my principal informants was Tomas Soi, a traditional healer who had become a Catholic. Soi, who died in 1986, could neither read nor write himself. . . . He had been a leader of a cult called *keveta pamo* (stone woman), which, in fact, was still active in Mararoko in the early 1980s, although he was no longer involved with it. Soi supplied me with information about the cult but asked that I keep the information to myself. Some of his information overlaps with that of other informants who placed no restriction on retelling it. Soi, who took a fatherly interest in my welfare, said that he gave me the information about *keveta pamo* because we had talked together about healing and he, therefore, wanted me to know about the role of the *keveta pamo* cult in ensuring the well-being of the community. However, Soi did not want me to disclose his information to the women, with whom I tended to spend a lot of time, and who traditionally were excluded from participation in the cult, or to other missionaries. I, of course, agreed to his restrictions. Since I did not ask whether I might tell his stories after his death, I still have a "Soi, restricted" folder among my South Kewa files.

. . . Knowingly, or unknowingly, Soi imposed two responsibilities on me. One concerns how to treat the information he provided on *keveta pamo*. To date when I have written about the cult I have used material from others and have refrained from using what he provided. The other responsibility is to take time to write more fully about Soi's healing practices. Lest I fail in the latter task I have left copies of notes of interviews with Soi in the Southern Highlands Archives and in the archives of the Melanesian Institute. However, I have not felt free to include the *keveta pamo* material. (MacDonald 2000, 163–64)

MacDonald, working at the time for the mission, was allowed access to information on an individual basis. Normally this knowledge would have been barred to her on grounds of both gender and occupation. Now, she allows us access only to the knowledge of the existence of this information, not to its contents. As such, she indicates both the nature and the extent of the dilemma that faces any attempt at repatriation of anthropological knowledge.

Anthropologists are no longer just gatherers and analysts of information about other cultures. Both the changed nature of the relationships in the field that no longer allow for the gathering of information based on the use of power and the increase of ethical consciousness among anthropologists themselves (Jaarsma 1998) have changed the appreciation that anthropologists have of their own knowledge.[9] They have become caretakers to some extent. While this is on the one hand basic to the dilemma facing repatriation, it is on the other hand also the reason why the need to repatriate ethnographic information is felt: it is no longer totally and unconditionally "our" property.

Knowledge and Audience

Repatriation does not take place in a vacuum. As indicated, both the field and fieldwork have changed, and, moreover, anthropology as a discipline has changed. Its institutional setting has become overwhelmingly academic since the 1960s, something that affects both its internal discourse and the way it relates to the outside world (Jaarsma 1998; Rohatynskyj and Jaarsma 2000). These changes that reflect processes of decolonization and globalization (Friedman 2000) may result in contradictory effects. Our attempts to create an identity for ourselves as an academic discipline on our own terms increasingly act as barriers toward our surroundings, professionally and nonprofessionally. Tendencies to aim anthropological discourse exclusively at anthropologists, inadvertently creating an ivory tower for ourselves, run counter to the effects of a more equal power base in the field and a more ethical appraisal of fieldwork and field materials.

We can appreciate the failure of such an exclusive focus on ourselves in the changing relationship with our audiences. Intentionally or not, we relate not only to larger audiences these days, but also to more diverse ones. Increasingly, we deal with more emancipated audiences that make demands as to what they are told about the people studied by the ethnographer. The diversity of our audiences can be seen to evolve in two main directions. On the one hand, we have gained a larger and more complex Western audience beyond our own discipline. An awareness of the nature of this audience will be a main asset to further evolve our identity as a discipline. As Dorothy and David Counts (chapter 1) suggest, addressing an audience can also become a factor of survival for the anthropologist-ethnographer.[10] We have long ignored the nature of our audience, something we can no longer afford to do. The use of new media also realizes new audiences, as Alan Howard (chapter 2) indicates, not only in the First World, but in the Third and Fourth World as well. The use of the Internet as a medium itself poses dilemmas of access, as it is hard to delimit access to private areas without also inhibiting the ease of use of public areas.

The changed use that is made of "culture" in the new nations of the Pacific adds to the different appreciations of ethnographic knowledge. This is a gradual process that started out—as Ron Crocombe indicates—as an anti-colonialist move: "In the years leading up to independence, many aspiring political leaders tried to redefine their culture as the antithesis of colonial culture. In this context, culture was often used to denote privacy, exclusiveness, and protection from external interference. The implication was that only biological members of the indigenous society could (or ought to) understand—whether they did or not. . . . The more important issue was power and once that was achieved, the emphasis on culture declined" (1994b, 24). While Crocombe is probably right in indicating that this "decolonizing" attention to culture was largely opportunistic, it is also true that it triggered the link between culture and identity on a previously unknown, national scale. This link still pervades the discourse on Pacific culture (see Linnekin and Poyer 1990). It drew in new audiences with their own agendas concerning Pacific culture. These agendas range from the recovery of indigenous rights by individual groups to the realization of purely commercial interests, such as the development of eco- and cultural tourism. In all of this, (knowledge about) culture plays a decisive role. Such knowledge—even for some indigenous groups—could be more easily and productively accessed through the products of academic discourse. As indicated again by Crocombe (1994b, 27) this second stage of interest in cultural issues most strongly developed outside the newly decolonized nation states:

> Probably the greatest effort in relation to cultural policies is in the countries where the indigenous people do not have independence. The expenditure on cultural matters per head of population is highest in Hawai'i, New Zealand, New Caledonia, and Easter Island. This is partly because the programs are largely financed by the central (predominantly non-indigenous) governments or other national resources, and per capita incomes are high, allowing funds to be used for these purposes. Partly it is a protective reaction by minorities working to assert their distinctiveness in situations in which they feel threatened, pressured, or marginalized. They also are in contexts where there is much more scope to earn a living from marketing aspects of creative expression to the nonindigenous population and to tourists in the form of song, dance, weaving, carving, art, teaching, adventure touring, and other income sources.[11]

Here, in fact, we see the first issues of "repatriation" arising, albeit focused first on material culture and readily recognizable cultural icons. An interesting example in this respect is the public debate occasioned by the preparations for the "Te Maori" exhibition that toured four major United States museums in the early 1980s. Adrienne Kaeppler (1996, 28) notes that "As a result of the 'Te Maori' buildup, the Maori leadership was, for the first time in the current generation, being asked to focus on the Maori content of museums. Also, for the first time, this leadership was having to confront the measure to which a major element of its cultural heritage was being interpreted and articulated—spoken for—by people who had little or no *mana*, or authority, in Maori terms." Nowadays indigenous rights of ownership of culture extend on occasion to ethnographic documents on specific Maori groups, resulting in attempts to influence their publication and contents (see van Meijl 2000).

A second aspect that Crocombe touches upon is the gradual commodification of culture. Indigenous culture as an item that can be sold is no longer limited to material culture, but is increasingly in demand as "entertainment" on a growing tourist market (Stanley 1998). The exploitation of the mud mask ritual described earlier is certainly not the only example in this respect. For that matter, ritual becomes subject to not only cultural, but also general economic policy development.

> National leaders often advocate economic development alongside the preservation of Melanesian custom and tradition. These two goals, on the face of it, might be seen as contradictory: preservation presumes cultural continuity; development and promotion demand change. But this contradiction is only apparent. A decision to preserve a custom necessarily transforms that custom, insofar as this now takes on new meanings and purposes as something valued that must be conspicuously appreciated and preserved. The effort to develop, promote, or enrich custom preserves certain cultural elements at the same time as it transforms others, in that change must build on what already exists within a people's cultural repertoires—whether this is old tradition or present-day custom. (Lindstrom and White 1994a, 17)

Requests for repatriation will have little or nothing in common with our own academic agendas. The indigenous agenda may run to laying claim on and copyrighting of cultural knowledge that may be of commercial value. Ethically, that is of an entirely different order. Each request or initiative for repatriation should then be placed in context and judged for possible consequences on a case-by-case basis. In that respect it would be advisable to develop some kind of impact analysis.

Repatriating Data

The basic question then is about means and motives for repatriation. I quoted a warning that "cultural research . . . is always susceptible to accusations of exploitation or paternalism" (Burt 1998, 97). Repatriating our field data does not resolve this issue. It might even place us in a double bind. We can be judged in these or very similar terms whether we return our data or not. Oles (chapter 10, page 193–194) clearly warns us of the dangers involved in the possible repatriation of anthropological studies to the island of Mokil. His final words leave little to the imagination: "The lessons to be learned from Mokil are that repatriated data are not necessarily welcome, and that the proper meaning and place of the data will be assigned in light of the local epistemological and social demands, regardless of the anthropologist's intentions. Therefore, I suggest that we view repatriated data not as a 'gift' based upon a Western moral imperative, but as an offering to the societies we study to be used, discarded, hallowed, or decried in accordance with local understandings and needs."

It goes without saying that we should cause no damage by returning our data. Just now, I signaled the need for an impact analysis. While this needs to be done on a case-by-case basis, some general points can be made here. These mirror to some extent the variables that Alan Howard set out earlier for his equation determining the fate of "hitherto inaccessible information" (chapter 2). My considerations, based on what was said before, fall into three categories: (1) what do we repatriate, (2) whom do we repatriate to, and (3) when do we take action. These questions, while not exhaustive, are basic to any setup of an impact analysis.

Both the questions of "what to repatriate" and "whom to repatriate to" involve aspects of ownership of the data and knowledge in question. The difference involves whose ownership or copyright we are speaking of. What we as anthropologists can repatriate divides into two parts. First, there is the data we originally collected, our field notes, audiotapes, films, and videos we made while in the field. Second, there is the interpretation of this material, the anthropological knowledge we produced based on the information we gathered. Here, Howard (chapter 2) makes good use of James Clifford's distinction (1990, 57) between transcribed and inscribed data. This has been laid down in ethnographic texts and other media we produced both for anthropological and general audiences. If we look at ownership in this respect, we should consider the transcribed data to be still owned by our informants. As indicated earlier, we are only acting as caretakers here.[12] The ownership of the inscribed material is another matter.[13] It certainly can be considered our intellectual property, whatever it may be based upon. Containing added value, it is a different product from its component parts. The result then is ambiguous, as it is nearly impossible to indicate a clear break between original material and interpretation on every occasion. The people we study and we ourselves both have valid claims on the ethnographic products and the data they are based upon (see Mary McCutcheon, chapter 4). It is an interesting paradox then that most anthropologists feel very few qualms about distributing their ethnographic publications, but are very protective of the data they originally gathered (Jackson 1990).

The question of who owns the original material becomes important when we actually return the data. The material should be returned to the original owners, the holders of the copyrights, or their heirs, if such rights can (and were) established. The problem here is the passage of time. Can we still identify these people or the heirs in question? If so, are they still in a position to enforce the copyright? Suppose the owner of a piece of religious knowledge converts at some stage to Christianity (see David Akin and Kathryn Creely, chapter 5). Will he or she (or his or her heirs for that matter) still be interested in holding the copyright on the notes we made on this religious knowledge? The example of the mud masks quoted earlier confirms the importance of the documented nature of the copyright. Similar aspects are touched upon by participants to this volume (the Chambers, chapter 9; Nancy Guy, chapter 11). The dangers of repatriating data when ownership has become meaningless are pointed out by Oles (chapter 10; compare Suzanne Falgout, chapter 6).

In actual practice we will probably be repatriating material to an institution set up for this or similar purposes.[14] Roger Keesing, for instance, indicated the need for "the creation of a small center, ideally in Solomon Islands College of Higher Education, . . . but perhaps jointly administered with the USP [University of the South Pacific] Centre, where materials such as [his] Kwaio tapes . . . and genealogies, and those gathered through the years by other researchers, can safely be lodged and used by young indigenous scholars studying their own cultural traditions" (1994, 194). The question of ownership then turns into that of controlling access. We need to determine what becomes publicly available and what remains in one way or another part of a private domain (Akin and Creely, chapter 5). The means by which such privacy can be attained are, of course, dependent on the local situation. We, together with the institution, and—if possible—the original owner(s) will have to determine to whom, why, where, and when access will be granted (see McCutcheon, chapter 4; Howard, chapter 2).

To return to the ambiguity I noted for anthropological ownership, we need to be aware that what we return as ethnographic data is not what the ethnographer originally saw. Even in the case of anthropologists' notes, we talk in terms of interpretation. Anthropologists cannot step out of their shadows to become absolutely objective. However, in the notes we will find less interpretation than in the later ethnographic documents. When the Tikopia quote to a newly arrived anthropologist Firth's writings on Tikopean culture, they can only reify Firth's interpretation further.[15] Yet in quoting Firth, they confirm their copyright on what is originally theirs in terms they consider comprehensible to us. Questioning their motives for using Firth's ethnographic material should not be an issue of debate; it should be an issue for further study.

The final question of when we should repatriate is probably the most difficult to get a grip on. There is as yet little experience with this phenomenon (see Howard, chapter 2; Akin and Creely, chapter 5). We should distinguish two possible scenarios for repatriation: (1) we act on a request from within the field or from representatives of the people we studied; (2) we initiate repatriation ourselves. Setting aside the ethical implications for the moment, the difference between the two lies in the background against which the demand for repatriation is made. In the first instance a demand for repatriation is present locally. In the second instance a demand for the repatriated goods will first have to be generated. Without such a demand repatriation would perhaps serve to absolve our ruminations about sitting on top of a heap of information that does not belong to us, but it serves little purpose otherwise. We should be acting on more than just our own moral imperative, as Oles notes. In either case an impact analysis will have to determine the possible risks involved, focusing this time specifically on the motives of the actors involved. A demand for the repatriation of anthropological knowledge and ethnographic information need not be limited to the owners of the original information. It can similarly be requested by larger factions within the society or by advocates acting in their interests. A third category that can initiate a demand "from the field" consists of local educational centers, museums, and government departments dealing with cultural policy. Any of these institutions can serve as depositories of traditional information.[16]

Throughout this section I have indicated an impact analysis as a possible way to flag various effects and problems of repatriating ethnographic data. But this analysis should be seen as an integral part of the process and not as an afterthought. Here the will, the need, and the dilemma of returning ethnographic materials come together. Repatriation itself occasions a research opportunity in its own right, and the impact analysis can be masked this way or even double as such. The return of data will—whether properly effected or not—cause reactions that are conceivably a worthwhile subject for study. In this respect it may provide sufficient grounds for Western academic institutions and research sponsors to support the process. Equally, the impact analysis can be used as a means to create a demand for the actual process of repatriation. While I indicated that the purpose of repatriation would be defeated when no local demand was first generated, it should be said that initiating repatriation of our own accord creates an ethical issue. Using an impact analysis to effect a local demand for repatriation poses an even bigger ethical problem, as we border on inflicting harm on the people we study. While there can be few reasons for making this kind of decision, it should certainly not be taken lightly, as the possibility for abuse is high.[17]

Repatriation Ethics

What then are the main ethical issues involved? First, any ethics we work with will of course be ours. We can perhaps surmise the ethics by which the people we study (have studied) decide they wish our anthropological knowledge and ethnographic data returned, but in the end we will respect their wishes according to our own ethics.

When we look at the recently approved "Code of Ethics" of the American Anthropological Association (1998),[18] it stresses a few very relevant points when describing the responsibility of researchers to the people they study (AAA 1998, 3.A.2–4, 6):

> 2. Anthropological researchers must do everything in their power to ensure that their research does not harm the safety, dignity, or privacy of the people with whom they work, conduct research, or perform other professional activities. . . .
> 3. Anthropological researchers must determine in advance whether their hosts / providers of information wish to remain anonymous or receive recognition, and make every effort to comply with these wishes. Researchers must present to their research participants the possible impacts of the choices, and make clear that despite their best efforts, anonymity may be compromised or recognition fail to materialize.
> 4. Anthropological researchers should obtain in advance the informed consent of persons being studied, providing information, owning or controlling access to material being studied, or otherwise as having interests which might be impacted by the research. . . .

6. While anthropologists may gain personally from their work, they must not exploit individual, groups, . . . or cultural . . . materials. They should recognize their debt to the societies in which they work and their obligation to reciprocate with people studied in appropriate ways.

To be added to this are the responsibilities to scholarship and science—specifically our own discipline—of which the relevant phrases here are (AAA 1998, 3.B.3, 5):

3. Anthropological researchers should do all they can to preserve opportunities for future fieldworkers to follow them to the field.
5. Anthropological researchers should seriously consider all reasonable requests for access to their data and other research materials for purposes of research. They should also make every effort to insure preservation of their fieldwork data for use by posterity.

Finally there is the responsibility to the public at large (AAA 1998, 3.C.1–2):

1. Anthropological researchers should make the results of their research appropriately available to sponsors, students, decision makers, and other nonanthropologists. In so doing they must be truthful; they are not only responsible for the factual content of their statements but also must consider carefully the social and political implications of the information they disseminate. . . .
2. Anthropologists may choose to move beyond disseminating research results to a position of advocacy. This is an individual decision, but not an ethical responsibility.

I have quoted the "Code of Ethics" in some detail here to show that it covers a lot of eventualities, even without mentioning the practice of repatriation. What differences there are do not outweigh the common denominators.

The essential ethical difficulties do not arise from the way we deal with people during the act of repatriation or from considering the provisions of care for what we are repatriating, but from *what* we are returning. The nature of what we return as well as the social context to which we return it have changed. We no longer return the oral tradition that we originally registered. We did not set out to buy our information over the counter in the local tourist shop, but what we are returning can easily be distributed through such a counter (and sometimes is). We return written material, films, and videos. Earlier on I referred to Michael O'Hanlon's book as an example of what can happen in this respect. Deborah Gewertz and Frederick Errington confront a very similar question when they comment upon the possibility of a dialogue approach to ethnography among the Chambri, whereby the "local people should at least be co-creators of the ethnographic text":

> Simply put, we cannot imagine Chambri reaching agreement on what such a text should contain. As will be evident, particularly in our discussion of literacy, . . . Chambri regarded their anthropologists as resources to be employed in local competition. Whose voice and hence whose partisan perspective became inscribed in written form was a matter of serious contention among Chambri. (It followed that contention among the Chambri became a potential source of resentment against us, the inscribers.) Nor can we imagine that such accounts, filled as they were with ancestral names and precedents, would in themselves have much intelligibility or significance for a Western audience, that audience that has the greatest power to affect Chambri lives. (1991, 19)

Imagine what the effect would be of repatriating ethnographic notes into this situation. However, between Keesing's conception of material on the Kwaio "used by young indigenous scholars studying their own cultural traditions" (1994, 194) and this potential field of contention among the Chambri there is a large gray zone where each situation needs to be studied carefully for its possible effects. As a matter of fact, Akin and Creely (chapter 5) show the Kwaio to be situated square within this gray zone with a considerable potential for abuse.

Problems and Pitfalls

Of course, we will not just be returning the original material. We implicitly return our Western interpretation, and this may add different dimensions to the material. Anthropological interpretation these days no longer stops at the village border. There is no longer just a holistic interpretation of what we found locally. Considerations of change are taken into account, larger infrastructures described. Again, I can profitably refer to Gewertz and Errington as they point out the limits of Chambri appreciation:

> There was much the Chambri did not yet understand about the world system. They did not fully recognize, for example, that this system was premised on such institutionalized inequalities as class and on the perpetuation

of underdevelopment. Although they did recognize that choice and the system in which choice was made both affected and reflected relations of power, they did not fully realize that, whereas they had some influence on their regional system, they would have virtually none on the world system. Yet, they were not entirely hapless. While the survival of their village economy might, indeed, serve to underwrite national and international capitalism (by absorbing many of the costs involved in reproducing the labor force), nonetheless, as the Chambri themselves knew, so long as the home environment was in working order, they would not be completely at the mercy of a precarious cash economy in a "developing" country. Stated in another way, they would not be hapless so long as they were successful in their efforts to maintain their subsistence economy, that most essential basis of autonomy. (1991, 14)

With our interpretation we are introducing vistas that do not necessarily have either meaning or reality as yet for the people we study.[19] Will the knowledge that they are underdeveloped affect the way people function economically now? It may or it may not, but it is worth giving some thought to these considerations. Previously I referred to the impression Firth's writings made on the Tikopia. The consideration might be extreme, but has the access to this anthropological knowledge frozen Tikopian culture in its tracks?

We also need to consider the passage of time. With time, culture will change, especially where it is under pressure from powerful economic and religious infrastructures to conform. This means that unless return of ethnographic materials takes place soon after the end of fieldwork or as an integral part of it, the original ownership structure will have changed beyond recognition. It will be hard then to determine whom to return material to, or whom to consult to determine possibilities for access.

Once a practice of returning field material becomes accepted, demands will arise for the return of field materials and anthropological knowledge "belonging to" anthropologists and ethnographers that are long since deceased. In fact, I expect that much of the local demand for repatriation in years to come will focus on this category of work, mediated by anthropologists currently working in the areas in question. Howard's work (chapter 2) is an example in this respect. In some cases the "distance" between the contents of the ethnographic material and present-day culture will be huge, which may perhaps resolve the problems I indicated in the previous paragraphs, but may also create problems with acceptance of this image of the past (see Oles, chapter 10).

Still, we can take nothing for granted here. As part of the ethnographic process the people we study will inevitably acquire the skills to appreciate questions about their culture and their way of life, and the basic reflexivity to be able to answer such questions. For repatriation to work in the sense that Keesing had in mind, however, for indigenous students to be able to study their own cultural patterns, a further jump in the ability to reflect upon one's culture will be necessary. In whatever way we translate this—level of education, literacy, development of socioeconomic or political infrastructure—repatriation will remain fraught with unexpected risks until that jump is actually made.

Mary McCutcheon

4

You Can't Die till You Clean Up Your Mess

Anthropologists, like most academics, reckon their achievements by their publications—by the length of the bibliographies attached to resumes. But how many stop to consider the treasure trove of unpublished material that might also have some enduring significance? How many more shudder as they imagine the boxes filled with jumbles of illegible field notes, mildewed photographs, and rusty ring binders full of esoterica that are somewhere in the attic?

This chapter is about the ways those field notes, manuscript drafts, photographs, films, journals, letters, and miscellaneous other mementos might very well come to life just as the anthropologists themselves are laid to eternal rest. It is worth stopping to consider what, if anything, anthropologists might want restricted from public access, and if anthropologists, their relatives, archivists, or the subjects of the research want to impose such restrictions, what are the options?

Because the focus of this volume is Pacific Island research, most of my examples will be drawn from that body of ethnographic work. I have also limited the discussion of legal issues to the United States, although many other nations are grappling with problems of information access, privacy, and copyright law. Furthermore, as is apparent in Nancy Guy's contribution to this volume (chapter 11), transnational legal problems are becoming more and more common.

This chapter serves first as a review of U.S. laws and policies pertaining to archives, second as a warning that anthropologists are not the only ones who might feel entitled to have a say in the disposition of their field notes, and third as an admonition to all anthropologists to tidy up their affairs.

It is not possible to predict how posterity is going to regard unpublished archives. The only thing that is nearly certain is that if one tells trusted loved ones to burn diaries, letters, and notes, they will not. Equally certain is that there is a lot of valuable material that gets burned because heirs, spouses, and employers do not know what else to do.

One researcher who had done botanical and ethnographic work in Polynesia in collaboration with his first wife divorced her and married another woman. He then died, leaving his research files in the possession of this unsympathetic second wife. So the first wife, hearing the news of her ex-husband's death, rightly worried that the widow would pitch the files in the trash out of spite or jealousy or both. The first wife sent a dispassionate person with a good negotiating style and a station wagon over to the house to retrieve the collection and take it to the Smithsonian where it would be made public. Upon looking closely at these field notes, however, the Smithsonian staff noticed that a large proportion of the material dealt with explicitly sexual subjects that were intimate and personal, and, in some cases, implicated Polynesian individuals. The scientist's meticulous and extensive lists of vocabulary words pertained to sexual subjects that are embarrassing perhaps to Polynesians, but most of all to the memory of this unfortunate researcher and his first wife. This example shows how bad intentions nearly destroyed this collection, but good intentions could have destroyed the reputation of the scientist and offended his informants. The collection is now in a small and uncataloged collection in the botany department of the Smithsonian where it is unlikely to be seen by anyone.

Restrictions Imposed by the Anthropologist

When anthropologists have the foresight to give their own research material to archives, they often anticipate the need to restrict access. There may be many reasons for doing this and just as many ways to impose restrictions. Obviously the manner chosen for exercising the restrictions depends in part on the reason.

Field notes have a lot of inchoate thoughts, bad information, and half-baked ideas that may not be borne out by intense research. How unfortunate it would be to be "credited," posthumously, for information that turns out to be all wrong.

Quite the opposite problem is created when the researcher is not given any credit at all for material that is obtained from archives where copyrights might be hard to enforce and where it is unlikely that anyone will be vigilant enough to notice the violation. Photographs, raw film footage, and audiotapes are perhaps more vulnerable to intellectual property theft than research data. Fearing this, donors might want to craft some restrictions to protect their interests even posthumously.

Raw data and notes jotted down in ways that anthropologists intend for themselves alone might be misinterpreted without proper explanation. Anthropologists writing in haste in uncomfortable postures tend to use shorthand. Unaware that anyone else may ever see the notes, the anthropologist might use nicknames for members of the community and places, and even include some editorializing that is not intended for other eyes. After thirty or forty years many of the anthropologists themselves have problems enough figuring out what they meant. Imagine the problems that others have. And imagine the unfortunate educated guesses that they might make about the things that are not clear.

Researchers who have gathered sensitive information might want to protect their subjects and informants from embarrassment and hurt by restricting access to field notes. Informant confidentiality is so important that the "Code of Ethics" of the American Anthropological Association (1998, 3.A.1) says

> "1. Anthropological researchers have primary ethical obligations to the people they study and to the people . . . with whom they work. These obligations can supersede the goal of seeking new knowledge."

Of the various aspects of this dictum, the following points are relevant to the problem of rights of privacy and access to archival documents (1998, 3.A.2, 4–5):

> 2. Anthropological researchers must do everything in their power to ensure that their research does not harm the safety, dignity, or privacy of the people with whom they work. . . .
> 4. Anthropological researchers should obtain in advance the informed consent of persons being studied, providing information, owning or control-

ling access to material being studied, or otherwise identified as having interests which might be impacted by the research.

5. Anthropological researchers who have developed close and enduring relationships with . . . individual persons providing information . . . must adhere to the obligations of openness and informed consent.

When correspondence between colleagues is donated to an archive, it is the recipient, rather than the writer, who has the power to prevent the exposure of the letter to archival clients. Anticipating this breach of privacy, the donor might stipulate restrictions.

Some anthropologists take notes or record tapes of information that include privileged secrets. Betrayal of these secrets is not so much a matter of personal privacy, but rather a matter of cultural privacy. Out of respect for the culture, researchers might suggest some limits on availability of these materials. How to restrict access is the next problem.

As long as the anthropologist is still alive, he or she can reserve the right to issue use permission on a case-by-case basis. Direct contact allows the donor and the user to discuss any limitations or caveats. The donor may name an executor to assume this authority after his or her death or simply close the collection entirely for a specified time period.

Carleton Gajdusek, who is still alive and the object of intense public curiosity for his allegedly improper interest in young boys, placed video footage of *kuru* patients and his journals in the Melanesian Archive at the University of California, San Diego. Other research material is at the Peabody-Essex Museum in Salem, Massachusetts. Partly to protect himself and partly to protect his subjects, these collections are now only to be viewed by individuals who have express written permission from Gajdusek. As far as I know, no one who has asked has been successful. Absent this permission, he wishes the collections to be inaccessible until ten years after his death.[1]

Restrictions against copying or citing the contents of unpublished material can be another solution. Richard Emerick, who worked on Pohnpei among the Havasupai and among the Inuit, gave many films to the Human Studies Film Archives at the Smithsonian, but reserves the right to restrict copying in order to prevent irresponsible commercial use.[2]

Restricting a collection for a certain period of time is a good way to resolve the problem of the sensitivities of individuals who are the subjects of notes or correspondence. While it is impractical to restrict material until the last informant is dead, a safe period of time might be seventy-five years, to allow for the youngest individual to live a fairly long time. Some donors feel that periods of five, ten, or twenty-five years are adequate. Nice round dates, such as the year 2000, are popular too.

Most troubling of all and hardest to implement is the categorical restriction against whole classes of individuals. This may seem like an appropriate solution when the material is composed of secret information exclusive to a group of people. Sometimes these items of information are personal confidences told to a trusted outsider, and sometimes these are secrets held by a subgroup of the society.

It should be obvious that restrictions based on the ethnicity, gender, or some other aspect of the client's identity are problematic, both legally and practically. They necessitate making sometimes quick and superficial assessments of the status of the visitor to the archives. Archivists are generally committed to treating all archival clients equally. Needless to say, such restrictions do not sit well with them.

William Lessa, many of whose interviews were confidential, gave his collection of Ulithian research materials to the Smithsonian in 1979 with a deed of gift stating: "It is the Donor's wish that the materials be made available for research as soon as possible, and to the fullest extent possible. At the same time, it is the Donor's wish to guard against the possibility of their contents being used to embarrass, damage, injure, or harass living persons. Accordingly, the Director shall have the materials reviewed and shall place under seal any material that may be embarrassing or damaging to living persons . . . specifically . . . journals, censuses, and other material that relates to the ancestry of Ulithians. *Such material will not be viewed by native-born Ulithians or their immediate relatives until the year 2000.*"[3] The restriction was duly placed on the collection, but Lessa could not have anticipated the burden that he placed on the receptionist charged with evaluating the ethnicity of each user.

Compounding this problem are restrictions based on the intended use of the material. According to Karen Peacock, Jack Tobin, a postwar ethnographer who worked in the Marshall Islands, gave his Marshallese genealogies to the University of Hawai'i Pacific Collection on the condition that they not be used for "any legal / political decisions."[4] It is not possible to respect this kind of restriction since the eventual use of the collection would not be known until it was too late, until the dreaded legal or political decisions had already been made.

Suzanne Falgout notes that Jack Fischer's material at the Bishop Museum is open to Ph.D.s for "academic purposes only," and he added that the notes "not be shown to missionaries or to Micronesians" (chapter 6). These are certainly unmanageable restrictions, so when his student and executor, Rick Marksbury, prepared the bulk of the original material for the Smithsonian's Anthropological Archives after Fischer's death, he chose not to impose any discriminatory restrictions at all on the notes, but did destroy the highly sensitive diaries.

To make reading his notes even more difficult for those who could misuse them, Fischer wrote some of them in an arcane code. When Marksbury found the coded notes, he was intrigued. Having all but given up hope of translating them, he happened to mention the problem to an FBI agent with whom he played handball. This agent arranged to have the code cracked by the FBI. Marksbury included the key to the code in the Smithsonian collection, figuring that coded papers, even with a key at hand, are enough of an obstacle to deter most casual users.[5]

When disputes about ownership arise, there are additional complications. Filmmaker Richard Sorenson and his assistants made many extraordinary films during the 1970s under the auspices of the Human Studies Film Center at the Smithsonian. Much of the footage was from the Central Caroline Islands in Micronesia. The Film Center evolved into the Human Studies Film Archive, and when Sorenson left, the films continued to reside in the archive. For years Sorenson fought to restrict any public access or use of them on the grounds that the films were his personal property and that the subjects of the film understood that he would be the guardian in perpetuity. He produced a letter signed by several chiefs in Micronesia stating that they had entrusted Sorenson exclusively with the film footage. The Smithsonian stood its ground and has on several occasions asserted its ownership by allowing open access, but has respected the wishes of the subjects by promising to notify them or at least their countries if any of the original footage is to be used in another film.[6]

Restrictions Requested by the Subjects

Archives generally negotiate with the donor of a collection when they create rules of access. The donor is most likely the person who produced the material or his or her heirs. Until recently, archivists did not hear much from the people about whom these field notes and other materials pertained. The subject population may not have been aware that the archive existed, much less have known what was contained in it. And even if people within the population had known, they probably did not feel empowered enough to protest access rules. The Native American Grave Protection and Repatriation Act (NAGPRA) of 1990 has brought about a new openness to discussions not only of physical repatriation, but also of the ways collections in museums and archives are used. Native American groups have been at the forefront of requesting access limitations, but indigenous Australians and most recently native Hawaiians have made similar requests. As a result, policies are evolving rapidly.

As is the case when anthropologists initiate restrictive rules, there are several different reasons that subject populations ask that restrictions be imposed: outrage at the incorrect information embodied in notes, photos, and films; suspicion that users may intend to profit somehow; fear that cultural secrets could be broadcast to cultural outsiders; anxiety that sub-cultural (gender, sodality, age grade, status, clan) secrets might be accessible to members of the culture who are not privy to those types of information; and concern that texts, films, and photographs that depict very sensitive subjects are tastelessly and insensitively available for view by others.

Bryan Oles (chapter 10) found that the people of Mokil object to the work done by Joseph Weckler and Conrad Bentzen more than fifty years ago not so much because of outright errors, but more because of the anthropologists' editorializing, their depictions of people that are embarrassing by modern standards, and their emphasis on scandal and discord that is too much a reminder of an unsettled past. The Mokilese are acutely aware of how "indelible" published ethnographies and films are. The physical permanence and the perceived authority of these media preclude selective uses of custom and history in changing contexts. While the Mokilese have not recommended that films and ethnographies be censored, they prefer not to be exposed to the offending material if they can avoid it.

Other groups of people who have been objects of anthropological study take a more active role in determining access guidelines. Having learned about misleading, offensive, sensitive, and secret material housed in archival collections, they are making requests that these items be repatriated, de-stroyed, or locked up. Native American groups, such as the Zuni and Hopi, have had mixed success in asking that certain photographs be kept from the public, but their requests have at least caused archivists to rethink accessions and restrictions.

Throughout the 1990s there have been a number of meetings composed of representatives of indigenous peoples to make recommendations on the issues of intellectual and biological property rights. At least two have been held in the Pacific Region. Hosted by nine Maori tribes, the First International Conference on the Cultural and Intellectual Property Rights of Indigenous Peoples was held in 1993 in New Zealand (Aotearoa). The "Mataatua Declaration" that emerged from that meeting encouraged indigenous people to assert their rights to intellectual property, to monitor any commercial use of this property, and to demand benefits that could accrue from such commercial use. The only mention of repatriation or assertion of control over materials that had already been expropriated focused on human remains and material cultural artifacts.

Two years later a similar meeting was held under the auspices of the United Nations Development Program (UNDP) in Suva, which culminated in the drafting of "The Final statement from the UNDP Consultation on Indigenous Peoples' Knowledge and Intellectual Property Rights." This document addressed the question of repatriation of intellectual property resources. In a long list of recommendations, it included

> 3.1. Encourage chiefs, elders and community leaders to play a leadership role in the protection of indigenous peoples' knowledge and resources. . . .
> 4. Recognize the urgent need to identify the extent of expropriation that has already occurred and is continuing in the Pacific.
> 4.1. Seek repatriation of indigenous peoples' resources already held in external collections. . . .
> 9. Urge universities, churches, governments, non-governmental organizations, and other institutions to reconsider their roles in the expropriation of indigenous peoples' knowledge and resources and to assist in their return to their rightful owners. (UNDP 1995)

While these statements have not been ratified by the United Nations, they exemplify the urgency felt by indigenous peoples who are increasingly aware of the volume of unpublished materials, photographs, films, and audio recordings housed in foreign collections. They are more and more conscious, too, of the potential commercial value of their property rights on songs, medicinal knowledge, plant varieties, and even cell lines.

Some collections may have no commercial value for anyone, but their existence in archival collections is upsetting to the people they pertain to. An example of this is the collection of photographs of Hawaiian skeletal material at the Bishop Museum. Edward Halealoha Ayau is the head of the project for the restoration and reburial of skeletal remains in the native Hawaiian organization, Hui Malama I Na Kupuna O Hawai'i Nei. He explained that excavating a human burial site is a form of desecration in Hawaiian custom. Photographing those remains is a double affront. The Bishop Museum in Honolulu apparently has a collection of such photographs, which Hui Malama originally asked to have destroyed or at least repatriated. Although the museum staff resisted total destruction and repatriation, they have agreed to restrict all access. Ayau has also asked that the location of burial caves and other sacred sites be restricted in order to protect them from vandals and looters. So far the Bishop Museum has been amenable to these modest requests.[7]

The Aboriginal and Torres Strait Islander Library and Information Resource Network (ATSILIRN) has issued a protocol in Australia detailing the need to restrict access to culturally sensitive materials and insisting that it be the indigenous people who retain the authority to determine what is and is not restricted (ATSILIRN 1995). Many Australian museums have agreed to comply with the essence of ATSILIRN's protocol.

Like many cultures, though, Australian aboriginal societies have sodalities, age grades, and other achieved or ascribed statuses that possess special secret knowledge. This poses an additional dilemma; it is not just indigenous people who should control access to the collections, but specifically members of the initiated minority. They must be entrusted with their own secret knowledge against not just the cultural outsider, but also the uninitiated cultural insider. The Victoria Museum in Melbourne says that "Aboriginal secret ceremonies—whether on still or motion film—are restricted to all but initiated people, whether men or women, and those who have been given specific approval to view that material. Sensitive scenes, such as a photograph or film of a person who is now dead, are also restricted and would not be shown to an Aboriginal relative."[8]

No social group is entirely homogeneous in its attitudes toward knowledge and secrets. When an individual in the group advocates the imposition of restrictions, obvious questions are who is this individual, does he or she speak with authority for the entire group, and, if not, what are the other points of view?

An example of the various perspectives that might be found within a community comes from the experience of David Akin and Kathryn Creely in their efforts to determine what kind of restrictions should be placed on the Roger Keesing collection once copies of the documents are repatriated to the Solomon Islands (see chapter 5). Akin spoke to members of the Kwaio community among whom Keesing worked and found that there are varying points of view. Some argue for exclusive access and others for a liberal openness. This situation calls attention to the factionalism and diversity present even within a small population.

Archival Policy

In addition to the anthropologists and the subject populations, archivists naturally have something to say about restrictions. They start by exercising their prerogative to reject the collection. Archives, with limited space and resources, cannot afford to accept every shred of paper and out-of-focus snapshot proffered to them. There are generally accession committees who evaluate the material and have to inform the donor (either the still-living anthropologist or the heirs) whether the bequest will be accepted.

Film is especially expensive and sometimes dangerous to store (such as cellulose nitrate film from before 1923). Much of it has to be copied and then kept in special accommodations. Pam Wintle of the Smithsonian's Human Studies Film Archive can only afford to accept exceptional ethnographic footage that is in excellent condition and does not duplicate other films in the collection.[9]

Archivists grapple constantly with the tug-of-war between the equally cherished opposing ideologies of free access to information housed in their collections and respect for both privacy and intellectual property rights of individuals. According to the Society of American Archivists "Code of Ethics" (1992), archivists should be committed foremost to open access and free use of collections, while considering institutional policies, legal considerations, and individual rights. Archivists are very reluctant to accept collections with any kind of discriminatory restriction. Instead they advocate that "Any portion of the collection that is restricted as a condition of donation should be closed to all readers and a clear end date to the restriction should be stipulated to facilitate eventual availability of the complete record" (Danielson 1989, 44).

It is probably safe to say that, as a rule, archivists are inclined to err on the side of free access rather than restrictions. This is, in part, because of their ideological commitments, but it may also stem from the fact that archivists simply do not have the time to comb through collections to find sources of embarrassment or violations of individual rights. Sometimes they get a sudden wake-up call.

The Sheldon collection is still the source of discussion at the Smithsonian. According to some accounts (cited in Marks 1995), William Herbert Sheldon was a staunch advocate of eugenics and an unrepentant Nazi sympathizer who coined terms many older anthropologists are familiar with: ectomorph, endomorph, and mesomorph. In the 1960s, under the pretense of studying somatotypes, he conducted a major project to photograph nude undergraduates from prominent East Coast colleges. The photographs ended up in the anthropological archives of the Smithsonian where they remained, largely forgotten, for thirty years. Now the middle-aged subjects have come into positions of power, maybe even in the White House. Several universities requested the return of the photographs of its own students, and Smithsonian legal counsel, determining that the ownership of the collection was in doubt, had the photographs of the students from those universities repatriated. They were presumably destroyed, while the rest of the photographs are still housed at the Smithsonian where access is strictly limited to "qualified researchers who can demonstrate a serious need to know."[10] If this disappoints you, take heart: the eccentric Southwestern anthropologist, John Peabody Harrington, had himself photographed nude, and these pictures are freely accessible in the National Anthropological Archives at the Smithsonian.

From the archivist's perspective some restrictions are impractical to implement. Restrictions that end with the deaths of donors, anthropologists, correspondents, informants, or subjects require that the archivist be a regular reader of obituaries. Although anthropologists and subject populations have suggested restrictions that are based on the identity or motives of the client, evaluating the ethnicity or intentions of each visitor to the archives is not only impractical, but also probably illegal. To respect the terms of William Lessa's restriction against anyone who is Ulithian, the receptionist had to ask, "Excuse me, but are you Ulithian?" to everyone who came in or, worse, inquire selectively of those who, judging from appearance, *might* have been from Ulithi (and how many receptionists know where *that* is). A Chamorro from Guam had to go through the inquisition and gave the receptionist a lesson in geography at the same time. Rob Leopold of the Smithsonian Anthropological Archives undertook a huge search to ferret out such discriminatory restrictions and apply them to all users, indiscriminately, while still respecting the original intent of the researcher. The genealogical parts of the Lessa collection are simply closed to everyone until the year 2000.

According to Akin and Creely (chapter 5), some Kwaio would like to keep Christians from seeing Keesing's field notes. If evaluating the ethnicity of an archival client is hard, imagine how difficult it is to tell the difference between a non-Christian and someone impersonating a non-Christian! Furthermore, a non-Christian (who might, under such a hypothetical restriction, have access to the collection) can easily turn into a Christian later in life.

Most archives will wisely refuse to accept collections with complicated discriminatory strings attached or will try to persuade the donor to close the collection entirely for a set period of time.

Freedom of Information and Privacy—Legalities

Anthropologists, the subjects of their research, and archivists are not the only ones with something to say about archival access. The archival client has a voice too, and this voice screams for disclosure and freedom of access.

When the research that generated the archives was funded by an agency of the United States government, that screaming client can invoke the Freedom of Information Act (FOIA) of 1966. The law, which applies to agencies of the federal government, and its equivalent laws, which apply to agencies of states (these are called "sunshine laws"), are on the whole a noble effort to open up government to the scrutiny of the citizenry.

Even the most ideologically committed advocates of free access to information, however, have to concede a few exemptions. Nine exemptions are written into the act and others have emerged in other legislation. Some limits to free access stem from obvious considerations of national security and criminal investigations. Other exemptions pertain to personnel and medical files of individuals and, interestingly, information on the location of certain geological features, such as wells.[11]

Because free access to information can lead to many abuses of personal privacy and individual rights, companion laws have been enacted that impose additional limitations. The Privacy Act of 1974 prohibits disclosure of any records pertaining to a living individual that are part of a system of records retrievable by name or individual identification number. It was crafted to give people some power over the collection and release of information pertaining to them.

As Suzanne Falgout (chapter 6) found, a clause was inserted in the Trust Territory Code in 1955 that privileges the conversations that anthropologists have with their informants. In section 342 title 7, chapter 1, section 2, it says:

> Subject to the limitations provided in this section, conversations held with an anthropologist in confidence in his professional character shall be privileged. No statement made in such a conversation nor the substance thereof shall be divulged without the consent of the person making it, nor shall the identity of any person making such a statement on any particular subject be divulged without his consent, except as provided herein. This privilege, however, shall not extend to the professional opinions or conclusions of an anthropologist even though they may be based in whole or in part on such conversations, nor shall it or the prohibition against divulging such statements or the identity of persons making them apply to admissions or confessions indicating that the person making them has committed murder in the first or second degree or voluntary manslaughter or is threatening to commit a crime in the future. (Trust Territory of the Pacific Islands 1970)

As far as I am aware only one anthropologist has ever invoked this privilege and this was in regard to a murder trial where the informant was *not* the suspect. Falgout notes that the clause was deleted from the Trust Territory Code in 1979, but I now wonder if anthropologists working prior to that date in the Trust Territory are exempt ("grandfathered") on the argument that their informants had an "expectation of privacy" when they spoke with the anthropologists at that earlier time.

It is also important to note that district or staff anthropologists and all other individuals working for the Trust Territory government were *not* employees of the United States government or any agency of the U.S. government. People wanting to use the Freedom of Information Act have sometimes tried to argue that they assumed the Trust Territory was part of the Department of the Navy or the Department of Interior. They are wrong: there is no extension of FOIA that applies to materials contained in Trust Territory records.[12]

The National Historic Preservation Act of 1966 as well as the Archeological Resources Protection Act of 1979 contain other qualifications that affect archives containing information on archeological sites on government land. These laws (described in Vogt-O'Connor 1998) are applicable to Hawai'i, Guam, and American Samoa. An agency that has records describing the locations of archeological or historic sites is not required to release those records if it is likely that the information might be used to harm archeological or historical resources.

Just to add extra power to this exemption and place the burden on the archival client, President Clinton in 1996 issued an executive order (President 1996) declaring that sites of sacred significance to Native Americans (including Hawaiians) should be kept confidential unless there is some salient reason that the information should be released.

Documents that were produced from privately funded research, even if they repose in federal document centers, such as the National Archives, are also outside the jurisdiction of FOIA and its companion laws. Like the National Archives, the Smithsonian Anthropological Archives is composed of a blend of privately funded and publicly funded research material and for most of its collections is free to forge its own policy on access.

Applying to all repositories of documents are a separate but related set of laws governing reproduction and appropriation of material. They are the copyright, patent, and trademark laws: the laws concerning intellectual property. These rules usually do not apply to mere access to documents, photographs, illustrations, audio recordings, and other archival material, but they *can* limit the means by which some of these materials are made accessible. Now that electronic means of cataloging collections includes imaging on CDs and videodiscs, these laws are becoming hard to interpret.

The University of Guam's Micronesian Area Research Center (MARC) has a lot of copies of documents whose originals are housed in Spain or in the Marshall Islands. There are restrictions on copying many of these that stem from agreements that the staff of MARC made with the originating institutions. Spanish documents are in the care of Marjorie Driver, who takes precautions against unauthorized copying. The collections of traders Jose DeBrum and Adolph Capelle and their descendants from the Marshalls are also not to be copied.[13]

The Copyright Act of 1976 allows intellectual property rights to be held by individuals and well-defined corporations for a limited amount of time. What the law does not address, however, is the problem of protecting intellectual property rights of ill-defined social groups that may be called "ethnicities" or "cultures." What about medicinal plant knowledge, a design element characteristic of a specific community, or a style of dance or music (see Guy, chapter 11)? These are ideas that can be derived from archival collections and appropriated for all kinds of sacrilegious or commercial purposes without requiring compensation of any kind. If any copyright law comes into play, it is usually the anthropologist or photographer or artist who holds the rights, not the source community or culture. The many meetings and conventions addressing the question of intellectual property rights of indigenous peoples may change this, but it will not be without a multitude of problems. Can and should the law protect access to and use of these kinds of property? If so, what is the duration of the "culture" that may own such rights, how is membership going to be defined, and how is compensation for release of rights or violation of rights going to be meted out?

The Freedom of Information Act (1966) seems to be well balanced by exemptions and privacy considerations, but new legislation threatens to destabilize this delicate balance and create many more practical problems.

Federal funds are given as grants from federal agencies to universities and research organizations to be spent by individual researchers on research that was either commissioned by the agency or proposed by the researchers. Proposals specify what the final product is supposed to be: a report on the research findings, an invention, a film, a museum exhibition, a design, or a solution to a burning problem. If raw data, miles of film footage, interview tapes, and individual survey forms happened to be generated in the course of performing the proposed job, that material is presumed to belong to the research institution or, as often as not, the individuals who performed the research. And those materials may reside in file cabinets or dusty boxes in the researcher's office or home to be dealt with, along with the rest of his or her personal possessions.

A study of diabetes medications conducted from the late 1950s to the mid-1970s produced controversial results. When rival researchers asked to see the original data, they were rebuffed. Eventually the case went to the Supreme Court (*Forsham versus Harris*, 1980), and the court determined that the final report satisfied the grant and was public while the raw data could be withheld from public scrutiny. It is this case that has, up until now, protected recipients of federal grants from having to forfeit any of their research materials to FOIA requests.[14]

But the United States Congress passed legislation in 1998 (U.S. Public Law 105–277) that effectively puts an end to the distinction between the final result and the basic research. Congress mandated that the Office of Management and the Budget (OMB) revise the guidelines (Circular A-110) for recipients of federal grant money to "require Federal awarding agencies to ensure that all data produced under an award will be made available to the public through the procedures established under the Freedom of Information Act" (U.S. Public Law 105–277).

The legislation, called the Shelby amendment, was short and ambiguous. As it was conceived, a FOIA request would be made to the funding agency. It would pass the request to the university or research organization. It, in turn, might have to seek out the individual researchers or their heirs to obtain the requested data. The agency would then evaluate the data to determine if it is subject to any of the nine FOIA exemptions or if it is subject to privacy or other restrictions. If not, it is released.

The threat of sudden, free, and possibly retroactive access to research materials, raw data, and notes precipitated an outcry from the scientific community. Among the organizations writing to voice an objection on behalf of its membership was the American Anthropological Association, which pointed out how destructive such free access to data could be to indigenous people and how problematic even the definition of the term "data" is in our field (AAA 1999).[15]

So on 8 October 1999, OMB qualified the language by limiting the application to those research projects that result in the development of an action "that has the force and effect of law" (OMB 1999b). They also stressed the many privacy limitations that would be used to defend restrictions.

Be Aware

A large cast of characters has an interest in and wishes to have a say in the extent to which people are permitted to look at, copy, or commodify the information we have stashed in file cabinets or deposited in archives. The issues of restrictive versus free access are complex and, for some archives generated by Americans, a matter not only of personal opinions and desires, but also of law.

To forestall the kinds of complications that make the life of an archivist difficult, it is best for us to know the issues before starting field research. Once in the field it is important for us to heed the advice of the American Anthropological Association and discuss ownership of information and consent to its use with our informants. We also should recognize that "the informed consent process is dynamic and continuous; the process should be initiated in the project design and continue through implementation by way of dialogue and negotiation with those studied" (AAA 1998, 3.A.4). Questions about the rights to publish photographs, play tape recordings in public places, show films, and publish direct quotes should all be answered before we leave for home and long before the FOIA requests come in.

In other words, it is best for us all to tidy up our affairs before it is too late.

Part II *Managing the Collected Past*

David Akin and Kathryn Creely

5

A Kwaio Case Study from the
Melanesian Archive

The field records of individual anthropologists are important to several constituencies: an increasing number of Pacific Islander scholars, scholars outside of the islands, the general public in the country of the data's origin, and, most important in ethical terms, the communities and individuals from whom data was obtained. To quote the late Roger Keesing, "even in those few Melanesian communities where traditional life seems intact and secure, the threat of cultural loss and breakdown is felt on all sides" (1994, 191). In such contexts, the preservation and repatriation of ethnographic records becomes an urgent, poignant necessity. The unpublished ethnographic record is a crucial primary source to which future generations will be able to turn. As Melanesian societies and cultures rapidly change, this data becomes an irreplaceable record of the past. Keesing continues,

> A researcher who has worked in a Melanesian community for many years
> will have recorded a rich knowledge of histories, genealogies, customary
> practices, and even traditional language and vocabulary that have been at
> least partly lost with the death of the elders with whom they originally

worked. In every Pacific Island village, the death of men and women over sixty or seventy brings the irretrievable loss of valued old knowledge . . . a scholar who began research twenty or thirty years ago or more is inescapably the custodian or repository, on behalf of present-day and future members of these communities, of valued knowledge with which they were entrusted by men and women long dead. (1994, 191–92)

There is a notable disparity between the wealth of ethnographic detail found in the primary unpublished anthropological record and its dearth in most anthropological publications today. The materials generated by anthropologists in the course of fieldwork (field notes, recorded interviews, correspondence, photographs, videotapes, and so forth) represent an impressive spectrum of data. But today, most scholarly journals and monographs emphasize analysis and theory, with ethnographic data summarized rather than detailed. This reflects shifts within anthropology itself and current financial realities of scholarly publishing. And yet the amount of data collected in the course of typical fieldwork is steadily increasing. In the words of one archivist, "Archaeological and anthropological records require a higher percentage of retention than do many other types of records. . . . nearly all of the available documentation is pertinent. Recent developments in field methodology accentuate this need. Field documentation has become progressively more systematic and, as a consequence, vastly more voluminous. The increase is dramatic" (Ruwell 1985, 1, 3).

When considering what to do with a corpus of fieldwork data anthropologists may find themselves troubled. Their discipline has been subjected to vociferous attacks, particularly regarding research carried out within colonial and postcolonial contexts (for example, Pels 1997). Ongoing debates over ownership of cultural knowledge and intellectual copyright are also germane to questions of field record disposition. These issues and critiques may engender confusion and philosophical anxiety about making appropriate decisions. They must, however, be thoughtfully weighed against other factors less often raised. In a recent article Michael Brown writes,

Anyone willing to look carefully at the historical evidence will be dissatisfied with blanket condemnations of ethnographic records. At the very least, we must acknowledge the agency of indigenous peoples—their strategic decisions to share ideas and stories and songs with inquisitive outsiders when, in their judgment, circumstances warranted. . . . This is hardly a history free of coercion, but it includes powerful elements of volition, and of cultural resistance through strategic sharing, that merit ac-

knowledgment and respect. . . . Today ethnographic records provide critical information that indigenous peoples use to revitalize their cultures and
to substantiate land and resource claims in courts of law. The species of naive presentism that judges historical actors by today's ethical standards
would, if given free reign, mandate the pious quarantine or even destruction of most of these important resources. (1998, 200)

In what follows we present a case study of some of the prospects,
problems, and decisions that can await anthropologists, archivists, and Pacific communities in managing and repatriating field materials. The materials in question are those of Roger Keesing, the community is the Kwaio
people of Malaita in the Solomon Islands, and the institutions are the Melanesian Archive at the University of California at San Diego (UCSD) and the
National Museum of the Solomon Islands.

The Melanesian Archive: Purpose and Procedures

One of the founders of the Melanesian Archive, anthropologist Donald
Tuzin, has written about the ethnographic record in terms of reciprocity:

Ethnography . . . is an intensely moral activity, engendering a distinctive
kind of commitment—indeed, identification—on the part of practitioners
toward their subject-matter. . . . When one has sojourned for years among
other people, depending on them for food, shelter, protection, information, and simple human contact, one is likely to form attachments to individuals and, at some intellectual remove, the values they hold. With
such involvement comes a sense of obligation to repay this generosity in
some way. For many practitioners, ethnography and the act of writing it—
whatever the scientific and professional incentives—is a gift in kind to the
people who made it possible. Never mind that they may not be able to
read it; their literate children or grandchildren will appreciate it as a
record—often the only record—of a way of life now lost to them, which
is generally the fate of peoples ethnographers have traditionally called
their own. Never mind, either, if no member or descendant of the group in
question ever reads the account; the gift is made by way of memorializing
to others, remote in space or time, this instance of cultural humanity. . . .
If it is true that one of ethnography's distinguishing features is the moral
cloak with which it wraps itself, then it is all the more surprising and
ironic that the record of ethnographic conduct is abysmal concerning the
preservation and dissemination of its findings. (1995, 23–24)

The Melanesian Archive was created in an attempt to address in a practical way issues surrounding the collection, preservation, and repatriation of unpublished ethnographic records from Melanesia. The archive was originally envisioned as a small project to be staffed by anthropology faculty in their spare time, but it quickly became apparent that a collaborative project with the library would be more appropriate. Beginning with a successful grant application for funding from the U.S. Department of Education in 1983, and mainstreamed into the regular library budget of the University of California at San Diego in 1986, the growth of the archive has accelerated in recent years and succeeded far beyond the modest dreams of its founders, Donald Tuzin and Fitz Poole. Clearly, the archive has struck a chord in the ethnographic community.

An important goal of the Melanesian Archive is the repatriation of unpublished anthropological materials to their place of origin. This is accomplished, with the anthropologists' written permission, through provision of free copies to fifteen libraries in Melanesia, with the original documents retained at UCSD. The copies are usually on microfiche, a medium chosen for several reasons: microfiche is low-tech, and so Pacific libraries need not divert scarce computer resources to use it; it is inexpensive to produce and distribute, which allows the archive to operate on a very modest budget; it is durable in archival terms, having a longer life expectancy than nonacid-free paper or electronic media; and, finally, it is compact and light so housing it does not place an undue burden on already-crowded shelves in Pacific libraries. To date, over 560 microfiche have been produced, representing some 370 items and 39,000 pages of text. Additionally, 36 reels of microfilm (some 18,000 frames) of the manuscripts of John Layard have been deposited with the Vanuatu Cultural Centre.

With the exception of the Layard papers, which contain extensive field records, most of the materials repatriated have been dissertations, unpublished conference papers, and an occasional book-length manuscript. Field notes and other field materials, which form a much larger component of the archive's collection, pose special problems. We can begin with technical and logistical obstacles. Notes are often handwritten, smudged, water-damaged, or otherwise illegible. Addenda inserted on small slips are difficult to keep in order. The paper may be too brittle to withstand the handling necessary for filming, or the ink may be too faded to copy clearly. Field materials are often idiosyncratically arranged, and this can make microform versions virtually impossible for researchers to use. Computerized data may be encoded in programs that are old, no longer available, or even unidentifiable, and therefore difficult to translate to newer software or even print out.

Ideally, arrangements for the long-term archiving of field materials should be made by the anthropologist who created the records. Contact should be made with the designated institution, and the decision should be recorded in a will or in written instructions to one's literary executor. Unfortunately, this is seldom done, and survivors are too often left with an office full of papers and no direction as to what to do with them. When an anthropologist dies, the Melanesian Archive staff will sometimes initiate contact with the family to find out what is being done with the scholar's papers. Families frequently greet this inquiry with relief. The library at the scholar's home institution or alma mater may already have turned down the collection. Research libraries and archives are often reluctant to accept an individual's unpublished materials unless he or she is famous or the materials relate to narrow institutional specializations. For example, at UCSD individual manuscript collections in the fields of modern poetry, history of science, oceanography, and Melanesian anthropology are actively sought and routinely accepted, but only rarely would papers relevant to other disciplines find a home there. Resources are simply too limited to house, process, and preserve (and in the case of Melanesian anthropology, repatriate) materials unrelated to subject areas of specialization.

It may also be unrealistic to assume that the national archive or university library of a Pacific Island nation will accept materials simply because the field research took place there. Archival repositories in the Pacific Islands and elsewhere in the developing world are particularly hard-pressed in this regard, given their low priority for government funding. Furthermore, these institutions must contend with high humidity (and the accompanying mold and insects), cyclones, the shortage of trained staff, the absence of proper equipment, a lack of space, and other obstacles generally less problematic outside the region.

The important point is this: as an anthropologist familiar with your own work and your special field, you know better than anyone else where your papers will be valued and welcome, and you should make arrangements for their consignment now.

Logistical matters aside, simply depositing one's papers in an archive does not solve another, thornier set of issues. That is, how does one protect informant confidentiality and respect host community rights of knowledge control, while at the same time providing as much access as possible to scholarly and other communities elsewhere? In making field materials available to scholars using the Melanesian Archive, and, through repatriated copies to audiences in their countries of origin, donors and staff must perform a balancing act (see also Mary McCutcheon, chapter 4). They must answer to the competing claims of rights of informants to privacy and rights of the cultural group studied, while observing the written and customary laws that may apply. But they must also consider their obligations to the academic field that trained and supported them, generated ideas that they employed to design and carry out research and analysis, and likely funded much of the data gathering and archiving itself (compare Sjoerd Jaarsma, chapter 3).[1]

Organizing the Keesing Collection: Listening, Labeling, and Confidentiality

We now turn to the case of Roger Keesing's field materials. It illustrates some of the complex logistical, ethical, and other issues that arise when making decisions about the consignment of field data, and who will access and control it. Roger died unexpectedly in 1993 at the age of fifty-eight and left a large body of field materials documenting his work with the Kwaio. In 1995 members of his family, several of whom belong to the anthropological community and were already aware of the Melanesian Archive, approached Creely, the archive librarian, about donating Keesing's field notes and other unpublished materials. The papers were gratefully accepted, of course, sight unseen. The family members elected to retain copyright to the collection, but they were enthusiastic about the possibility of repatriating copies of materials in an institution in the Solomons. Long before the collection actually arrived in San Diego, the authors of this chapter began discussing how to address problems inherent in its repatriation.

Akin himself has spent well over five years living in the same larger Kwaio community where Keesing worked, most recently during a fifteen-month postdoctoral study from 1995 to 1997. By that time, Keesing's papers had already been offered to the Melanesian Archive, and family members had requested Akin's help in mediating their placement there and in re-patriating parts of the collection to the Solomons. Akin was able to person-ally inform the Kwaio of the plan to archive the papers and to consult with a range of Kwaio people about how they thought the materials should be handled.[2] He worked with them to devise a plan whereby a selected set of the materials will be placed in the Solomon Islands National Museum in Honiara, with access controlled by a committee of Kwaio leaders. Several Kwaio have had a good working relationship with the museum in the past, and nearly everyone agreed that the materials should be kept there rather than in Kwaio itself, where there are no appropriate facilities.[3] Museum Director Lawrence Foanaota readily agreed that his institution would re-ceive the papers and help the Kwaio administer them.

Before this arrangement could move forward, the Keesing materials had to be processed and inventoried, and decisions had to be made as to exactly which materials the Melanesian Archive will duplicate and send to Honiara. Some have already been copied and are about to be sent, while others are still being reviewed and processed. Let us briefly summarize these undertakings before turning to the thorny issues surrounding who should have access to different parts of the collection.

In the summer of 1997, soon after returning from the Solomons, Akin spent three weeks in Montreal helping Christine Jourdan, Keesing's widow, to sort his materials before their shipment to San Diego. Jourdan was particularly concerned that papers of a confidential nature, such as sensitive personal correspondence and letters of recommendation or refereeing, be separated out. In the fall of 1997 staff in the Mandeville Special Collections Library at UCSD (where the Melanesian Archive collections are housed and administered) began processing the collection. A basic inventory was prepared, and preservation tasks, such as transferring materials to acid-free containers, were completed. During this phase many problems were identified and the relevant materials set aside for Akin's attention. The following spring Akin spent several weeks in the archive working with staff to identify and order the Keesing collection and deal with the problems identified in the preliminary processing. He spent a further three weeks working on the collection, particularly Keesing's photographs, in March 2000. In the course of this work, issues arose that can serve as cautions to other researchers.

Keesing's collection was unusual in that the archivists charged with managing it could rely on help from a second anthropologist. Akin had worked in the same community, was fluent in the language, knew most of the informants personally, and had discussed the collection's archiving and repatriation with the host community. Yet even with his background, the tasks were daunting. Like many of us, Keesing had not labeled most of his materials with the idea of someone else having to navigate through them.[4] Dozens of files were unsorted, and some had no labels or evident topical focus; few of the many hundreds of photos were identified, and, outside of correspondence, little was dated (some things were dated by only month and day, since the year was obvious at the time of labeling). Endless hours were spent deciphering, sorting, labeling, and filing these materials, and, after the weeks of work by Akin, and several months more by library staff, the job is still incomplete. Keesing himself, familiar with the material, could have accomplished the task in a fraction of the time.

The most formidable parts of the collection were the 180 cassettes and 150 reel-to-reel tapes of interviews with Kwaio people (as well as some music), dating back to the early 1960s. Some of these were labeled as to the interviewees, some had a date, and a few bore sketchy topical notes. Many of the labels and nearly all of the tape recordings themselves were in the Kwaio language. Between Montreal and San Diego, Akin heard and indexed over 200 hours of tapes, listening to many of them while working on other materials. The most pressing need was to determine which of the interviews contained sensitive or confidential information and should therefore be somehow restricted.

We do not recount these problems to criticize how Keesing organized his materials. Suffice it to say that Akin's most common thought while working through them was "Yikes! I've got to do this for my own materials (tapes, field notes, photographs, transcripts, genealogies, pig censuses, et cetera) when I get home!" He has discussed this with several colleagues who have extensive field data and each has expressed similar concerns.

We cannot overemphasize the importance of immediately labeling material that is, or may become, sensitive, and to which access should be restricted to protect individual informant or host community interests. Akin's in-depth knowledge of the subject matter of Keesing's work makes this an exceptional case. More typically, an archive will not have anyone at hand with the linguistic and cultural fluency to review your field materials once you are gone.[5] The result may be that sensitive materials are left unprotected, or, conversely, restrictions are unnecessarily placed on valuable research materials. "The archivist's goal is to save materials and to make them available for use, that is to provide access to as many potential users as possible" (Parezo and Person 1995, 173). In the absence of restrictions imposed by anthropologists or other donors, an archivist will almost always choose to not restrict material.

Who Will Have Access?

One of the most problematic aspects of the Keesing materials is that nothing in the collection is marked as being "confidential" or sensitive in any way. It was agreed by both Roger's family and the Melanesian Archive that Akin was in the best position to decide which materials should be restricted and, in consultation with Kwaio, what the conditions of restriction should be. Some Kwaio, too, were anxious that potentially troublesome materials might be opened up to the community; no one person knew everything his field data contained. Local leaders, too, asked Akin to determine on their behalf what should be restricted and what should be returned to the Solomons.

Thus, Akin was left to make difficult decisions. First of all, whether information is sensitive varies widely with context. For example, an interview about a community member's sexual transgressions may be rather innocuous in the hands of a foreign library researcher who will never know the principals involved. But the same interview might cause significant embarrassment and social damage to both subjects and informants if returned to the community. In an earlier time such a distinction might have been employed to decide how to handle such data; that is, make it available to researchers in California or London, but do not repatriate it to the Pacific. This is no longer realistic, however, and today one must assume that someone from the local community, perhaps a young Pacific researcher (see below), may eventually visit the archive and hear the tapes or read the transcripts. Anthropologists applaud and often try to facilitate such new opportunities for Pacific scholars, but, in terms of protecting confidentiality, it means they must manage their data more carefully than did their forebears.

Most of Keesing's materials are, on the surface, unproblematic. His interview questions were constructed mostly in terms of hypothetical situations, except for accounts of historical and Kwaio-wide political events (particularly relating to the assassination of District Officer William Bell in 1927; see Keesing and Corris 1980, Keesing 1992). His taped interviews only rarely dealt with case studies of a personal nature. All of the listening revealed that only a handful of the recordings contained material that raised privacy issues. The field notes (which are mostly in English and are currently being worked through) are more difficult since they contain more accounts of actual cases. We are considering making a second copy of these specific notes for unrestricted access, with certain personal and place names blacked out to protect those involved.

But even this is trickier than it appears at first glance. Kwaio resembles many other Melanesian cultures in that people often downplay or ignore certain illicit behaviors so long as they are not publicly revealed (see, for example, Malinowski 1982, 77–80; Akin n.d.). Simply removing names from an infamous case will not necessarily disguise it, and repatriating field notes that explore such cases could cause considerable social distress by placing (or returning) the matter into the public arena. But there are deeper quandaries involved here than questions of personal privacy, scandal, or illegal activities. Questions about access to Keesing's materials may well become entwined with larger sociopolitical issues in Kwaio, involving local ideas about the power of knowledge and its control.[6] These issues are, in their specifics, singular to Kwaio, but they are nonetheless broadly instructive because similar complexities are likely to present themselves in other Pacific communities. The Kwaio situation can be elucidated by presenting sketches of three different Kwaio individuals with whom Akin has discussed the Keesing collection. All three view the materials and their return in quite different ways, illustrating different problems regarding questions of access.

The first is Tome (all names are pseudonyms), a highly respected political leader of the non-Christian bush Kwaio community. Tome has an impressive intellect, including a photographic memory, and in later years he became Keesing's major informant. Nearly one-third of Keesing's cassettes are recordings of interviews with and monologues by him. Tome's father was also a close friend and informant of Keesing (as well as Akin). Tome is enthusiastic about the return of the Keesing materials and will be a key member of the committee that will oversee how they are used and by whom. When Keesing wrote in various publications that Kwaio saw his research as a joint project to preserve aspects of their traditions, he likely had Tome in mind. He sees Keesing's field materials as a treasury of traditional knowledge, one that, as already indicated, he himself had a significant role in constructing. Tome is determined that there will be tight control over access to the materials when they are returned to Honiara. Like many bush people Akin spoke with, he is concerned to protect them from those who might misuse them, particularly evangelical Christians.

Most often cited regarding these concerns is Tome's cousin, Jackson. During Akin's early years in Kwaio, Jackson was the main priest for a shrine for key ancestral spirits of his kin group (which included Tome). Then, in the mid-1980s, Jackson's sister became ill, and, despite the sacrifice of many pigs on her behalf by himself and others, her ancestors took her life. Jackson, in his anger at the spirits, left his mountain community and moved to the coast to become a member of the South Sea Evangelical Church (SSEC). He has since become involved in an SSEC movement that performs *kasiaoto* (casting out devils) rituals intended to drive ancestral spirits from Kwaio and their non-Christian descendants to God. Some participants in these rituals are former bush people, and they perform them partly by drawing upon their knowledge of the ancestral religion, particularly the highly taboo names of ancestral spirits. Recent converts may be directed to desecrate the spirits they have left behind. Most commonly, a new female convert will sleep on top of a piece of paper upon which have been written sacred ancestral names, names forbidden for even a priest to utter except in shrines. A friend of Akin's explained to him how mountain Kwaio perceive the rituals to work:

Some of our relatives . . . have gone to the mission, and those church teachers [that is, church leaders] there told them, "Say the names of your ancestors." And so they told out the names of all of their ancestors. "Tell us the ancestors that give you pigs, and the ancestors that you call upon when planting taro or yams. And those ancestors to whom you plant shrubs to protect you and insure stability. The ancestors that grant you wealth. Tell out all of their names, and give them to us." Those teachers wrote down the ancestral names as they said them. When they had them on paper they prayed over them, then they took all of those things of our *kastom* [traditions] and they put them underneath women. And then the women took the paper to the women's toilet area and they defecated on it. . . . The Christians defile those ancestors so they will abandon us, and they thereby take our pigs away from us, and our good living. In the past people lived to a ripe old age before they died. But now Christians rip the ancestors apart and spoil them so that they can no longer be strong. That's why people nowadays are dying all the time without any reason.

A fear expressed to Akin by Tome and several other non-Christians was that Keesing's papers concerning sacred things might fall into the hands of Christians who would employ them as a weapon of ethnocide, to attack the ancestors and force everyone to flee to the Christian churches. Jackson, currently one of two leaders of SSEC *kasiaoto* activities, is the son of another of Keesing's key informants. His relatives' words fill many of Keesing's cassettes and transcriptions. Should Jackson be given the same access to this material as Tome?

Tome and other bush people say Jackson's access should be strictly limited. They assert that, by becoming Christian, Jackson and others have forsaken their ancestors and also their right to the knowledge associated with them. Some point out that they, and often their parents, worked with Keesing to strengthen *kastom*, not to undermine it. For them to give Jackson and his associates access to the ancestral names or other religious knowledge in Keesing's notes would, they believe, be suicidal. Jackson himself did not know how to respond to Akin's questions about what he thought should happen to Keesing's material. His initial reaction (the only one Akin was able to elicit) was that he now belongs to God and ancestral things are thus forbidden to him. The situation is further complicated because in the early 1990s Jackson led a local Christian effort to prevent Keesing from returning to Kwaio. Keesing was a vocal critic of Melanesian Christianity in his publications and more generally in the Solomons, and his sentiments were well known throughout Kwaio. Non-Christians now cite this legacy to justify their maintaining sole control over his field data. At present there are no Christians on the Kwaio committee to control the Keesing materials.

But some Christians are interested in Keesing's materials for other reasons. Most conspicuous are several young, well-educated men who have spent much of their lives away from home and are now anxious to learn more about Kwaio culture. Our third individual, Biri, is one of these men. He is a quite liberal SSEC member who was until 2000 the head teacher in a government secondary school on another island. In 1996 Akin received a letter from Biri asking if he might visit Akin's mountain hamlet to learn to properly record genealogies. Upon arriving, he opened his attaché case and sheepishly produced materials from his project to document his family's history—some two dozen cassettes of interviews, meticulous Kwaio transcriptions of them, and several genealogical diagrams. All were indexed in minute detail, and the undertaking was clearly a labor of love.

Biri is now back in Kwaio, has continued his ethnographic and ethnohistorical work, and is seeking a place to publish some forty ancestral myths he has collected and transcribed. He is excited that Keesing's materials will be returned to the National Museum, and he hopes they will help him to delve deeper into Kwaio culture and eventually perhaps to write a book. But whether Biri will have access to Keesing's materials is unknown. Thus far, he has only been able to work closely with members of his own extended family, especially a brilliant uncle (now Christian) who was also one of Keesing's most prolific informants. Most other Kwaio have declined to work with Biri because they fear that he might use their knowledge to become wealthy. This raises a broader issue: while we might conceive of Keesing's work as a collection of material about "Kwaio Culture," Kwaio themselves often perceive it as several bodies of data collected from the different "Kwaio cultures" with whom he worked. That is, he gathered knowledge from and, most important here, belonging to many separate kin groups. If Biri explores Keesing's material, he will be delving into the knowledge of groups to which he does not belong, groups who will likely object. This dovetails in interesting ways with current debates about who is indigenous, who speaks for indigenous communities, and how the memberships of those communities are being defined (Beteille 1998).

Biri will have problems not only because he is an outsider to most of the kin groups who have contributed to Keesing's data, but also because he is a Christian and outside of the mountain community that will control that data. Furthermore, as an educated man who has spent much of his life away, he is another kind of outsider, seen by some as culturally more attuned to the streets of Honiara than to Kwaio. We might think that Biri is the ideal beneficiary of returned field materials, a budding Melanesian scholar with an enthusiasm for anthropology. But if Keesing's materials are controlled solely by non-Christian mountain chiefs, it seems unlikely that Biri or, for that matter, any other government- or mission-educated man (let alone a female scholar) will be given access to Keesing's materials in the near future. If the non-Christian community continues its gradual decline there will come a time when, as in neighboring Kwara'ae, it will be a tiny isolated minority.[7] One wonders who will control the Keesing collection then, and to what purpose.

The Anthropologist's Responsibilities

Although these conflicts and concerns are specific to Kwaio, the broader issues involved are also pivotal in other parts of the Pacific, particularly in Melanesia. Across the region we encounter individuals and groups vying for control over the legitimacy granted by tradition, *kastom*, or culture, *kalsa*. Many evangelicals are hostile to symbols of pre-Christian indigenous cultures, and we often find growing community divisions between traditionalists and modernists, rural people and urban, educated elites. We expect that the quandaries that we are facing regarding Roger Keesing's papers will present themselves in related forms elsewhere.

These are not the kinds of decisions that anthropologists or archivists want to be making for Melanesian communities, although, as in the Kwaio case, those communities may ask that they make them (compare Alan Howard, chapter 2; Keith and Anne Chambers, chapter 9). We can return here to the responsibility researchers have to decide what will happen to their own data, both now and after they are gone. The complexities of local culture and politics are beyond the realm of archivists or even other anthropologists who have not worked in the same community. Even within the narrow Kwaio context, Akin finds repatriation and confidentiality decisions far easier to make for his own materials than for Keesing's.

There are obviously no perfect solutions to these issues, and to a certain degree we will have to deal with the complexities involved on a case-by-case, culture-by-culture basis (compare Howard, chapter 2; Jaarsma, chapter 3). We should prepare ourselves by questioning our own procedures, educating ourselves about relevant cultural practices and laws, and talking with others to build a shared understanding of what these issues mean for host communities, anthropologists, and archivists.

Suzanne Falgout

6

Archiving Jack Fischer's Micronesian Field Notes

The issue of cultural property has increasingly come to the forefront of discussions of anthropological research. Once, anthropology was considered to be a humanistic endeavor that would serve to heighten awareness of cross-cultural diversity, enlarge the discussion of human nature, and preserve knowledge of traditional cultures for posterity. More recently, anthropology's collection of other people's cultural properties has come to be regarded as a form of cultural imperialism, expropriation, or even outright plunder.[1]

The concept of cultural property itself raises a number of complex and interrelated questions. First, what is cultural property? Next, who is its rightful owner?[2] And, to whom within the culture of origin should the cultural property be given access or returned, or should other forms of restitution be made?

A number of other relevant issues have been given only scant attention in this debate. First, answers given to all questions of cultural property raised above have tended to be phrased in Western terms. What is the meaning of cultural property, in general, to the indigenous people who possess it?[3] Also, most of the attention paid to cultural property has centered around the removal of tangible forms of culture—human remains, archaeological sites, and artifacts.[4] Far less attention has been given to the issue of intellectual cultural property.[5] Next, how does intellectual cultural property differ from tangible cultural property? In what way are tangible and intellectual property linked to the people of the culture who possess it?

An additional complexity pertains to shifts in the epistemological, ethnographic, and political contexts of cultural knowledge. These contexts have changed for both anthropologists and indigenous peoples over time. Given these shifting contexts, what is the status of cultural knowledge collected in an earlier context, under very different understandings and even policies regarding cultural knowledge, today? Should recent understandings of cultural knowledge and its ownership automatically take precedence in deciding who owns cultural knowledge? To what degree should understandings in existence at the time of the original collection be considered relevant? Furthermore, whose understandings—the anthropologist's or the indigenous people's—should prevail?

This chapter will argue that both the anthropologist's and indigenous people's understandings of cultural knowledge, within the full context of original collection, should be included in considerations of ownership of cultural knowledge today. It will consider these issues in the case of an anthropologist who worked in Micronesia in the early United States Trust Territory (USTT) period of administration of the area. John (Jack) L. Fischer worked in an advisory capacity as a district anthropologist in Chuuk and Pohnpei in the early 1950s; later he served as an island affairs officer in Pohnpei. He also served as a "friend of the court" in Pohnpei, providing information on traditional cultural practices for use within the American judicial system.

For reasons discussed below, Jack Fischer, like other anthropologists of his time, worked with his Chuukese and Pohnpeian informants under conditions of extreme confidentiality between researcher and informant during the USTT period. But today, the political context has changed. Most of the various Micronesian islands included in the former administration have successfully negotiated the Compact of Free Association with the United States.[6] Chuuk and Pohnpei (along with Kosrae and Yap) are member states in the Federated States of Micronesia.[7] This new Micronesian nation is itself in charge of its own internal affairs, including its own cultural properties and anthropological research. Questions now arise about the status of intellectual cultural properties collected by earlier American anthropologists, such as Jack Fischer working under the USTT, and deposited in American archival collections at the Bishop Museum and Smithsonian Institution (see also Mary McCutcheon, chapter 4).

Here I will give primary focus to Fischer's research in Pohnpei, where he worked more extensively and where I have since worked as an anthropologist. I will also give attention to Fischer's field notes, deposited in the Bishop Museum in Honolulu. To answer the questions of access, I will first examine what kinds of intellectual cultural properties were collected, from whom, under what circumstances, and for what purposes. It becomes relevant to know how Fischer and his Pohnpeian informants understood cultural knowledge, its ownership, and its dissemination. Once this knowledge had been collected and recorded by Fischer, who then was thought to own that knowledge of the culture? Who was to be given access to this data? Who was to decide these questions, and on what basis?

American Anthropology in Postwar Micronesia

Anthropological field research in Micronesia was initiated shortly after the United States forces took possession of the former Japanese mandated islands at the close of World War II. Although the American administration shifted three times over the next six years,[8] the stated U.S. goals for governance of the area would remain largely the same: the establishment of American institutions and democratic ideals, but with sensitivity to Micronesian customs (Leibowitz 1989; Poyer, Falgout, and Carucci 2001). Yet the U.S. had fought and won a war in this area with very little knowledge of the peoples and cultures of Micronesia. The area had been closed for decades behind a Japanese bamboo curtain (see Falgout 1995; Kiste and Falgout 1999).

The usefulness of anthropology had been proven for the American war effort in Micronesia, as elsewhere. During the war, anthropologists had assembled the little information available on Micronesia for the Yale Cross-Cultural Survey, produced military handbooks for the postwar administration of the area, and even helped to train officers who would assume the immediate postwar governance of the territory (see Falgout 1995; Kiste and Falgout 1999).

The postwar period presented the opportunity for professional anthropological fieldwork on still little-known Micronesian customs. This work was considered to be important. Although researchers were guaranteed academic freedom, nevertheless the results of their findings were expected to be useful to the U.S. administration of Micronesia in culturally sensitive ways. The number of American anthropologists working in postwar Micronesia research projects was significant. A total of forty-four anthropologists worked on three major research projects:[9] U.S. Commercial Company (USCC; 1946); Coordinated Investigations of Micronesian Anthropology (CIMA; 1947–1949); and Scientific Investigations of Micronesia (SIM; 1949).[10] Then, just prior to the switch of the U.S. Trust Territory from Naval to Interior Department administration, the government began to hire a staff anthropologist (SA),[11] an administrative-level appointee who was to report directly to the high commissioner. The Trust Territory government at the same time hired district anthropologists (DAs),[12] who worked as field consultants specifically to assist the local civilian administrators, and who typically had very little knowledge of the area.

The position of district anthropologist attracted a few anthropologists who had worked on earlier Micronesian projects. Most, however, had little prior experience in Micronesia, but they were attracted by this opportunity for employment combined with the promise of approximately one-third of their time for their own independent research. Many saw it as a means to complete their doctoral research in anthropology (Falgout 1995).

The role of American anthropologists as consultants was almost without precedent (see Kiste and Falgout 1999). From the outset of this venture, some potential problems were recognized and attempts were made to clarify the anthropologist's role in administration. Homer Barnett, experienced in earlier Micronesian research and the first staff anthropologist in the High Commissioner's Office, sought a means to preserve the anthropologist's role as an objective and neutral researcher (1956). Barnett insisted that the anthropologists were only technical specialists—neutral, intermediate links between islanders and the administration. They were to collect information on Micronesian customs; they were to advise on the culturally appropriate implementation and success of administrative programs. Anthropologists were not to be involved in any policymaking (Barnett 1956).

But the U.S. administration's understanding of the anthropologist's role and use of this cultural information was not always easily accomplished. The relationship between administrators, anthropologists, and islanders varied throughout Micronesia, but at its worst extreme there was poor communication and a lack of respect between administrators and anthropologists, and there was also an ethnocentric attitude on the part of some administrators toward the Micronesians (Falgout 1995; Kiste and Falgout 1999; Poyer, Falgout, and Carucci 2001). Formal restatements of the anthropologist's role were made at the 1952[13] and 1957[14] conferences in Palau (USTT Archives 1950–1960). The anthropologists' most serious concerns centered on the protection of their sources and the inappropriate ways in which cultural knowledge was sometimes sought or actually used by some administrators. Several serious disagreements regarding the confidentiality of sources resulted in the eventual addition of section 342 to the *Code of the Trust Territory of the Pacific Islands.*[15]

Jack Fischer: Consultancy and Fieldwork

It was within this postwar context, specifically during the USTT/ Department of the Interior period of anthropological consultation, that Jack Fischer conducted his work on Chuuk and, even more extensively, on Pohnpei. According to the job description, most of his effort was to be devoted to research on "hot spots" or especially difficult problems for the administration. As elsewhere in Micronesia these problems tended to center on topics of enduring local controversy—land tenure (requiring research on traditional and contemporary notions of land use, land possession, land ownership, inheritance, kinship, adoption, and residence), traditional politics (including research on social organization, succession, roles of the chiefs, dispute resolution), and courtship, marriage, divorce, and adultery. In addition to helping Micronesians with problems, Fischer worked in support of the new American administrative directives by participating in field trips to outlying islands, resettlement of outer-islanders in the district center, conducting censuses, levying "dog taxes" to control mischievous mongrels, and the like (USTT Archives 1950–1960; Fischer n.d.).

The remainder of Fischer's time was to be spent on his own interests in Micronesian culture—principally magic and medicine and folklore. However, in a series of memos to the administration, and also at the anthropology conferences, Fischer added his complaints to those of other district anthropologists about the lack of time to accomplish their own work (see USTT Archives 1950–1960). These complaints apparently met with some success (see USTT Archives 1950–1960).

Fischer's very well-organized and fruitful ethnographic work can be seen in his research and field notes deposited by him in the Bishop Museum Archives in 1984. I was directed to the notes on Pohnpei by Fischer himself in an interview I had with him in his office at Tulane University in 1985. His research notes consist of two boxes of typed carbon copies, with penciled corrections. Each item is carefully dated and gives the informant's name; the notes themselves are often organized according to topic headings. These notes only occasionally discuss the context in which the information was collected and recorded; however, some contextual clues can be inferred from other information.

It seems that most of the information contained in these field notes was gathered during Fischer's work as field consultant, working as an advisor to troubled Micronesians and on administrative "hot spots." It is clear from even a cursory reading of his research notes that these issues had become especially complicated by Fischer's time. His advice was sought by Micronesians who had difficulty sorting through the complex maze created not only by varying traditional customs, but also by the differing Protestant and Catholic church regulations and by four successive colonial regimes that had been in place over the previous sixty-five-year period. Further contributing to the confusion had been statements by American liberation forces that Micronesians were now "free." Many Micronesians thought this meant "anything goes," and they did not realize there were American laws until they had broken them (Poyer, Falgout, and Carucci 2001). A smaller amount of data appears to be the result of Fischer's participant observation, principally at Pohnpeian feasts. A still smaller amount of data seems to be the result of largely ad hoc conversations that took place with his research assistants or with others in his work as consultant or participant observer.

The data contained in Fischer's research notes is most often presented as a third-person English summary, but first-person conversations and local language texts are sometimes also included. The data are carefully indexed according to the audiograph discs (these seem quite mixed according to date and topic; they were not deposited at the Bishop Museum and their current whereabouts is unknown to me), the date, informant, ethnicity, and topic.

By using the index to locate various topics over the past decade, I have found Fischer's research notes to contain information on almost every aspect of Pohnpeian culture. The notes are not only broad in scope, but also rich in the depth of the information presented. What is particularly impressive is the degree to which his informants are forthcoming about their own lives. Pohnpeians are typically very reluctant to divulge personal information, especially that which is not socially approved; it is told only to the most trusted of confidantes. Most frequently, Fischer's informants discussed those matters in which they were one of the principle participants, but they also occasionally discussed concerns of others, which also significantly impacted their own lives. Indeed, as can be observed in his research notes, this is the manner in which Fischer seemed to typically work—from the particular cases of a number of named individuals to more generalized statements about the culture. While this may have been his personal research strategy, I believe it was also a function of his work as district anthropologist in helping Micronesians with their individual problems.

A third box contains a typed carbon copy of Fischer's actual field notes, again well-organized with headings that indicate location, date, topic, and informant. These field notes differ from Fischer's research notes in several ways: they are chronologically organized; they contain more information on the context in which they were collected and recorded; they sometimes contain Fischer's personal appraisal of his assistants, informants, or events; they have more transcriptions of texts in local languages, with or without translation; they contain topics more varied and more focused on those related to his own personal interests; and some documents are labeled "confidential." In short, these field notes seem to be more personal; they contain materials considered to be more important, private, or sensitive, to both Fischer and to Pohnpeians. They are indexed in a manner similar to the research notes; in addition, they are indexed according to the manner in which they were collected.

The chronological organization and contextual notes contained in these field notes are even more revealing about the manner in which Fischer worked. It becomes clear that many of the Chuukese tales recorded by Fischer were collected after he relocated to Pohnpei by working with Chuukese who were resettled there. It also seems that many of the Chuukese and Pohnpeian tales were given to Fischer either from or through his research assistants (in Chuuk, Kin; in Pohnpei, Kuhrekohr) and their family members, neighbors, and friends. Others had been recorded and translated by his wife, Ann Fischer,[16] who had worked on the earlier SIM program in outer-island Chuuk and who had accompanied her husband to Pohnpei and there worked with her own assistant (Iowanis). Later, additional tales seem to have been given to him from those he had worked closely with on important cases. These networks of personal relationships are similar to those used by Pohnpeians in garnering knowledge of important oral traditions, yet Fischer's collection is far more extensive than any one Pohnpeian would be expected to possess.

In fact, the amount of important oral traditions collected by Fischer toward the end of his research and contained in his field notes is truly astonishing. As I expected, the collection contains transcriptions and translations of parts of the written volume of Luelen Bernart held by members of his family. This manuscript was collected from Luelen's descendants and later published along with another volume of annotations by Jack Fischer, USCC and Staff Anthropologist Saul Riesenberg, and District Anthropologist John Whiting's wife, Marjorie (Bernart 1977; Fischer, Riesenberg, and Whiting 1977). What was unexpected was the recording of several other manuscripts and collections of oral traditions given to Fischer by other informants. This, I believe, is another instance of remarkable cooperation given to Fischer by his Micronesian informants.

The Rationales and Results of Collecting Cultural Knowledge

How can we evaluate Fischer's anthropological work—a humanitarian endeavor in support of enlightened colonial policy, or a rip-off of indigenous cultural property? In the context of his times, I believe Jack Fischer was engaged in a bit of both. The job description of a district anthropologist implied a clear distinction between consultations for the administration and private research. In the abstract, sometimes Fischer's work was expressly designed to benefit Micronesians; at other times, it was expressly designed to benefit himself. Yet, I believe that in the field these two aspects increasingly began to blend together in his work, in the minds of Jack Fischer and his informants.

Fischer's role as their liaison and advocate meant that what they told to him was understood to be for their own benefit, either immediately or ultimately. Thus, Jack Fischer was "helpful" in a Micronesian culture for which this behavior is very positively valued; he was also "helpful" in a context when Micronesians truly needed his assistance. Furthermore, Fischer was a well-respected and sympathetic authority figure within this neocolonial context, one who promised informants confidentiality. In short, I believe informants saw in him someone who asked probing questions for a good, beneficial purpose; they also saw in him someone they could trust with their personal secrets. This includes much information contained in his notes that, if made public, could prove deeply embarrassing in a culture for which shame is highly marked. It also includes some information that could be potentially harmful to individuals living under a measure of American scrutiny today.

I believe the rapport and trust Fischer gained working as a district anthropologist gave a tremendous boost to his personal research on magic and medicine, and especially on oral traditions. Fischer's name is still known, and he still enjoys a very good reputation for the high quality of his research among many of those with whom he worked in Pohnpei. Even today, I have heard some Pohnpeians refer to him as a *soupoad*, "master historian." This is a label of high praise used in reference to those who have an in-depth knowledge of Pohnpeian oral history. This knowledge is considered to be especially important, valuable, precious, and sacred. The ultimate locus of this knowledge is with the revered ancestors; it is initially communicated from them to a chosen descendant through the medium of dreams. Subsequently, it is conveyed from the chosen recipient to only one or a few within a limited genealogical unit of inheritance or other very special relationship. By keeping this knowledge relatively secret, Pohnpei's master historians have kept concentrated the power of this knowledge. This power is in turn imparted to those who possess it and manifested by their enhanced life force, status, title, and *manaman* (power and authority) relative to others in Pohnpeian society (see Falgout 1984).

I believe that Fischer's unusual success in collecting Pohnpeian oral traditions, then, is a testament to his special role as a district anthropologist in the USTT / Department of Interior context in Micronesia. But it is also a testament to the special relationships he was able to develop in working as a district anthropologist with several Pohnpeians, who happened to also be historians. In a very real sense, the DA and informants were being "helpful," in their different ways, to each other. While this scenario could be cast in terms of colonial exploitation, or even mutual exploitation, I believe that this would be a Western, and a very limited, understanding of the nature and quality of this relationship. I believe it was also a relationship of mutual respect for differing areas of expertise and of generosity in using this expertise on behalf of others.

Another important consideration in the cooperation of his informants, as discussed by Fischer in his field notes, was his outsider status. Several of his informants stated that they felt less reticent to reveal these stories to him than to Pohnpeians. As a cultural outsider, Fischer was not in a position to reap the benefits of this knowledge in traditional ways. Thus, his possession of this knowledge was a less serious matter than if it had been given to a Pohnpeian.

It was in his role as an unusually "helpful outsider" in this postwar Micronesia context that Jack Fischer came to possess far more traditional knowledge than any single Pohnpeian could ever hope to achieve. Perhaps, to a somewhat lesser degree, this is a common result of intensive ethnographic fieldwork. Although usually considered a successful research outcome, it produces a host of additional ethical issues that include ones regarding the anthropologists' subsequent academic use of these materials and the granting of access to their field notes to others.

Academic Use of Pohnpeian Cultural Knowledge

In the overall context of anthropological fieldwork consultation in postwar Micronesia, Jack Fischer went on to enjoy a particularly successful academic career. Only half of the district anthropologists who worked in

Micronesia eventually earned their Ph.D.s; fewer still went on to academic careers.[17] In contrast, Fischer completed his dissertation, "Language and Folktale in Truk and Ponape: A Study in Cultural Integration," at Harvard University in 1954, just one year after his return, and assumed a lifelong position at Tulane University shortly after.

Over the course of his life, Fischer's publications on Pohnpeian culture were numerous and well regarded by his colleagues. They included articles on kinship, gender roles, residence, language, folklore, religion, et cetera. He also published three books. One is a useful reference text, *The Eastern Carolines*, written with the assistance of his wife, Ann Fischer, and published by the Human Relations Area Files Press in 1970. The other books are the aforementioned *Book of Luelen* and the *Annotations*, co-authored with Riesenberg and Whiting.

Yet some in Pohnpei have been ambivalent about Fischer's use of Pohnpeian historical knowledge. While acknowledging his "help" as a district anthropologist and admiring his command of Pohnpeian oral history, they are somewhat disapproving of his publication of the *Book of Luelen*. At issue is not Fischer's knowledge of or continued possession of this oral history; rather it is the issue of access. When Fischer, Riesenberg, and Whiting published Luelen's manuscript, this made a very highly regarded version of Pohnpeian oral history available for purchase and possession, not just by numerous cultural outsiders, but also by Pohnpeians as well (see Hanlon 1992). This widespread public distribution is culturally understood to dilute the power of the knowledge and the benefits that accrued to those who rightfully possessed it. And some voice their concern that Luelen's descendants were not completely aware that this would become public knowledge.[18] The publication of important Pohnpeian cultural knowledge by other outside researchers was not without precedent. The collection and publication of oral traditions by Paul Hambruch (1932–1936; completed by Elliers) during the German period of administration is the best-known example. Hambruch's collection of oral traditions is thought of as literally exhausting one informant, depleting the life force imparted to him by his possession of secret knowledge and resulting in his death. Reportedly, after a very long session of storytelling, the informant left in his outrigger canoe for home, but was found dead in his canoe in the lagoon the next morning.

Although originals of this text are limited in number, a copy is contained in the collection of the local college library and photocopies have also been made. On more than one occasion, recent anthropologists have speculated that the source of their informants' knowledge has been gained from a copy of this work.

More recently, the Department of Education has sponsored the Old Age Program, charged with collecting and compiling important cultural knowledge from Pohnpeian elders for publication and use as part of the classroom curriculum. While many see this culturally relevant part of the curriculum as an improvement over an emphasis on George Washington and other American "heroes," they also complain about the widespread access being given to secret knowledge (see Falgout 1992).

The New Context—Anthropology in the Federated States of Micronesia

Fischer's work as a district anthropologist in postwar Micronesia was conducted in two contexts that necessitated confidentiality about cultural knowledge—American and Micronesian in the 1950s. Perhaps for these reasons, when he placed his research and field notes at the Bishop Museum Archives, he restricted access to them. They are for inspection by Ph.D.s for academic purposes only. Following the USTT code, he asked that access be denied to any government employees. He also asked that they not be shown to missionaries or to Micronesians.

But so much changed since Fischer worked as a district anthropologist in Micronesia. Chuuk and Pohnpei are member states in the Federated States of Micronesia under a compact of free association with the United States. This political status guarantees their own control over internal matters, but agrees to grant the U.S. rights to external security matters in exchange for some funding. The former code of confidentiality between anthropologist and informant was stricken in 1979 as being anachronistic and paternalistic. It was also criticized for privileging Micronesian conversations with outsiders above those between Micronesians themselves.[19]

Clearly, there are issues of power here—who is considered to be important, and who is in charge. Today, Micronesians are firmly in charge of their own governance and of their own cultures. Here, they are arguing against the hierarchy of privilege granted to Americans in the old USTT days and codified in this section of the code. In striking this section of the code, they make a statement to themselves, and to the world, that today they have assumed the power to determine their own fates.

This responsibility is being shouldered by a new group of American-educated Micronesian leaders today. Education for Micronesians, just beginning in Fischer's day, has grown tremendously. Today, several Micronesians have earned Ph.D.s and are working in new government positions. A Pohnpeian who holds a Ph.D. in anthropology now heads the Federated States of Micronesia Historic Preservation Office.

Anthropology has also changed since the postwar period in which Fischer and his compatriots worked in Micronesia. Shortly after Fischer deposited his field notes at the Bishop Museum, he met an untimely death in 1987. The executor of his estate, a former student, was charged with disposing of a multitude of other research notes that remained in Fischer's Tulane office. Operating under a newer, different set of understandings of cultural property, these additional research notes were placed at the Smithsonian without restrictions. Mary McCutcheon (chapter 4) reports though that the Smithsonian is now reevaluating the access it offers to its portion of Fischer's field notes. What about Fischer's research and field notes at the Bishop Museum? Should their restricted status be removed or kept in place?

This is a very difficult question to answer. Clearly, the opinions of many are needed—those of a variety of anthropologists and those of a variety of Pohnpeians. However, in this final section, I wish to raise several issues that I think should be addressed in reaching a final decision. And, in doing so, I will express my own opinion on the status of Fischer's research and field notes.

First, in a very fundamental sense I think that questions about the status of cultural knowledge should not be completely abstracted from the original cultural and political contexts in which the knowledge was acquired by the anthropologist because the information provided to and collected and recorded by the anthropologist was shaped by that context. The context, then, as well as cultural knowledge, is very much a part of what is encoded in any collection of anthropological data.

The lingering presence of original context can be clearly seen in Fischer's research and field notes. As a district anthropologist researching "hot spots," the information provided to Fischer was by definition on culturally and politically controversial topics. Then, in his role as mediator between the American administration and Pohnpeians, Fischer's informants expected him to be sympathetic and to use the information they provided in ways directly or indirectly helpful to them in solving problems. Finally, the information was collected and the notes were written under the assurance of confidentiality. As such, informants were more open, and perhaps also more partisan, in their discussions with Fischer on a range of very sensitive topics. Fischer himself provided at times a very candid, and sometimes uncomplimentary, assessment of what he learned. In short, much that is included in these notes would be very embarrassing to many and potentially even harmful to some if revealed. And, although more than forty years have passed since this information was collected, a number of these people are still alive today. I believe that making this information publicly available would be regarded by Pohnpeians, still today, as a breach of trust given to

anthropologists in general, and Fischer in particular (compare Alan Howard, chapter 2; Bryan Oles, chapter 10).

In addition, I think that the culture's epistemology is fundamental to
considerations of ownership of the content of cultural property. Related to
indigenous epistemological concerns is the difference between tangible and
intangible aspects of cultural property. It can be argued that the separation of
tangible from intangible property is somewhat arbitrary, since the production of tangible items entails cultural knowledge. And tangible items, once
removed, can be recreated by the cultural knowledge of their manufacture.

Nevertheless, the removal of tangible cultural property creates an absence of the items from the original context; this absence is only rectified by
the items' return to their original owners. This differs significantly from
the removal of cultural knowledge, which although removed also remains
largely intact in the original context.

The oral histories that are recorded in Fischer's collection were removed
from Pohnpei by him, but this did not create their total absence. First, these
stories are likely still known and kept relatively secret among select members of the culture today. Unlike tangible cultural property, these stories are
still possessed, told, and retold at the storyteller's will. In telling the stories,
the stories are not lost, either to the storyteller or to the culture. It is true
that Pohnpeians believe that the stories and the life force they convey to the
storyteller become diluted in the process of being told. This is why the
storyteller very carefully chooses to reveal his knowledge only to someone
who is known to be closemouthed. In short, the collection of oral histories
by Fischer created a weakening, but not a total loss, of this form of cultural
property. And, ultimately, the "original" form of this knowledge remains
stored with the ancestors; they may choose to bestow this knowledge at
their will to another chosen one.

"Returning" these stories by opening this collection to the peoples of
Pohnpei, furthermore, would not rectify the situation. Rather, in Pohnpeian
understanding, it would exacerbate the process of weakening. Although
many in the culture who are denied traditional access might like to learn
these stories, those who are the rightful owners of this knowledge might be
appalled to have it widely given away without their consent. It is considered
to be their right to possess this knowledge and their responsibility to pass it
on to individuals of their own careful choosing. Granting open access to
Fischer's field notes would allow the reader to immediately overcome the
traditional Pohnpeian considerations of genealogical connection, personal
relationship, character, and a long period of apprenticeship. Instead, the

reader could gain immediate knowledge of a range of secret knowledge far beyond anything previously obtained by any one Pohnpeian.

In short, while much has indeed changed over the past fifty years in Pohnpei, still the issues of privacy in candid discussions and secrecy in the transmission of cultural knowledge in oral histories live on. For now, I believe that in both American and Pohnpeian understandings, a promise is still a promise. Two misguided wrongs (first collecting and then "returning" these candid discussions and oral traditions) will not make a right.

Karen M. Peacock

7

Returning History through the Trust Territory Archives

life must be understood backwards; but . . . it must be lived forwards.
SØREN KIERKEGAARD
Journals and Papers

There is no future, there is no past . . .
Hurry, hurry, this is the last, . . .
STEPHEN V. BENÉT
John Brown's Body

To be able to look backwards and understand life, one must have the records—the tangible evidence, the source material. Archives and records are not solely a Western concept, but for the Pacific Islands, with its oral history, the paper path to the past is relatively new. At the same time the importance of colonial records is evident in the exciting new developments in rethinking Pacific Islands history, politics, and culture. Pacific Islanders themselves are turning to archives for just such academic research, as well as for information needed for government studies and for personal family history.

I do not deal with issues of repatriating field notes here, or theoretical examination of the ownership of knowledge, or the ethical dilemmas of confidentiality of informants. Instead, in this chapter, I offer a case study of an attempt to capture the records of a colonial past and return them to the people of Micronesia. To make the process clear, a fairly detailed background of the history of the Trust Territory Archives will be given. Subsequently, I turn to the problems of developing archival programs and the specific criticisms and rumors that have haunted the Trust Territory Archives. I should offer another disclaimer: I was an active participant in the events described. I coordinated the University of Hawai'i Library's role in assisting the Trust Territory Archives project. The reader should bear in mind that my involvement with the Trust Territory Archives over the past eighteen years has given me detailed knowledge of the initial program and the records with which it dealt, but has also made me to a great degree a defender of the project, though I readily admit its faults and weaknesses.

Creation of the Trust Territory Archives

The United States administration of Micronesia, the Trust Territory of the Pacific Islands, covered the period from 1947 to 1994. Immediately following World War II the islands were under the control of the navy, but administration was transferred to the Department of the Interior in 1951. Government headquarters, originally in Honolulu, moved to Guam and later to Saipan, where they remained until the end of the trusteeship. For administrative purposes the Trust Territory government organized the islands into six districts, based on earlier colonial precedent: the Marshalls, Pohnpei, Chuuk, Marianas, Yap, and Palau, with the later addition of Kosrae. During the trusteeship, programs in economic, social, educational, medical, and political development sought, with widely varying degrees of success, to fulfill the United Nations trusteeship charter. After many years of intense and complex negotiations on the political status of the area between representatives of the United States and the Congress of Micronesia, new entities emerged: the Republic of the Marshall Islands, the Federated States of Micronesia (Kosrae, Pohnpei, Chuuk, and Yap), the Republic of Palau (Belau) in free association with the U.S., and the Commonwealth of the Northern Mariana Islands (Saipan, Rota, Tinian, and the northern islands). The trusteeship ended when Palau's long and torturous path to status resolution concluded with free association in 1994.

As the new entities began to emerge and assume their autonomous government, the United States scaled down its operations in the region, anticipating an end to its administrative involvement in the 1980s. Concerns arose over the issue of preservation of the records of the trusteeship, and this concern was highlighted by the destruction Saipan experienced from a typhoon that hit in 1979, leaving water damage in some government office files. Sam McPhetres, a member of the high commissioner's staff, proposed the creation of a program to preserve the Trust Territory's files through indexing and microfilming. It should be noted that although the region had seen considerable development in its public library system, no official gov-

Digitizing of Trust Territory Archives photos at University of Hawai'i in 1992 (University of Hawai'i Library)

ernment archives existed, nor were there any district archives upon which the new Micronesian nations could build.

As no one in Washington seemed to know just how long the Trust Territory would continue to exist as an entity, a desperate sense of urgency pushed concerns about government records forward—government officials and academics alike feared the possible loss of a treasure trove of information and felt that a last chance existed to rescue the past.

After consultation with University of Hawai'i Professor Emeritus Norman Meller, as well as other university faculty and library administrators, Acting Deputy High Commissioner Daniel J. High issued Executive Order 128 on 12 June 1981, establishing a Trust Territory Archives Committee and Program. The program sought to provide the newly formed governments of Micronesia with important research and documentation concerning the history of their lands and peoples and to offer primary source material for scholarly study. Because four governments now existed that would have a need for the official records, microfilm seemed an option that would allow each new government to possess a copy of the archives of the entire Trust Territory government.

The University of Hawai'i Library sent Aggie Quigg, then on the library faculty, to Saipan to serve as a consultant and work with Sam McPhetres. Together they surveyed and evaluated all existing files in the various headquarters departments, determining the extent of preservation required and establishing the framework for creation of a computerized index to the records. Quigg and McPhetres devised an archives survey form to provide the data for a computerized index. For each file examined, archives staff recorded the agency responsible for producing the material (or holding the material produced by another entity or individual), a bibliographic citation (author, title, and date of publication, if any), subject headings assigned to the file or document, span of years covered, appropriate geographic areas concerned, format, quantity (number of pages or files), and final disposition of the original documents.

Having secured the support of the Trust Territory government and conducted a survey of records, McPhetres negotiated an agreement with the University of Hawai'i whereby the library would hold a master copy of all microfilm. Through funding from the Department of the Interior, the library would copy all film produced on Saipan to provide complete sets of microfilm for each Micronesian government. The library also made copies for public use at its Manoa facility and made its services available to duplicate microfilm for interested persons and government agencies.[1]

A set of microfilm would also be sent to the National Archives of the United States.[2] The disposition of the original files and documents caused some considerable concern. As stated earlier, there was no existing Trust Territory Archives facility, nor was there any national library, although the Trust Territory's Library Services program had worked with the district governments to develop high school and public libraries and had been involved with the library of the (then) Community College of Micronesia. The National Archives, the University of Hawai'i, and the University of Guam's Micronesian Area Research Center all declined, albeit reluctantly, the offer of becoming the final repository of the original files, largely because of space considerations. Housing these materials would have required a warehouse-sized structure, and none of the agencies contacted had the space or the funds to acquire a new facility. Consequently, the Trust Territory Archives team decided to deposit materials with each government based on area covered therein.

Materials described as "routine, general files of government offices" were destroyed (McPhetres 1992a, 11). Rare or unique materials that required special handling, such as an eighteenth-century voyage account, were sent to the Micronesian Area Research Center at the University of

Guam. The Trust Territory government retained files regarding "matters which would be involved in future litigation" (McPhetres 1992a, 11). Some files of particular historical interest were deposited at the University of Hawai'i Library, although in these cases each government received a full microfilm copy.

The microfilm project encompassed an enormous bulk of materials, and consequently the majority of files were processed on 16 mm film as a more economical measure. The maps, blueprints, and other oversized documents went on the 35 mm film that allows better viewing. The Trust Territory Archives also incorporated and indexed documents filmed in the 1970s under an earlier project.[3] Microfilm produced by the archives project is of varying quality and readability. When work began in 1981, the equipment available was old and subject to frequent breakdowns. Lack of repair facilities on Saipan created delays, and the camera and processor were often in use even when the resulting film did not yield good-quality products. It is important for users to know that some microfilm is difficult to read because of the poor quality of equipment available during the early stages of the project, and because at times staff were filming thermofax paper, faded dittos, or third-generation colored carbons that did not reproduce well. The team quite rightly felt that it was wiser to attempt to preserve important documents that might be at least partly legible on film. It is in such cases, a small percentage of the total film produced, that the disposition of originals becomes a pressing concern.

Arrangement of files on microfilm was determined by availability of processed documents, and thus the index is essential for access. In the ideal archival system records from one agency would be kept together, but the practical necessities of the program did not allow for such a methodology. It might be argued, although archivists would surely contest the point, that a computerized index alleviates the need for traditional record maintenance.

A target sheet to indicate the beginning of a new entry prefaced each file filmed. The archives survey sheet that described the file was filmed next, providing a "title page" for the material that follows. The data entered in the computerized index indicates both the reel number for each file and the frame number for the set. As odometer readings vary on different equipment, it is necessary to scroll carefully through the approximate vicinity of the frame indicated by the index. Unfortunately, frame numbers are not cited on the "pages" of the microfilmed records.

As the materials were processed, the Saipan Archives team sent microfilm to the University of Hawai'i Library. The original microfilm sent from Saipan became an archival set, with a second set of negatives created to use for copying. A set of positives was made available for library users at the university. At the end of the project, complete sets of all microfilm were sent to each of the four Micronesian governments.

A Path to the Past: Indexing the Archives

As material was organized on Saipan, the archive survey forms were entered into a computer database, and from this data a printed version of the index provided the initial access for users.[4] When the archives project was completed in 1988, the library received the computer tapes of the index, which were then transferred to the MARC format used in the library's on-line catalog system.[5] The transfer of data from one index type to another has created some unavoidable confusion, as the category of author used in MARC format replaced the label of "Primary Branch, Dept. or other office producing materials" originally designated on Saipan. This might seem at first reading a logical category to name as "author." However, in the organizing of the archives the Department of Public Affairs might have had a copy of a study by anthropologist Leonard Mason in its files, for example. Under the new University of Hawai'i data-entry style, Public Affairs becomes the author, and the use of individual names such as that of Leonard Mason in an author search becomes meaningless. The most useful search mechanism for use of the Trust Territory Archives on-line index is the keyword approach.[6] One can also limit the search by date.[7] Despite some of the difficulties involved in searching the index, numerous students, researchers, and community users from Hawai'i, the United States, Australia, and the Micronesian nations have been able to successfully access information from the archives, either at the library terminals, through the Internet, or via the library's web catalog.

After the Trust Territory Archives work was completed, archives in the Micronesian governments (which had the original Saipan index) requested copies of the University of Hawai'i version that could be utilized from computer disks. The library complied with this request and set up memoranda of understanding with each government, whereby in return for the disks of the library's index each archive would supply copies of future microfilm to the University of Hawai'i for preservation in environmentally controlled storage. One of the major components of the Trust Territory Archives project was to establish an archives unit in each government, supplying these units with microfilm equipment and training so that work could proceed to further preserve the records and files being created by the new governments.

Unique Images: Trust Territory Archives Audiovisual, Map, and Photograph Collections

The Trust Territory Archives on-line index also covers three unique collections, most of which are not found on the 2,169 reels of microfilm that make up the document collection. A small number of filmstrips, audiotapes, and videotapes were deposited with the University of Hawai'i Library and can be reproduced on demand. A large collection of maps and aerial photos, not all of which were microfilmed, are indexed and available in the Library Map Collection, where they are filed geographically. At the end of the archives project, the library received the photograph and slide holdings of the Trust Territory government. This unique resource of over 50,000 photos and over 2,000 slides documents the history of the American period in Micronesia (1947–1988). Thanks to the vigorous efforts of Sam McPhetres, Deputy Director Jones George, and other staff members, photographs were retrieved from various government files. The largest portion of the collection contains work done by government photographers and other employees, often for use in Trust Territory publications such as the biweekly newsletter *Highlights*, the quarterly magazine *Micronesian Reporter*, and the annual report to the United Nations. The archives project staff made every effort to identify persons shown in the photographs (which often were unlabeled) and ran copies of elusive scenes in the Saipan newspaper, asking for community help in identifying individuals and locations.

In 1991 the library received a Title II-C federal grant to create a digitized database of selected photos from the Trust Territory Archives collection. The task involved inventorying and selecting photographs of important historical and cultural significance. As Pacific curator I was responsible for surveying the entire holdings. I identified over 6,000 images, for which I created descriptive information to enhance the existing index records. The original indexing had grouped photos together under general headings. Thus a set of photos labeled "Photos of High Commissioner Elbert D. Thomas in Hawaii, 1951–1952,"[8] also contained images of other administrators and of naval personnel. The added descriptions for images to be scanned were entered into the database. Photographs and slides selected were scanned to produce a digital image file, which was then linked to the on-line catalog record. This effort sought to preserve the photo collection by allowing users to search and view images with less handling of original works and also to provide enhanced and faster access for users. The database that emerged has been available only at workstations in the Pacific Collection, although the index information is available to anyone able to dial-in to the library's on-line catalog or to access the catalog via the Internet.[9] In 1995

Political parade in Palau prior to the 1978 referendum on future status (Trust Territory Archives, University of Hawai'i Library)

I published an article concerning the library's work on the Trust Territory Archives photograph collection,[10] and I discussed progress on the digitized database with librarians and archivists during my travels in Micronesia to such events as the 1996 Pacific Association of Libraries and Archives conference held in Majuro, Marshall Islands.

In October 1998 the library received a federal grant from the Institute of

Museum and Library Services that allowed the entire digitized database to be made available on the World Wide Web, moving access to an international level and, most important, providing resources to the growing number of Micronesian government offices, libraries, schools, and individuals having Internet access. Web access to the full collection of digitized images should be available by 2001.

Problems, Pitfalls, and Possibilities: Evaluation of the Archives

The Trust Territory Archives is a monumental achievement that has given both the world of scholarship and the community at large a resource of immense value. In my role as Pacific curator at the University of Hawai'i Library, I have assisted in providing access to this collection. Students, faculty, Micronesian government officials, lawyers, business people, and the general public have found in the microfilm files and the photographic images information on history, culture, land tenure, economic development, education, art, political process, and a host of other topics. A number of prominent authors have based their research on documents from the Trust Territory Archives, and they have used its photographs to illustrate their work.[11] Despite the unprecedented achievement of placing nearly all records of a colonial government on microfilm and insuring preservation and access, a number of problems and issues illustrate some of the difficulties in this repatriation of resources.

The first issue to be discussed continues to create controversy, and that is the matter of disposition of original documents. The question could be posed as, Who inherits the past? As noted earlier, no external agency was prepared or able to take on housing the original records, files, and documents that were microfilmed by the Trust Territory government. Consequently, much of the material was sent to the four Micronesian governments. As the creation of archives was still in process, the safe disposition of records was uncertain. In the case of the Marshall Islands, the Alele Museum became the repository for the microfilm and printed documents. In Pohnpei, capital of the Federated States of Micronesia, the College of Micronesia was able to obtain large amounts of Trust Territory publications and documents included in the materials sent out from Saipan to the Federated States of Micronesia. A new and impressive College of Micronesia campus in Palikir includes a fine library, and Director Dakio Syne has hopes of seeing the Trust Territory Archives materials formally organized. The Federated States of Micronesia government also has the advantage of a very experienced archivist, Jones George, who was deputy director of the original Trust Territory Archives project, and who possesses intimate knowledge of the database and records. The official archives office is currently located under the Department of Health, Education, and Social Affairs. The Commonwealth of the Northern Mariana Islands is fortunate to have the knowledgeable services of Herbert Del Rosario, also a former Trust Territory Archives team member, working with the microfilm and index, which is part of the holdings of the Northern Marianas College Library located on Saipan. In Palau, archives responsibility has shifted with reorganizations, and at the moment (September 2001) Naomi Ngirakamerang is national archivist, with her department a part of the Bureau of Community Services, which falls under the Ministry of Community and Cultural Affairs of the national government.[12]

Without a doubt, and based on all standard archival practice, the best course of action would have been preservation of all original records. This is particularly true given the difficulty in deciphering a portion of the microfilm. The problem lies in the lack of established archives in the various governments of Micronesia. It is certainly possible to criticize the former Trust Territory government for its failure to create either centralized or district-level archives, but the fact remains that as the Trust Territory moved to closing its offices, McPhetres and the archives team were faced not only with the Herculean effort to preserve records on film, but also to find the means to create offices and train staff for archival functions in the Republic of the Marshall Islands, the Commonwealth of the Northern Mariana Islands, the Federated States of Micronesia, and the Republic of Palau. As McPhetres has stated, it was very much a salvage operation, geared toward preserving what otherwise might be forever lost, with a second goal of setting up ongoing archival programs (1992b, 3).

Concurrent to the development of the Trust Territory Archives project, the Pacific Regional Branch of the International Council on Archives (PARBICA) held training seminars in 1981 and 1985 in which some Micronesian librarians and archivists participated. This group's excellent work in the development of Pacific Islands archives is well known, and contact had been established between the archives organization and the Trust Territory Archives operation on Saipan. As mentioned earlier, the secretary general of the Pacific Regional Branch of the International Council on Archives visited Micronesia in 1987 and met with Sam McPhetres, as well as with archivists and librarians throughout the former Trust Territory. Indeed in 1988 *Pacific Archives Newsletter* published an article by Sam McPhetres describing the Trust Territory Archives project (mentioned in Cleland 1989, 33). The 1989 issue of *Pacific Archives Journal* contains an article describing to readers the full history of the Trust Territory Archives project (United States Trust Territory Archives Project 1989). In 1990 former Trust Territory Archives

Deputy Director Jones George contributed an article, "Federated States of Micronesia Country Report," in which he referred to the archives project, the disposition of records, and the existence of microfilm sets at the University of Hawai'i, the United States National Archives, and in the four Micronesian nations (George 1990).

In 1989 I made mention of the fact that damage from a 1979 typhoon on Saipan created the idea of a need for an archives program (Peacock 1989, 168). As part of a description of the process entailed in creating the microfilm archives, I also stated, "Many of the records now on film were destroyed after filming, although those relating specifically to one of the current governments of Micronesia were sent to the appropriate government" (Peacock 1989, 170). I based this statement on my knowledge of the Trust Territory Archives project, and this was later substantiated when McPhetres wrote that records were "destroyed if they were routine, general files of government offices" (McPhetres 1992a, 11).[13]

At the 1991 Pacific Regional Branch International Council on Archives conference, Peter Orlovich, an archivist from Australia, brought my article to the attention of the group and quoted the section cited above. He went on to raise two issues, "which he felt should be of major concern to PARBICA members" (PARBICA Minutes 1992, 64). The first issue was that, according to Orlovich, the article "revealed—apparently for the first time for many members of PARBICA, including those from the former Trust Territory islands, that a formal agreement was drawn up between the University of Hawaii and the Trust Territory of the Pacific Islands Government in 1982" (PARBICA Minutes 1992, 64–65).[14] Orlovich went on to note that the agreement provided for a set of Trust Territory Archives microfilm at the University of Hawai'i Library, with copies made for the four governments of Micronesia.

In the discussion that followed, described in the PARBICA Minutes, Nancy Lutton (National Archives of Papua New Guinea) spoke of her knowledge of the Trust Territory Archives project and "saw no objection to microfilm copies of the records being in Honolulu" (PARBICA Minutes 1992, 65). Eamonn Bolger of New Zealand expressed concern that vitally important records should have been destroyed and asked whether criteria for the selection of archives were adopted. The ensuing deliberations are of sufficient interest to the evolution of the controversy surrounding the Trust Territory Archives to merit full quotation:

> *Peter Orlovich*, in concurring with this view, said that much of the article appeared to reflect an approach to the task of preserving the US Trust Ter-

ritory archives which attached more importance to their value predominantly as information, to be manipulated for research scholars, than as the records of a complex government administration, which formed a legitimate part of the archival heritage of all the nations that were formerly comprised within the Trust Territory of the Pacific Islands. *Jones George* said that destruction of records of the US Trust Territory have resulted from the closure of the Trust Territory Archives, and not from the effects of a typhoon in 1979, as might be implied from the article. He said that no thought had been given to the provision of long-term storage accommodation of the archives until the impending closure of the Trust Territory Government, and the question arose as to who would take care of them. In describing the archives he said that a computer generated form accompanied every record that was microfilmed, and the forms were used as the basis for the computerised index to the archive. Provision was made at the end of each sheet for a decision to be made by an "Evaluator" as to whether to (I) distribute the archives to the governments of Palau, Federated States of Micronesia and Commonwealth of Northern Marianas; (II) destroy the records; or (III) retain the records. These forms were then initialled by the Evaluator, and microfilmed with the records. His own view was that the evaluation decisions were "really valid," and that some destruction was unavoidable because there was nowhere to deposit the millions of records involved. *Hermana Ramarui* [Palau] asked whether all of the Trust Territory records had been microfilmed. *Jones George* responded that two sets of master reels had been made, one being deposited with the National Archives in Washington, and the other with the University of Hawaii. Duplicate copies had also been deposited with each of the four governments of the former Trust Territory. In response to a question from *Hermana* as to who had determined the distribution of copies, *Jones George* replied that the Trust Territory archives were public records, and therefore should be available for public access.

Hermana said that the existence of the Agreement of 1982 between the University of Hawaii and the Trust Territory Government was not known to Archivists in the individual states because it had been executed prior to their achievement of independence, consequence of which no consultation took place.

She thought that PARBICA should represent the interests of the individual states in seeking more information about the Agreement. *Jones George* emphasised that the files belonged to the High Commissioner, who was the United States representative in the Trust Territory. *Sam Kaima* [Papua New Guinea] asked whether the Federated States of Micronesia had a copy of the Agreement of 1982. *Hermana* asked whether it was not too late to re-negotiate the Agreement. *Gabriel Gerry* [Papua New Guinea] enquired as to when the destruction of records referred to by Karen Peacock occurred. *Jones George* stated that microfilming project was completed in 1988 or 1989. He did not think that records of archival value were destroyed, but had not been consulted on the matter. In fact, he understood that most of the original records had been sent to the respective governments of the former Trust Territory. In response to a question from *Eamonn Bolger* [New Zealand] who asked whether criteria for the selection of archives were adopted, Jones replied that they had not, adding that "archives" was a new concept for the Trust Territory administration at that time, and that the project was undertaken in a rush. *Sam Kaima*, noting that several issues had been raised, enquired as to what PARBICA should do.

Sam Kaima asked whether copies of the Agreement of 1982 could be sent to all Archivists in the Federated States of Micronesia jurisdiction so that they had copies. *Michael Piggott* [Australia] suggested that, as *Nancy* had a lot of information from *Sam McPhetres*, and as the Pacific Archives Journal was published in Port Moresby, *Nancy* and *Tukul* [Papua New Guinea] might include a copy of the Agreement of 1982 in the report of PARBICA V Conference. *Hermana* thought that as Palau was closer to the countries concerned, the matter should be pursued from there. *Tukul* asked *Jones George* if he could draft a report on the various issues and concerns, which had been expressed in the foregoing discussion.

George Panlani [Cook Islands] concluded the discussion with a suggestion that it be recorded in the Minutes that the Conference notes with great concern the factors involved in the Trust Territory archives microfilming project, and that other countries in the region with archival interests in the project be urged to pursue further enquiries about it with their own governments. (PARBICA Minutes 1992, 65–67)

At this same conference, during the period devoted to biennial reports of members, Belau and the Marshalls both cited information relative to the Trust Territory Archives. In the Belau report, reference was made to the receipt of the microfilm from Saipan. In more extensive comments, Alfred Capelle of the Marshall Islands (at that time head of the Alele Museum in Majuro) noted that the Trust Territory Archives microfilm included German records for Micronesia and added that his understanding was "that after the original records were microfilmed, they were sent to Hawaii. A lot of the material, which had been deposited with the Hamilton Library, University of Hawaii, appeared to have been destroyed. Duplicate copies of the microfilm were made and sent to the islands formerly comprising the Trust Territory of the Pacific Islands. If, in fact, the original records were destroyed [and there was some speculation on this matter], he conjectured that they were destroyed because their value was not fully appreciated" (PARBICA Minutes 1992, 54).

Given the Pacific Regional Branch International Council on Archives' earlier contacts with the Trust Territory Archives project, and that a synopsis of the archives work had appeared in the organization's own journal, it does seem strange that my article generated such controversy. It is also puzzling that the representative from Palau professed ignorance of the project and that the Marshalls' representative would assume that the University of Hawai'i had destroyed any records. McPhetres's communications and consultations with each government and with the archives units that were formed are contained in a large file of correspondence and reports.[15] Capelle had a long history of contact with the University of Hawai'i and its library and knew the emphasis they place on preservation.

How did the Trust Territory Archives come under attack at the 1991 PARBICA conference? I would suggest that a multifaceted explanation answers this query. The lengthy period of time of the archives project (1981–1988) saw a considerable turnover in personnel from the four governments in communication with Saipan, and this in itself may have contributed to the confusion by 1991. However, the conference where the questions arose had in its midst the former deputy director of the project, Jones George, and he attempted to explain the process and the decision to destroy some records. He did take issue with my reference to the 1979 typhoon as the catalyst for the commencement of a preservation program. Here I feel that I was at fault in failing to footnote my source, an introduction to the Trust Territory Archives by McPhetres, in which he wrote of water damage to files from a 1979 typhoon on Saipan. This raised the issue of the future of the Trust Territory government's files, especially in light of a then-anticipated closedown of the government in 1981 (McPhetres 1992b, 3).

Although George clearly attempted to explain the background and the work of the Trust Territory Archives, the tone of comments from participants seemed hostile to the entire concept. Part of the problem may have arisen from a sense of rivalry between the institutions of the United States, Australia, and New Zealand, although I hasten to add that in my visits to and dealings with colleagues in all countries, relations have always been most cordial and cooperative.

Reading between the lines I sense that what is truly behind the controversy is a quite logical fear on the part of Pacific Islanders and those working with them that historical documents bound with their past had been destroyed or removed without their knowledge, and that the University of Hawai'i—being a United States institution—represented yet another high-handed colonial power. Given the past appropriation of artifacts and the current work for repatriation in the museum field, such sentiment is understandable. It is clear also that once an issue has been raised, and misinformation conveyed and even printed, the fears are hard to put to rest. In 1996 Australian archivist Peter Orlovich again referred to the Trust Territory Archives, "The archives of the administration of the United States Trust Territory of the Pacific Islands . . . were transferred to the custody of the University of Hawaii at Manoa for microfilming" (1996, 8), citing McPhetres (1992b) as his source for this information. In fact, the user's guide (McPhetres 1992a) clearly states that the microfilming was done by the Trust Territory on Saipan, with microfilm sent to the University of Hawai'i Library for duplicating for the four governments. McPhetres does make reference to some files (already microfilmed) being sent to the University of Hawai'i, as were the audiovisual and map collections. The role of the "outside" institution (in this case the library), once inserted into the dialogue as an appropriator of materials and knowledge, is difficult to dislodge.

In reviewing this material it has become clear to me that despite years of work with archivists and librarians in the Micronesian governments, misunderstandings still exist regarding the University of Hawai'i's role in the creation of the Trust Territory Archives. The library did create a brochure ([Peacock] 1994) describing the Trust Territory Archives and photo collection, which was disseminated to Pacific Islands institutions and libraries, but it seems that further work is required to clarify the situation. I propose to write a brief report that states clearly that the microfilm at the University of Hawai'i is also held by archives in each of the Micronesian nations, and that lists what files and collections were deposited with the library (stating also that none of the latter have been destroyed). Perhaps a communication outlining its holdings will put to rest any misunderstandings that still persist.

Electronic Repatriation

The microfilm at the University of Hawai'i Library is duplicated in holdings in archives in the Micronesian nations, but the photograph collection is held only at the library in Honolulu. These images have immense historical, cultural, and personal value for Micronesians, and there has been considerable interest in the collection. As stated earlier in this essay, in the early

Laying out coconuts to sprout, Trust Territory Farm Institute, Pohnpei, c. 1970 (Trust Territory Archives, University of Hawai'i Library)

1990s the library received a federal grant to create a digitized database of selected photographs from Trust Territory Archives holdings. The Institute of Museum and Library Services grant obtained in October 1998 will make possible the transfer of that database to the World Wide Web and will also fund a CD-ROM of the images. As of 2001 the Trust Territory Archives' digitized photographs are available on the Internet through the University of Hawai'i Library's website. Micronesian schools, libraries, and individuals will be able to access the images and print copies. The originals remain in the Pacific Collection at the University of Hawai'i Library and can easily be duplicated if high-quality copy is needed for a publication. While some may question how readily Micronesians have access to the technology for either Internet or CD-ROM usage, it is my experience that technological resources have become a prominent feature in the libraries, schools, and offices of Micronesia.[16]

Technology has made it possible for the images to be returned to the people. Although the digitized database represents only 12 to 15 percent of the total photograph collection, most of the images not digitized were either duplicates or very similar shots of a person, event, or structure, or a series of photos that dealt with topics not of great interest to the general public or the researcher, for example, photos showing the laying of sewer lines. Web and CD-ROM access to the digitized images will not give Micronesians complete access to all of the photo collection, but this access does provide immediate viewing and printing capability for the most historically significant photos. As has always been the case, users will be able to search the index and request that university staff inform them of relevant contents of photo files not represented in the digitized database and arrange for reproduction of photographs. Hopefully increased Internet availability for those in Micronesia who wish to search the index for photographs or documents on microfilm will resolve problems that have occurred with access to local versions of the Trust Territory Archives index.[17] Using funds from the Institute of Museum and Library Services grant, University of Hawai'i librarian Martha Chantiny, a computer and systems expert, and I presented a workshop for the Pacific Islands Association of Libraries and Archives on Guam at their fall 2000 conference. Grant funds allowed us to sponsor at least one participant from each country in the Micronesian region, and a large number of conference attendees also came to the workshop. The Guam program gave us an opportunity to explain how to access the Trust Territory Archives on the Internet and to share our experiences with a major digitizing project. I also used this occasion to discuss the history of the University of Hawai'i's involvement in the Trust Territory Archives with a Micronesian Library and Archives audience.

Ongoing Archival Programs—What is the Future of the Past?

When McPhetres, George, and the Trust Territory Archives team devised the archives project, it was with the understanding that there was an ongoing need for archival work throughout the Micronesian nations. In order for the final product to be usable, each archive requires equipment: a reader-printer and computer capability for the index. Department of Interior funds made this possible, and the department also funded cameras and film processors for both the archives and the fiscal departments of each government (the latter were seen as an area that would require careful storage and retrieval of documents whose extent made long-term housing of originals impractical). Training sessions were held for Micronesian archives staff, and McPhetres assisted with in-country setup of the new archives programs. As has been noted above, some of the archives were fortunate enough to have experienced staff who had been part of the original Trust Territory Archives project (Federated States of Micronesia and the Commonwealth of the Northern Mariana Islands).

Unfortunately, the salvage operation that created the Trust Territory Archives microfilm, while in my opinion a praiseworthy and essential contribution to both Micronesia and the world of research, evolved into an organization that microfilmed documents rather than preserved them in their original form. Keeping in mind that archives as such were a new concept for the nations formerly comprising the trusteeship, it is quite understandable that the various archives would follow the practice of the only known model—the Trust Territory Archives project. In fact, the equipment and training received were designed to perpetuate the microfilm project approach. Given the lack of adequate facilities, storage limitations, problems of climate control, and weather hazards such as typhoons, it might be argued that microfilm of essential documents is the most appropriate measure for Micronesian archives preservation. However, one could equally well make a case for the importance of preserving government records in their original form and order, as is traditionally done in archives worldwide.[18]

In the Micronesian region, looking at the microfilm aspect alone, there has been very limited success. The Federated States of Micronesia and the Commonwealth of the Northern Mariana Islands have been able to create some microfilm of important government records and publications, following the model of the Trust Territory Archives project. Equipment breakdowns, lack of repair facilities, staff turnover, and financial difficulties have plagued the Marshalls archival effort, and, to my knowledge, no microfilm has yet been produced. The Alele Museum was able to obtain a building to house both the archival documents received from the former Trust Territory government and the microfilming station. In 1995 *PARBICA Panorama* editor John Wright reported that "virtually all of the original filmed material for the Marshall Islands, sent from Saipan following filming, has been destroyed by water damage." As of 1998 Palau's national archivist was preparing a three-year plan to establish a records center. The plan also covered microfilm projects that would involve the records of the *Olbiil Era Kelulau* (national legislature), records of the 1979 Constitutional Convention, journals of the House and Senate, among others (Wright 1998). It would seem that, as Micronesian archivists have stated in the past, one of the most pressing needs is for education, to ensure that government leaders understand the need for maintaining archival records, and for legislation to structure a record-keeping process.[19]

When the University of Hawai'i Library made its version of the Trust Territory Archives index available to the archives of the four Micronesian

governments, it did so through a memorandum of agreement that stipulated that the university would in return receive copies of microfilm produced by the new archives.[20] The university, in addition to providing the
index, would ensure safe housing of a master copy of any such film. The
University of Hawai'i Library would also undertake to add newly received
data to the index. To date only the Commonwealth of the Northern Mariana Islands has deposited some microfilm with the University of Hawai'i,
but the university has never pressed the issue, understanding that the situation in the Micronesian archives is still evolving.

United States National Archives—What Is the United States' role?

Access has been a problem since the completed set of the Trust Territory
Archives microfilm was deposited with the National Archives.[21] First came
the problem of format: most of the Trust Territory Archives collection is on
16 mm microfilm, and at first there was no reader for its use. That problem
has, I understand, been resolved, but the reader does not have a print
capacity. Much more serious is the lack of access to the index. The computer
tape index supplied to the National Archives was the original Saipan version
and, to my knowledge, has not been loaded for use. The problem is perhaps
resolved by the existence of the University of Hawai'i's on-line index to the
Trust Territory Archives, which is available from the library's homepage on
the web.

The National Archives is a vast organization with a huge scope of operations that suffers from budget and staff shortages. Understandably, a matter
such as the Trust Territory Archives has taken a back seat to other priorities.
Most mainland users tend to contact our Pacific Collection staff for research
assistance and for reproduction of film in print or microfilm. The question of
access goes further, however, in terms of what source materials on microfilm may be only available at the National Archives. A case in point is the
War Claims Records for the Trust Territory government, that is, documents
for cases for reparations to Micronesians who suffered damages during
World War II. These were microfilmed but not distributed to the University
of Hawai'i or to the Micronesian archives. This presumably was material
that fell into the category of items that might have been under litigation in
the 1980s and therefore was not released by the Trust Territory government.

Recently an occasion arose in which the library was queried about the
War Records. Having contacted the Department of the Interior and found
that the microfilm should be with the National Archives, I approached its
reference staff via e-mail. After considerable effort, I was able to establish

personal contact with a staff member, who located the War Claims microfilm.[22] The University of Hawai'i Library ordered a complete set (TTA reels #241–76).[23] Upon receipt of the reels, I wrote to all Micronesian archives to let them know that the set is available at the University of Hawai'i Library and to provide full order information, should they wish to purchase a set from the National Archives. I was able to discuss this with Federated States of Micronesia Archivist Jones George recently, and he was pleased to learn that the War Claims documents on microfilm had been located. I learned at the conference on Guam in November 2000 that at least one of the Micronesian archives has ordered the War Claims microfilm from the United States National Archives, and doubtless others will follow suit.

Repatriation: Strategy for Salvage or Strategy for Power?

The University of Hawai'i Library's participation in the creation of the Trust Territory Archives may seem to some observers the long arm of metropolitan power reaching into the affairs of island peoples. It seems that such criticism or misunderstanding may be an unavoidable aspect of any repatriation project. I maintain that the University of Hawai'i involvement came about through the efforts of a number of concerned faculty, responding to a plea for "salvage archival work" that would rescue the records of an era in Micronesian history. The library stood to gain by becoming a repository for the valuable microfilm, but in return the library contributed a substantial amount of staff time in organizing, inventorying, and duplicating microfilm for the archives in the Marshalls, the Federated States of Micronesia, Palau, and the Commonwealth of the Northern Mariana Islands. The University of Hawai'i made a long-term commitment to reference service and access for the Trust Territory Archives, one that has consumed considerable time and effort over the past eighteen years.

Again, the University of Hawai'i may be criticized for holding unique materials that more properly belong in Micronesian archives. The fact is that the library was initially reluctant to accept any materials other than the microfilm. I was present at the meeting where Sam McPhetres, on behalf of the Trust Territory government, offered the library the audiovisual, map, and photograph collections. My predecessor, the distinguished bibliographer and curator Renée Heyum, did not want to take on this material, as the Pacific Collection had, at that time, not ventured into visual holdings. I agreed with her, as I did not feel that we had the staff or funds to handle a large photograph acquisition. University librarian John Haak, however, felt strongly that this valuable resource would be a most significant addition to the Pacific Collection, and given the uncertainties of preservation measures available at that time in the region, Heyum put aside her opposition. I hope that this anecdote illustrates the true nature of the library's role in regard to the Trust Territory Archives. Its goal was then and is now to work to preserve the records of the American colonial period in Micronesia and to ensure that these records are available to the people of the islands, in their national archives and through images caught and conveyed on the Internet.

In the Pacific Islands region the libraries of the larger academic institutions have for many years worked to promote library and archives development. The University of the South Pacific Library has had extensive involvement in library training, which has created extension courses and distance education that has been profitable for many, particularly given the acute need for professional training. These efforts have expanded to include courses being offered in the Republic of the Marshall Islands. The University of Guam's Robert F. Kennedy Library now serves as a hub for reduced rate interlibrary loan for the entire Pacific Islands region, with the University of Hawai'i Library participating in providing materials not available in Guam but needed by researchers and the general public. The University of California, San Diego (UCSD), Melanesian Studies Resource Center and Melanesian Archive have worked to repatriate research products. The goal of the Melanesian Archive is "collection, preservation, dissemination, and repatriation of unpublished materials on all aspects of Melanesian society, culture, linguistics, and history" (Creely 1992, 210). Through this program microfiche copies of unpublished research materials have reached libraries in Papua New Guinea, the Solomon Islands, Fiji, Vanuatu, New Caledonia, and Irian Jaya. In one example of this collaborative effort, UCSD librarian Kathryn Creely worked with the Papua New Guinea National Archives to index and microfilm patrol reports and station records, which make up an invaluable primary source for scholars. Despite the ever-present problems of low budgets and insufficient staffing, the major libraries in the region or those with substantial Pacific collections have made valiant efforts to promote library and archives development. Libraries and archives in Australia and New Zealand have been actively involved through regional organizations, such as the Pacific Regional Branch International Council on Archives, and through training efforts and exchange programs at individual institutions.

The University of Hawai'i Library's Pacific Collection has participated in training efforts, exchanges of publications, cooperative preservation programs, and other work to enhance access to resources for the entire region. While much of the effort has been in resource sharing through distribution of Pacific Islands–related books and serials to regional libraries, the Pacific Collection has also become involved in professional development through such activities as the Center for Pacific Islands 1998 conference on Pacific libraries, organized by the library's Pacific Collection staff. In the more delicate area of repatriation of resources, the University of Hawai'i's focus has been on the Trust Territory Archives as its largest and most visible archival resource. The library is also undertaking enhanced access to resources through digitizing projects that make available Hawaiian-language newspapers essential to historical research and the Hawai'i War Records Depository photographs that reflect the impact of World War II in Hawai'i. Although we may never completely ease the fears that *"They* have *our* history," the continued close contacts with Pacific Islands libraries and archives and the electronic repatriation now possible will go a long way to resolve the need for access. While there is great room for growth in collaborative ventures with our colleagues throughout the Pacific Islands, the University of Hawai'i Library's history has been one of cooperative endeavors. The library has entered the twenty-first century with a renewed commitment to participating in Pacific Islands archives and library development.

Amy Ku'uleialoha Stillman

8

Resurrecting Archival Poetic Repertoire for Hawaiian Hula

Unpublished manuscript collections held by library and archival institutions in Honolulu contain thousands of items from the poetic repertoire for performance as Hawaiian hula dance. While many of the collections were compiled by individuals for personal souvenir purposes, some were the result of deliberate collecting efforts during field research. A majority of the presently available archival material had been institutionalized by World War II. Because most of these archival collections became separated from the hula community, processes and problems of resurrecting poetic repertoire for hula crosscut numerous facets of repatriation.

This chapter is written at a very specific historical juncture, in the context of a vigorous resurgence of interest in hula that commenced in the 1970s and subsequent efforts to resurrect back into performance the substantial amounts of institutionalized poetic repertoire. Prior to the 1970s, much of the hula in active circulation was of the westernized "modern" type that provided entertainment in tourist venues as well as in community and family celebratory functions. Knowledge of older styles of hula was held by a small group of elderly masters who were highly revered throughout the community. Although these older styles were considered by many to be antiquarian and esoteric, the cultural resurgence of the 1970s stirred renewed interest in them. Under the auspices of a variety of community-driven initiatives, many elderly masters taught their repertoire in workshops and symposia to the new generation of teachers and students, thus ensuring its continuity in practice.

However, while the existence of archival collections of poetic repertoire was known in the hula community, the specific contents of those archival collections was not known, owing to circumstances of institutionalization. Over time, the contents of those archival collections acquired an aura of mystery and secrecy. By the 1980s, though, members of the hula community turned to these archival resources to augment what had been taught to them by their teachers. In drawing upon a repertoire that had been separated from practice for decades, teachers and choreographers were in effect engaged in repatriating objects of cultural patrimony back into the community. The emergence, in the 1990s, of historical scholarship on the hula tradition has contributed to facilitating access into the contents of archival collections (Bishop Museum Audio Recording Collections 1997; Kaeppler 1993; Smithsonian Folkways 1989; Stillman 1996b, 1998; Tatar 1982, 1993). These publications play a major role in bringing sources previously unknown or neglected to the attention of the hula community. Yet those publications have also placed scholars and authors into the role of brokering knowledge.

The desired outcome, it would seem, is reunification of performers and poetic repertoire. The journey, however, traverses intertwined issues of materiality, agency, institutionalization, deinstitutionalization, and moral imperatives.

Materiality

Fundamental distinctions can be drawn among at least three types of material that accrue during fieldwork. First, there are the raw data themselves. This includes quantifiable information compiled about the community such as censuses and genealogies, oral histories that often embed mythical origin tales, physical descriptions of landscape, geography, flora, and fauna, and taxonomies and vocabularies of social and occupational practices. Second, there are interpretive remarks, judiciously recorded in field notebooks and logs, through which processes of understanding can be traced over the fieldwork period. Third, there are objects of material culture, whose accumulation is the special focus of museum collections. Among objects of material culture, those of everyday functional use can be further distinguished from those possessing "cultural capital" by virtue of serving non-quotidian or extraordinary ceremonial or symbolic purposes. In the United States, material objects having "ongoing historical, traditional, or cultural importance" have been defined legislatively as objects of "cultural patrimony" in the landmark Native American Graves Protection and Repatriation Act (NAGPRA), passed by Congress in 1990.[1]

Materials generated or accumulated during the process of fieldwork are distinct from products that emanate out of processes of scholarship, namely ethnographic books and articles. Ethnographic writings have the potential to attract tremendous interest within the communities studied. Through the existence of studies from earlier decades, community members can access a diachronic perspective that, over time, comes to exceed the recollection capacities of living generations. Even when communities have neither interest nor proficient literacy capabilities at the time that scholarship is generated (see, for example, Dorothy and David Counts, chapter 1), we cannot yet know whether and how the vagaries and passage of time might bring together communities and scholarship about them in the future. There are cases of communities having successfully accessed published scholarship for extremely vital politico-economic ends, such as the case of Native Americans in Mashpee, Massachussetts, who used ethnographic research to support claims of tribal existence and continuity in order to legitimize land claims (Clifford 1988, 317–18). There are also cases of communities in which an educated intelligentsia participates in the discourses of scholarship and contests what are claimed to be misrepresentations of cultural or social practices, such as the reactions voiced by Haunani-Kay Trask (1986) to the analyses of rural Hawaiian social organization and exchange practices by Jocelyn Linnekin (1985; see also Trask 1991).

In performance traditions, there are potentially numerous items of material culture that can be an integral part of performance. Such objects would include musical instruments, costume items, and dance implements, as well as other contextual ("stage") props prescribed by the tradition. Performance traditions may also entail the use of other material objects that are not used during actual performance, but are integral to the instructional setting, or to the ritual practices surrounding safekeeping of knowledge, or to the initiation of specialists.

Central to performance, and having a tangible—though not necessarily material—existence, are items of repertoire, of which enactments in sound and movement enable performance to occur (see also Nancy Guy, chapter 11). There exist various possibilities for visually representing items of repertoire through systems of musical or dance movement notation, or simply writing down poetic song-texts. While performers and performance scholars alike understand that such representations are not equated with their actual enactments in performance, such representations do point to the ontological existence of discrete "works" of repertoire. Through their representation via literate means, or the documentation of performances on audiovisual recordings, items of repertoire can be accumulated into collections. Individual performers can also simply accumulate items of repertoire in memory, without the aid of notational technologies.

A further distinction can be made between objects and knowledge about those objects. Having an object, either by possession or simply holding it in hand, does not necessarily entail knowing all of its attributes, or how it should be used "properly." Often, knowledge about an object is imparted from expert to novice in an instructional setting. Whether that knowledge is inscribed in writing or remains in the sphere of oral transmission or dissemination, knowledge about proper use of an object can be stored, encoded, and maintained in some way separate from the object itself, and knowledge about objects can take journeys separate from the material objects. An additional consideration about knowledge is that it can be frozen when it is captured in written form, removed from the sphere of potentially changing with each telling.

In the case of the Hawaiian hula tradition, the poetic text is absolutely central to performance as recited song and enacted dance. The dance combines hand and arm gestures that depict selected aspects of the poetic text with repetitive, named lower-body patterns through which a dancer maintains rhythmic coordination with the musical accompaniment. Dance performance requires the recitation of the poetic text, in either chanted melodies that descend from the indigenous performance tradition, or westernized sung melodies associated with "modern" hula that emerged in the late nineteenth century. Poetic composition is the domain of poets, who are called *haku mele.* Poets as a group are separable from hula masters, called *kumu hula,* whose domain is to create choreographed routines to chosen poetic texts.

Both poets and hula masters can accumulate collections of poetic repertoire, either in memory or in personal notebooks. Since the late nineteenth century, collections of poetic repertoire have been published in over two hundred songbooks, most containing notated musical scores of westernized, "modern" Hawaiian songs (Stillman 1987). Thousands of poetic compositions were published in Hawaiian-language newspapers between the 1860s and the early 1920s. Other collections of poetic repertoire have remained unpublished and privately held. Some collections, especially those associated with members of the nobility (many of whom were themselves poets), have passed into the care of institutional archives, especially the Bernice Pauahi Bishop Museum in Honolulu.

Because poetic texts are necessary prerequisites for musical and choreographic composition in hula, poetic texts represent a form of cultural patrimony. To a great extent, collections of poetic texts from times past can be read as historical chronicles. Poetic texts are conveniently grouped into named categories according to their subject matter. Thus honorific *mele inoa* (name songs) and *kanikau* (laments) laud physical attributes of beauty, symbolic dimensions of rank, and celebrated exploits of contemporaries to the poet; intimate relationships are celebrated—anonymously—in *mele ho'oipoipo* (love songs); and affection for particular locales, especially birthplaces, is registered in *mele pana* (place songs). During the political turbulence of the final years of the monarchy in the 1890s, numerous poets from all over the kingdom expressed proroyalist loyalties in nationalist *mele lāhui*, hundreds of which were published in newspapers. Because a poetic text inscribes sentiments that prevail at the time of composition, the perpetuation of poetic texts from past times affords performers and audiences alike opportunities to engage with people and events long after they have passed. And because poetic texts can be choreographed anew, they constitute a resource that is usable without being consumed, remaining available for renewed use, either in subsequent performances or through interpretations by other hula masters as presented by other performers.

Materiality in the hula tradition, then, includes not only items of material culture such as musical instruments used by musicians who accompany dancers, but also dance implements used by dancers in self-accompaniment for seated dances and costume items that include attire and plant adornments worn by dancers (and musicians) as *lei* wreaths on the head, neck, wrists, and ankles. The poetic texts that are the basis for choreographic interpretation are themselves tangible objects that can be accumulated into collections by poets, hula masters, dancers, musicians, enthusiasts, scholars, and researchers conducting fieldwork.

Accessing poetic repertoire, however, does not necessarily entail accessing knowledge about that poetic repertoire. This holds particularly for poetic texts that have become removed from transmission by a teacher. Poetic texts collected from performers during fieldwork are more prone to be accompanied by notes that illuminate aspects of performance or subject matter categorization than those poetic texts collected by poets and enthusiasts for their own souvenir purposes. At the same time, not all dimensions of poetic texts collected in fieldwork were made explicit to fieldworkers. Thus aspects that may be crucial to a poetic text's interpretation may be absent from the documentation. This leaves open the possibility that resurrecting a poetic text from a written form may be subject to misinterpretation, because crucial information about a given poetic text has become separated from it. Complicating the potential for misinterpretation is the fact that the fragments of contextual information captured by fieldworkers cannot be identified as fragments until they can be compared to information held elsewhere or captured through other means.

Knowledge about hula practice documented in ethnographic fieldwork exists on yet another plane. Because of historical circumstances that compromised continuous transmission of much repertoire in practice, many knowledgeable masters took substantial amounts of knowledge about poetic repertoire with them as they passed away. This results in high cultural capital being attributed by hula performers to information documented in ethnographic studies of hula, such as those authored by Nathaniel Emerson (1909), Helen Roberts (1926), Mary Kawena Pukui (1936, 1942, 1943), Adrienne Kaeppler (1993), and Elizabeth Tatar (1982, 1993). Repatriation of this information has taken place through publications that are readily available in the Hawaiian community.

Agency

Tensions in agency that propel repatriation efforts forward stem from initiative, direction, motivation, and purpose. As pointed out by Sjoerd Jaarsma, initiating the repatriation of materials collected during fieldwork is not solely the provenance of the fieldworker: "with an increasing role played by cultural identity in all kinds of (geo)political debates, indigenous peoples will increasingly take action on their own behalf."[2] Within the hula community, the cultural resurgence known as the "Hawaiian Renaissance" that began in the 1970s reignited interest in reviving older repertoire. The recollections of elderly masters provided an impetus for upcoming instructors to explore what other historical resources survived to the present. Thus they turned to archival collections in the Bishop Museum, in search of links through poetic expression to people and places of past times.

Inherent in the notion of repatriation is a unidirectional flow inward from somewhere external. In the case of data and materials that result from ethnographic fieldwork, at present it is often the good intentions of fieldworkers that initiate the flow of materials back into the communities studied. What is becoming a mandate among contemporary fieldworkers to return research results is closely related to trends in either formal written research permits or agreements with communities studied that now stipulate the deposit of copies of materials in places accessible to those communities. More and more, however, peoples from societies studied in earlier years are also seeking out and drawing upon materials and knowledge gained from ethnographic fieldwork. Considered directionally, the conveyance of information still flows inward from some location external to the community.

Despite the unidirectional flow of materials, the difference in initiating position—from within the community, as opposed to from agents external to the community—corresponds with an identifiable distinction in motivation. While field researchers are concerned primarily with making materials accessible and available, community members who seek out ethnographic information and materials from the past often do so with specific purposes in mind to which that material will be put. This distinction in motivation can be formulated as a tension between description and prescription. While ethnographers are concerned with describing, representing, analyzing, explaining, and interpreting objects and practices, community members are interested in putting information to practical use, to prescribe actions or outcomes. Put another way, while ethnographers are interested in accumulating information, community members are more often interested in how that accumulated information can be used.

The poetic repertoire for hula offers a concrete example. Researchers would be interested in cataloging collections of repertoire in order to carry out analyses. Topics for investigation might include surveying different kinds of subject matter, analyzing relationships between subject matter and kinds of melodies used to perform poetic repertoire, and finding patterns of historical development over time, in subject matter, use of vocabulary, use of patterns of format, or other such structural concerns. Hula masters and performers, on the other hand, are interested in performing the repertoire and need to know how that repertoire might be interpreted choreographically. Thus, while much of the research enterprise is driven by the "what is it?" of description, the performance enterprise is driven by the "how to?" of prescription.

Institutionalization

Institutions archive information in the form of tangible, material objects, as inscribed in written documents or as captured on sound or moving-image documentation. These include objects of cultural patrimony, as well as information about such objects—when available. The mission of archival institutions is preservation; thus the continued existence of objects placed in their care is presumed. Because tangible objects outlive people, these objects remain available to subsequent generations of descendants. Yet the capacity of archived objects to evoke sociocultural processes among users, and what uses are actually made of archived objects, depends entirely on whether objects remain accessible to users.

In the case of poetic repertoire for hula, while some collections passed into the care of the territorial archives (now Hawai'i State Archives), the vast majority of materials went into the holdings of the Bishop Museum. It was founded in 1889 in honor of Princess Bernice Pauahi Bishop, the last direct descendant of the Kamehameha dynasty that had ruled the kingdom until 1873. The mission of the museum included scientific investigation of cultural and natural history. Because of the chiefly association of the museum, the personal effects—including substantial collections of poetic repertoire—of many members of nobility came to be housed in the Bishop Museum. And because of the museum's participation in numerous fieldwork expeditions, especially throughout the 1920s and 1930s, materials generated in field research came to coexist alongside personal effects and collections compiled by individuals for souvenir purposes.

The two most important collections of poetic repertoire generated from field research are the Roberts and Kuluwaimaka collections. The compilation and organization of materials in these field collections fared better than the personal souvenir books, as they benefited from external funding and more structured input by museum staff.

The Roberts collection of mele contains the materials collected by Helen Roberts, an ethnomusicologist from Yale University. Over an eleven-month period in 1923–1924, Roberts sought out performers on three islands (O'ahu, Hawai'i, and Kaua'i), made audio recordings, and collected many more poetic texts in written form. This field research was commissioned by the Hawaiian Legend and Folklore Commission, a territorial agency; Bishop Museum staff members aided in organizing her notes and editing her monograph, *Ancient Hawaiian Music*, published by the museum in 1926.

The Kuluwaimaka collection resulted out of the initiative of Bishop Museum staff anthropologist Kenneth Emory, in collaboration with Theodore Kelsey, a community scholar. Emory organized a series of recording sessions in 1933 with master chanter James Kapihenui Pālea Kuluwaimaka, a highly esteemed performer who was associated with the court of King

David Kalākaua (r. 1874–1891). Like the Roberts collection, the Kuluwai-maka collection includes many more poetic texts collected in written form in addition to those documented on sound recordings.

Once collections of poetic repertoire passed into the care of the Bishop Museum, they were subject to institutionalized management, which was constrained by limited financial and staff resources. For decades, the personal souvenir books languished in near obscurity; over time, their contents became separated from the hula community. This is how it happened.

The personal souvenir books were only minimally cataloged in the library. Books that primarily contained poetic repertoire were grouped together and numbered in one sequence; that grouping has since come to be referred to as "the mele books." In the card catalog, only one entry was made for an entire volume, and there was no index of contents. At some later point, a separate first-line card index was created. However, the card index remained a working tool and not a public access tool; it was kept in a workroom that was off-limits to the public and was consulted by staff librarians on behalf of patrons. This minimum amount of cataloging did not enable exploration in the archival collections; patrons had to know about the existence of particular pieces of repertoire in order to inquire about them. There was no subject index, and it is evident that some sources were not included when the card file was compiled sometime between the 1930s (when the Kuluwaimaka collection was compiled) and the 1970s (when I began my research and enjoyed the privilege of learning about the card file and its quirks).

The field collections were fully cataloged by 1978, following the 1977 appointment of ethnomusicologist Elizabeth Tatar to the staff. However, complete and systematic cataloging of the contents of the personal souvenir books was undertaken only in the early 1990s, with the financial support of the federally funded Native Hawaiian Culture and Arts Program. Accessibility into those contents was finally realized when the Bishop Museum Mele Index became available online through the University of Hawai'i Library catalog in 1993. With the possibility of subject and keyword searching, community members can now explore the contents of the archival collections to a historically unprecedented extent.[3]

In the years between the 1920s and 1930s, when the two major field collections were compiled, and the 1980s, when they were finally fully cataloged, the hula community did enjoy one channel of access through the work of Mary Kawena Pukui, a Hawaiian scholar and translator. Pukui collaborated with researchers affiliated with the Bishop Museum and in 1937 was finally appointed to the museum staff as a translator. Over the next five decades, Pukui participated in the production of a dictionary (Elbert and Pukui 1986), a major ethnography (Handy and Pukui 1958), a two-volume compendium of Hawaiian customary practices for social workers (Pukui, Haertig, and Lee 1972), translations of historical lore published in Hawaiian-language newspapers (Ii 1959; Kamakau 1961, 1964, 1976, 1991), and a major collection of proverbial sayings (Pukui 1983). While Pukui worked extensively with translating poetic repertoire in the field collections (Pukui 1995), she dipped into the personal souvenir books only as time permitted. Through an examination of her notes compiled into a separate series called "Hawaiian Ethnology Notes" (affectionately known as "HEN"), it has become apparent that Pukui's forays into the personal souvenir books were not systematic. She worked with some sources more than others; furthermore, some sources with the potential to contribute clarity to the nineteenth-century repertoire evidently remained unfamiliar to her (see Stillman 1996b). Pukui was herself a hula master, and as such she served as a point of contact between the poetic repertoire in the museum and the hula community outside the museum by answering questions, providing translations, and delivering public lectures (Pukui 1936, 1942, 1943; reprinted in Barrere, Pukui, and Kelly 1980). Through her efforts, the hula community came to some understanding of some of the treasures hidden away in the museum.

With poor accessibility of the mele books and virtually no Hawaiian-language expertise on the museum staff beside Pukui until the 1980s, it becomes easy to understand how the poetic repertoire institutionalized in the Bishop Museum became separated from the hula community. The museum appeared to be an institution with locked secrets. Hula masters came to rely on Pukui and to accept her purview of what the collections contained. Indeed, for them there was no alternative.

The poetic repertoire institutionalized in the Bishop Museum fell out of practice over a long period of time. The history of hula throughout the 1920s, 1930s, and 1940s can be characterized as a time when new poetic repertoire kept appearing and eclipsing older repertoire in popularity. However, two events are seminal to refocusing attention on older, pre-1920 material, much of which was institutionalized.

First, a shift in the community's historical gaze from the monarchy era—the subject of community pageantry in commemorative holidays such as Kamehameha Day and May Day (see Stillman 1994; Friesen 1996)—to the precontact era, when the islands were still independent rival chiefdoms upheld by indigenous ritual observances, can be accounted for in the context of the establishment of the Aloha Festival in 1947. Honolulu businessmen conceived this festival as a means of stimulating tourism in the off-peak month of October. Founders linked the festival theme with the precontact autumn harvest festival known as *Makahiki*. This particular focus stimulated community interest in antiquarian knowledge that could be incorporated into pageants, a format that enjoyed popularity in the community since the early 1900s. In the wake of the successful launch of the Aloha Festival, the translation of David Malo's *Hawaiian Antiquities*, originally published in 1901 and long out of print and an important resource for pageant organizers, was republished in 1951 (Malo 1951; for a new translation see Malo 1996). Renewed interest in precontact antiquarian practices also brought back to view a revival of the oldest and most sacred *hula pahu* repertoire for presentation in pageants, thereby stimulating new interest in maintaining what was left of hula from that period (Nelson 1947; Kaeppler 1993, 49–53). However, the hula that was brought back into circulation was that which had remained in supposedly continuous transmission; performers did not, for the most part, draw upon institutionalized materials that had fallen out of continuous transmission.

Second, the resurgence of interest in cultural practices that began in the 1970s brought of age a new generation of hula masters and instructors who asserted determination over matters of cultural patrimony. Concomitant with the increased training of hula teachers and the opening of new schools and venues of instruction was the establishment of hula competitions, which addressed needs for visible and prestigious performance opportunities (Stillman 1996a). With hula competitions came the need for original choreography and thus for poetic repertoire on which to base new choreography. In the 1970s, although a revival of Hawaiian language was nascent, there was not as yet a critical mass of composers who possessed knowledge and skills in poetic composition to provide sufficient quantities of new compositions that could meet the demand for poetic repertoire. Thus hula masters turned to institutionalized collections of repertoire.

A side issue arises from the fact that institutionalized collections of poetic repertoire include objects and knowledge about those objects collected during fieldwork, and also materials that were privately held. This raises a central question of ownership: does institutionalization of material make it then publicly accessible by anyone who enters? At the time of composition, poetic repertoire is the property of individuals. Formerly within the indigenous Hawaiian system, a dedicatee became the "owner" of honorific name songs composed for him or her by others; this is in contrast to United States copyright law, which Hawaiian composers adhered to as early as the 1870s, that considers the composer as the owner of rights in a work.

Either way, poetic repertoire was individual property, and not, thus, subject to direct regulation under legislation such as the Native American Graves Protection and Repatriation Act. Yet in the present climate of the cultural resurgence, all repertoire that survived to the present has become cultural patrimony in the sense of enabling native Hawaiians as a group to make connections with the past.

The extent to which hula instructors were able to access institutionalized poetic repertoire, however, depended on many factors. For some, the mere act of entering the Bishop Museum Library was a border crossing, from the world outside that operated on interpersonal relationships, to the rarefied—and discomforting—atmosphere of scholasticism. As a university student conducting research for an advanced degree in the late 1970s, I watched hula masters enter the library's reading room. They sat in silence as librarians consulted the card file, then sat respectfully before treasured manuscript books opened to the page of the item sought. Some came to verify versions of pieces they had received from teachers, hoping to glimpse furtively on other things in the process. Others came hoping to discover unfamiliar repertoire, and were astonished to learn that no subject index existed. Some left having achieved their purpose; many others wondered how much else there was in the museum collections and how these things might be revealed to them.

Those who persevered encountered the mechanisms of institutional control. The audio recordings, for example, were kept in the Anthropology Department, which made them accessible to the community, by appointment, by the late 1970s. However, the accompanying written materials, housed in the library, were not made available to patrons as they consulted the audio recordings. Kalani Akana, an award-winning chanter, is widely credited with revitalizing a specific chant style called *ho'āeae*, together with his teacher, John R. Kaha'i Topolinski. In the early 1980s, this chant style was heard only infrequently. Akana is fond of relating his experience in consulting the audio recordings in the Bishop Museum, without seeing the accompanying textual materials. He describes it as such: "I would listen for a little while, then run out to the car and try to write down the words. Then I went back and listened some more, then ran back to the car to write down some more words. [laughter] It's my favorite story; I tell all my students. . . . I couldn't see the words. Those days, it wasn't open to the public. Before Betty Tatar came, even the tapes weren't open to the public."[4] Yet Akana concedes: "I was so happy just to be able to listen."

Issues of institutional control and access apply whenever institutionalized safekeeping is involved, regardless of whether the institution is at a point of origination outside the community (see, for example, David Akin and Kathryn Creely, chapter 5), or whether, as in the case of the Bishop Museum, the institution is situated within the community. As the case of poetic repertoire for hula demonstrates, institutional accessibility is an entirely separable matter from repatriation that either begins or ends with institutionalized location—and control—of materials.

Deinstitutionalization

In the case of hula, processes of reaching into institutionalized holdings and bringing objects of cultural patrimony back into the community raise some key questions about repatriation processes. At what point is repatriation accomplished? When objects and information reside outside the community, a return of those objects and information to someplace within the community is clearly a goal (but see Bryan Oles, chapter 10). But is physical location sufficient? Is repatriation accomplished with the physical return of objects and information to the community? Located in Honolulu, the Bishop Museum is in spatial proximity to the hula community; yet owing to institutional practices, there have been psychological barriers to entering the museum in order to access its holdings. Clearly institutional proximity is separate from deinstitutionalization of holdings and their reintegration back into the stream of daily life.

What relationships ensue, then, between repatriation and deinstitutionalization? Are they overlapping or distinct processes? Is it sufficient to repatriate poetic repertoire by simply making it available to hula masters for reinterpretation? Or is repatriation completed only when objects and information are resurrected from an institutionalized state, deinstitutionalized, and put back into use or circulation? In the case of poetic repertoire, is it sufficient to hold a tangible material document in hand, or is repatriation accomplished only with the reanimation of poetic expression in performance?

In performance traditions, tangible objects such as poetic repertoire can enable processes of performance, but knowledge about the objects is what enables deeply insightful enactments of those processes of performance. Thus there are important distinctions to be made between repatriating objects, repatriating knowledge about those objects, and reintegrating those objects back into daily life and artistic practice.

In the case of the hula, the poetic repertoire long institutionalized in the Bishop Museum took on renewed value as cultural patrimony in the context of the cultural resurgence, ongoing since the 1970s. In many ways, though, the meanings this repertoire held during and since the 1970s are not the same meanings held at the time of its creation, or institutionalization, or even deinstitutionalization. Poetic repertoire being resurrected from archival sources is being brought back into circulation within vastly altered sociohistorical circumstances.

A major impetus that stimulated historical research into poetic repertoire for hula came from one event in particular, the Merrie Monarch Hula Competition. Established in 1971, it quickly became the largest and most prestigious annual competition event in the hula community, attracting some twenty-five to thirty groups each year. The groups compete over two nights. On the first night of group competition, groups perform in the older "ancient" style that had by now acquired a term—*hula kahiko*. Dances were performed in a more robustly vigorous style, to the accompaniment of indigenous percussive instruments. On the final night, groups perform in the westernized "modern" style known as *hula 'auana*, to the accompaniment of stringed instruments such as guitar, 'ukulele, and bass.

Until the early 1990s groups were required to present two dances in the *hula kahiko* division. One was of the group's choice. The other was a "competition chant"—one poetic text that all entering groups were required to set musically and choreographically. Women's groups all set one piece, while men's groups all set another piece. The competition chant was eliminated after 1992, in order to allow time for more groups to enter. In some years the competition chants were original compositions by contemporary poets. A majority of the competition chants, however, were late-nineteenth-century pieces taken from contemporary archival sources by a handful of knowledgeable people (most—if not all—of whom were close associates of Bishop Museum staff member Mary Kawena Pukui) who possessed some familiarity with those sources.

The solutions presented in performance during the competition are revealing. On the one hand, the fact that hula masters were able to choreograph routines to an unfamiliar poetic text meant that knowledge of hula practices was sufficient to do so. On the other hand, the presentation of a wide range of choreographic and melodic settings also meant that knowledge about those poetic texts was vastly uneven and subject not to direct transmission, but to politics of access on multiple levels. Those who persisted found their way into archival sources, though more frequently into the Roberts and Kuluwaimaka collections of field materials than into the personal souvenir books. They did so, moreover, at a time when there was as yet no understanding that materials in the field collections were but a fraction of the contents in the older personal souvenir books, and when the contents of the personal souvenir books were still not yet comprehensively cataloged. And because the older souvenir books lacked virtually any kind of descriptive annotations as contained in at least some of the field materials, those who made their way to the souvenir books were left to their own devices as far as coming to creative interpretations and conclusions.

In the process of locating materials relevant to the competition chant, however, hula instructors took advantage of the opportunity to discover other treasures. In this way hula masters became informed about the potential of the archival collections in the Bishop Museum and began to draw on those resources for their choice chant and for other performance opportunities, as well as for information on the assigned competition chant. Their exploratory efforts were focused largely on the field collections because of their relative accessibility, but also because the field collections offered direct connections to past generations of performers, many of whose voices could be accessed as well in audio recordings.

Moral Imperatives

When considering issues of repatriation, deinstitutionalization, and resurrection of objects of cultural patrimony, how is the repatriation and restoration of knowledge about those objects to be handled? This is pertinent when recovery of knowledge comes about through historical research and involves compiling knowledge in such a way as it was unlikely to have existed prior to the intervention of research. And this brings me to the roles and responsibilities of researchers as brokers of knowledge.

In the context of discussing repatriation of ethnographic materials that would enable their resurrection in performance, scholars are faced simultaneously with two dilemmas. First, integrity becomes triangulated among the scholar, the community, and the material itself. While scholars harbor an ethical sense of responsibility to the community in which research is conducted, many scholars do find themselves in the curious position of harboring responsibility for material entrusted to their care—on behalf of those individuals who entrusted the materials. This becomes an issue with the passing of one generation who granted the materials, and the emergence of spokespersons in the next generation who wish to reclaim said materials, but whose interests may not be congruent with those of their elders. Moreover, if the younger generation had become separated from the materials, then it is probable that they have also been separated from knowledge about the materials. It follows, then, that availability of the materials does not automatically include access to knowledge about those materials.

Second, scholars may be confronted with the fact that their intentions, goals, and values in reconnecting communities with ethnographic items of cultural patrimony may not be congruent with the goals, values, needs, and intentions of the community in resurrecting that material back into circulation (Meyer 1998; Smith 1999). Scholars aspire to understand performance repertoire at the time of its composition; reaching such an understanding often involves peeling back subsequent layers of interpretation. Performers, on the other hand, strive to present materials in ways that are relevant to contemporary audiences; to do so, they build upon those very layers of interpretation that historians would peel away. Thus the historian's goal of historical reconstruction may not necessarily be shared entirely by performers, whose interests include exercising performative creativity and license for the purpose of addressing contemporary, rather than past, interests and needs.

Deinstitutionalizing archived materials adds another layer of separation. Those who would access such materials must first work through institutional procedures for access. There is thus, for hula, a significant role for historical research that the hula community must be able to put to its own use. By virtue of providing a roadmap, of identifying what materials exist, scholars can contribute to lowering barriers to access.

What are the roles and responsibilities of scholars to fill in the blanks of background information? Simply put, scholars occupy an intermediary role as brokers between the community and the institutionalized resources. Scholars can make a valuable contribution by identifying and locating resources and by sketching the broader background that contextualizes individual pieces within a larger whole. Yet scholars also have the responsibility of making not only the material available, but also any knowledge about it. This is because the resurrection of knowledge would enable the restoration of performative creativity, in turn allowing performers to exceed mere repetition of repertoire and engage in creative interpretation and composition. By providing access to interpretation, insight, and knowledge, scholars can extend integrity to the material as it embarks on a new journey back into the life of the community that values it.

What happens when knowledge about objects is not readily available, and those objects are reanimated in ways that potentially compromise their original integrity? Two false issues arise with such a question. One has to do with using an "authentic past" established by the scholar-historian to discredit contemporary practices by performers as an "inauthentic present." This strategy has been documented in situations of colonial domination: administrators, in the guise of scholars, pursued antiquarian study in order to establish a glorious past from which present-day subjects had degenerated; this scholarship was then used as a justification for establishing and maintaining colonial rule (see, for example, Cohn 1996; Said 1979; Trasoff 1999). Implicit in this issue is the assumption that cultural practices and artifacts from the past must be preserved in some kind of pristine state. In reality, living traditions breathe and change, and formerly colonized peoples, engaged in processes of decolonizing, are actively using international forums to assert rights of self-determination over cultural practices. Relevant statements can be located in two prominent international documents. The United Nations' Working Group on Indigenous Peoples developed the "Draft Declaration on the Rights of Indigenous Peoples" over an eight-year period, from 1985 to 1993. Part 3, article 12 reads as follows (see Venne 1998, 107–34; the complete text of the "Draft Declaration" is on pp. 205–16; see also Posey and Dutfield 1996, 181–88): "Indigenous peoples have the right to practice and revitalize their cultural traditions and customs. This includes the right to maintain, protect and develop the past, present and future manifestations of their cultures, such as archaeological and historical sites, artifacts, designs, ceremonies, technologies and visual and performing arts and literature, as well as the right to the restitution of cultural, intellectual, religious and spiritual property taken without their free and informed consent or in violation of their laws, traditions and customs." The "Mataatua Declaration on Cultural and Intellectual Property Rights of Indigenous Peoples," drawn up by attendees at the First International Conference on the Cultural and Intellectual Property Rights of Indigenous Peoples in June 1993, is more succinct on the matter of indigenous peoples exercising creativity in cultural practices. Article 2.2 called upon states and national and international agencies to "recognise that Indigenous Peoples also have the right to create new knowledge based on cultural traditions" (Posey and Dutfield 1996, 207; see also Mead 1998–1999, 18).

The other issue is related to matters of authority: does the authority to proclaim a performance "wrong" belong to a community member who claims cultural patrimony as his or her own? Or does it belong to a scholar whose conclusions are likely to be based on a wider range of sources than might be readily accessible to the community? Implicit in this particular query is the assumption that "scholars" are not members of indigenous communities to whom institutionalized materials are being repatriated. Thus, what of the scholar who, like me, is a member of the community, but for whom the conflict of historical verification versus creative license is likely to have much more salient emotional charge? On the one hand, for example, through my historical research I have reached understandings of how certain categories of repertoire were classified as sacred, and how ritual safeguards protected that sacredness (Stillman 1998); on the other hand, as a native Hawaiian, I applaud hula masters who take poetic texts that have been dormant for over a century, breathe life and voice back into them, and animate them once again onstage.

The issue of authority is a nonissue. At issue are the rights of indigenous peoples to self-representation and creativity. Repatriation of resources provides the means through which indigenous peoples can decide how they will then be put to use. Scholars have a potentially important role in making resources accessible and in contextualizing those resources as broadly as possible through scholarship. Scholars have an additional responsibility to foster indigenous scholars through whom indigenous perspectives can be articulated (Meyer 1998). Once that is accomplished, scholars must exercise courage in letting go of the material. The community members must make of those materials what they will—whether it be reanimating pieces of poetic repertoire or turning their backs on baggage from the past that they decide is best left in the past.

Should repatriation be considered a moral imperative (Keith and Anne Chambers, Alan Howard, chapters 9 and 2 respectively, as opposed to Bryan Oles and Mary McCutcheon, chapters 10 and 4)? In the case of hula, when the life of a performance tradition hangs in the balance, yes. But the moral imperative to "do no harm" applies not only to the community to which material is being returned, but also to the integrity of the material being resurrected. In this vein, anthropologists and scholars stand in a unique position to serve as intermediaries and brokers, not only to the people in whose information they traffic, but also to the information itself.

Part III *Transformation, Interpretation, and Ownership*

Keith S. Chambers and Anne Chambers

9

Ethnographer as Taker and Maker in Tuvalu

In the canonic model of fieldwork, exemplified since Malinowski by the meticulous data gatherer who took and crafted (but rarely devoted much energy to giving back), ethnographers did not need to be overly concerned with the return of their materials to those who originally provided them. A host of implicit assumptions clothed the ethnographic enterprise. These included assumptions about who read and was concerned with the representations created, as well as assumptions relevant (and oblivious) to intellectual property rights. These assumptions helped to render invisible the creative process of ethnography itself. Today, a more reflective approach requires that the implicit and explicit dimensions of fieldwork be examined so that we can fully understand the process of ethnographic representation.

Return of ethnographic materials to the people on whom these focus is now inevitable, with or without the ethnographer's assistance. This fact makes it even more important to build-in the return of information as a more conscious and intrinsic part of the fieldwork process. This chapter draws on our research experience of more than a quarter century in Tuvalu, focusing on the efforts we have made thus far to return research materials to

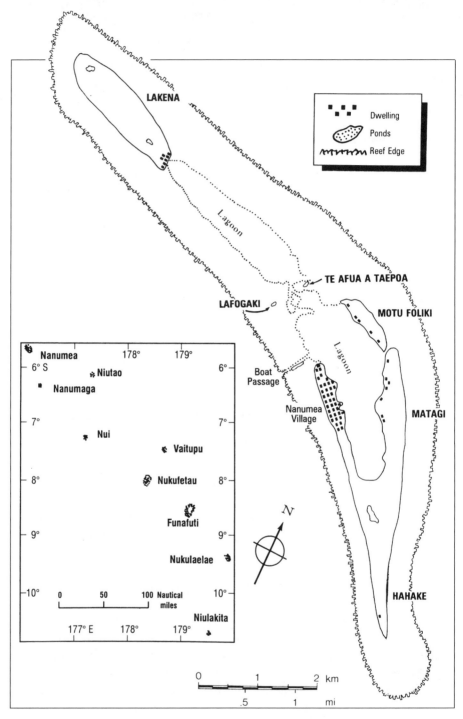

Map Nanumea Atoll with Tuvalu insert (Keith S. Chambers and Anne Chambers 2001, 23).
Courtesy of Waveland Press.

our hosts. Our goal here is to raise and explore some of the questions and dilemmas created for all participants in the drama of long-term fieldwork. We argue that the process and semantics of "return" are more complex than they might first appear, and that the repatriated materials (and even the repatriation process itself) alters the local culture and research context forever after.

We first conducted ethnographic research in Tuvalu in connection with an applied socioeconomic project funded by the British government in 1973–1975. At that time, the Gilbert and Ellice Islands (now the separate independent nations of Kiribati and Tuvalu) were administered together as a colony by Great Britain. We have returned for two additional periods of fieldwork, six months in 1984 and two months in 1996, as well as a brief visit by Keith in 1998. We intend to maintain a long-term relationship with the Nanumean community in particular and with Tuvalu in general. We have always intended our ethnographic work to make a positive contribution to Nanumea / Tuvaluan life, going beyond the simple production of academic writing.

This chapter discusses the efforts we have made to return ethnographic materials to the Nanumean community. We first describe the materials that have resulted from our field research, local interest in them, and the context of ethnographic collaboration that resulted. We then go on to discuss issues that have become important in the last twenty-five years as we have tried to return ethnographic items to the Nanumean community in ways that were appropriate to our relationship. These include our role in "making" local tradition, the problems of homogenizing competing versions, the issues involved in "freezing" fluid oral traditions, and the questions of accessibility and ownership.

Ethnographic Collaboration

Over the years we deposited (and redeposited) copies of our publications in the National Library and gave copies to government departments, individuals whom we felt might be interested, the Nanumean Island Council, and local schools and leaders of the Nanufuti community in the capital. We also went to some lengths to provide most of Nanumea's 150 households with a copy of our 1975 report to the government, a return of information that was unconventional in the colonial context. This report (A. Chambers 1975, republished as A. Chambers 1984) contained several sections that have proven to be of particular interest to Nanumeans. One section summarized local views about the island's settlement and well-known stories of the precontact era, such as local feuds and attempted invasions. Another section

describing traditional sociopolitical groupings (extended family corporations and chiefly descent groups) was also of local interest. Neither grouping
had been active at the time of our research in 1973–1975, but Nanumeans
regarded both family corporations and chiefly descent groups as key institutions and saw them as shaping the social context in which past events had
unfolded.

While this report was written as part of an applied project intended to
help the colonial government plan toward a postcolonial future for the
Gilbert and Ellice Islands, we assumed from the outset (and in fact made
promises to this effect) that we were incurring an obligation to return, in
some form, our "data" to the community. It was clear, too, from the considerable interest people expressed in some of this material during our work in
Tuvalu that its future return would be valued. However, during our initial
fieldwork in 1973–1974, we felt that few community members really understood our ethnographic intentions, even though we spent considerable effort attempting to explain our research objectives to them. Because people
had not heard of anthropology and were not familiar with scholarly research, they had no frame of reference to contextualize or make sense of our
ethnographic fieldwork. People did seem to appreciate our role as providers
of a conduit for communication to the colonial government, and they were
pleased at the prospect that they would become known to the wider world
through our writings. Our efforts to record oral tradition, to collect genealogies, and to learn the language were welcomed. On many occasions people
commented approvingly (or appeared to us to be understanding) about the
positive value of recording traditional history and describing indigenous
institutions. These aspects of life were associated with a past heritage that
most Nanumeans recognize as old and treasured (*taaua*), and as providing a
basis for the community's distinctive identity within Tuvalu.

As David and Dorothy Counts have noted (chapter 1), an ethnographer's
gathering of oral or visual material differs from the act of removing physical
items. People can, and do, repeat their statements, so that simply recording
oral materials does not make them lost to the community. In fact, by
recording and making this information more permanent, we ensured that it
would not be lost when an elder died. Though people also willingly provided us with detailed information about work patterns, exchanges, and
food consumption, our unflagging interest in such mundane aspects of their
lives largely mystified them. When they thought we were not listening,
people joked about our fascination with such things, wondering why we had
come hundreds of miles only to ask them about trivia.

This same painstakingly collected "trivia" constituted the parts of our writings that were most valued by the government, slotting into practical and policy questions for which administrators needed answers, or at least useful data. By contrast, administrative readers proved quite uninterested in the sections of our report that summarized traditional history. Nor did they have much interest in our description of the social groupings that had once structured precontact Nanumean life, viewing these as effectively supplanted by missionary and governmental changes. Extended family residential corporations (*kopiti*), consisting of household clusters of patrilateral kin living on a named land plot, had been located in the same area as the contemporary village. These residential groups had fragmented before the turn of the century due to contact pressures. They were replaced by a rectilinear village of smaller households, laid out on each side of the Congregational church. The family corporations had also been the locus for worship of ancestral spirits. But like other indigenous religious practices, care of ancestors' spirits had become both problematic and redundant when the last "pagans" converted to Christianity in the early 1920s. By the time of our fieldwork in the 1970s, *kopiti* had become a vague memory for most Nanumeans. Just a few elders still recalled the old residential locations or the organizational details of *kopiti* life.

While the disappearance of *kopiti* groups seemed to have been accepted with little regret by Nanumeans, loss of the community's political system of traditional chiefs lingered on as a critical (though disempowered) commentary on its replacement, the elected and government-instituted Island Council. The chiefly council (*kaualiki*) was drawn from specific traditional lineages, each of which had a designated leadership role to play.[1] Stories of heroic deeds and past power struggles provided rationales for the political roles allocated to some lineages. In recent history, at least, two lineages alternated in the high chief role while the remaining five were charged with supporting responsibilities. The system was consensus based, despite the use of the term "chief" (*aliki*), and never fit well with the British need for authoritative political leadership that could enforce the colonial government's edicts. By the time of our first research in the 1970s, the chiefly system had been proscribed, an elected island council had been created to handle government funds and decision making, and the chiefs, very much alive but without either power or responsibility, were left with a small bank account, but no designated role in island affairs. We tried to understand the covert power struggles and factional splits that became apparent through our research on traditional history and genealogy as complementary to the unified cooperation that the community showed to the wider world. Similar processes were clearly implied in the community's traditional history. We tried to be mindful of the complex issues of representation involved in reconstructing traditional practices, as well as the possibility of "invention" of tradition (Hobsbawm and Ranger 1983).

Information that may be dismissed as peripheral by one audience can be of vital importance to another—and this proved to be the case with our writings on traditional history and the chieftainship. Our ethnographic accounts have gradually become "official" records in a sense, available to all members of the community and apparently regarded as a sort of definitive compilation of the memories of the elders with whom we are known to have spent time a generation ago. As we will discuss below, substantive public (written) versions of the community's history have never existed before. However, in defining themselves as the "Children of Tefolaha," descended together from Nanumea's legendary founder, Nanumeans have been using the generalized version of their traditional history as a symbolic statement of their unity as a community for some time. This unity apparently served in the contact era (just as it continues to serve today) as the accepted context within which the ongoing challenges and dialectics of community life are acted out.

Nanumean cultural emphasis on its corporate unity has structured the way in which our relationship with the community evolved. One of the first questions we had to answer about our fieldwork was whether our research and presence on Nanumea was to be seen as "of the island," with the community as its primary beneficiary and patron, or as "of the government," in which case it would be seen to have a primarily governmental orientation and commitment. Following the advice of local leaders and our research assistant, we opted for the first classification. This choice prompted the community to provide logistical assistance to our fieldwork, which continues down to the present day. In response, we took care to align ourselves with the community as a whole and felt an obligation to avoid exclusive ties to any single grouping, community faction, or family, lest these limit other peoples' access to us. Though we did inevitably develop personal relationships with particular individuals, these were spread widely across the community and seem not to have undermined the whole-community orientation that Nanumeans valued.

Looking back, it seems to us that Nanumeans and we ourselves were collaboratively engaged in creating a community-oriented fieldwork relationship, with both sides responding to what they believed to be each other's assumptions and subtle wishes, in a semiconscious way. As Michael Ashkenazi (1997) and others have pointed out, both the community and the anthropologist play determining roles in creating an ethnographic part-

Keith Chambers with Noa, reigning chief [*pulefenua*], 1996 (Keith S. Chambers and Anne Chambers)

nership. Each side's expectations affect the way that information is managed and the form that the fieldwork relationship assumes. From this perspective, it seems likely that our focused relationship with the community as a whole has informed not only our approach to fieldwork, but also the orientation from which we interpreted the information shared with us. For example, we realize that we initially took a generalizing approach to the community's history, an approach that was later corrected as we learned the importance of contested, dissenting versions of the charter stories. More positively, this same orientation encouraged our sense of obligation to the community and our determination that the results of our research be useable by, and equally available to, all its members. But looking back on our repatriation decisions, it is clear that over time some of them came to lag behind current realities, and that contextual changes made some of them more problematic than they initially appeared to us. Situational complexities such as these have spawned the questions that we discuss in this chapter.

The Anthropologist as "Maker"

By 1996, when we returned to Tuvalu twenty-three years after our first fieldwork, virtually the whole generation of elders who had contributed information about precontact social organization had died. Apparently, much of their knowledge had not been passed on through informal channels. Perhaps as a result, our writings had come to be seen as a source of authoritative information about traditional institutions.

By this time, very few of the one hundred copies of our first report (written in English) still survived in the community. People expressed pleasure when we presented copies of another of our publications: a thesis that included two versions (in Tuvaluan) of the community's legendary founding, as well as details of traditional social organization and an analysis of the contemporary uses of historical narratives. Possession of this volume was widely sought after and parts were read enthusiastically by a number of people during our stay. Some of these readers commented in their speeches during community gatherings in the public hall that the book finally allowed them to see some usefulness in our work. In effect, members of a new generation had been provided with materials about themselves (and ostensibly from themselves) in a community and country where there is little written material people consider directly relevant to local life. However, though these materials were accepted as the community's own, not all of them had been authored directly or completely by Nanumeans.

Our fieldwork in the 1980s had made us aware of the contested nature of Nanumean tradition. This was reflected in the dissertation's orientation to the community as an enduring social group. The importance of differences in families' versions of founding stories had also been recognized, however, and the dissertation discussed the way that these divergences resonated with contemporary political maneuverings. By writing at this level of generalization, one consistent with anthropological analytical conventions, we ourselves had become involved in a subtle "making" of the community's traditional history. Our written accounts expressed our own particular orientation to the Nanumean past. This orientation was indisputably based on the large repertoire of accounts shared with us, but through the normal process of ethnographic analysis, this information had been digested into an account oriented around our understanding of Nanumean social organization and our anthropological interests and concerns. As Roy Wagner (1975) pointed out, this maker's role is inherent in anthropological fieldwork and a characteristic feature of ethnographic writing.

But while our writings faithfully encapsulated a version of the information that now-deceased elders had given us, it inevitably could not include the full range of implicit, political meanings that each elder's separate account would have held for its listeners. Missing, in large part, in our reformulation was the living context of these materials. Our process of distilling and recasting had not been oblivious to these contextual dimensions, but rather our own goals necessarily limited how this ambient material was considered. Historical narratives or discussions of them arise in many situations besides elicitation by an ethnographer, including orations in the meeting hall or more casual banter during work parties. In all contexts the audience influences the information and its emphases and critically evaluates the "performance" based on its own foreknowledge. With contested, politically sensitive materials, some of this evaluation will include private dismissal of the truth value of the account. Such rejection is rarely made public at the time of presentation. As outsiders we are only partially aware of the depth of cross-referencing, community memories, political ambitions, and influence seeking involved in the transmission of materials of this sort. For all of these reasons, the written versions that we conscientiously "gave back" and that the community appears to have accepted as authentic tradition had been influenced in a host of subtle ways by our involvement. As far as we have been able to ascertain, Nanumeans have not yet raised questions about the nature of this influence and shaping of "their" material.

We inadvertently took on yet another "maker" role in 1996, when we brought back two rolls of genealogical data as a gift to the community. These large, photocopied pages, with information gathered a generation before, generated great interest and comment. We originally had intended to computerize the genealogies, thinking that they would be most useful in this form to ourselves and the community, but we have not found the time needed to input and analyze the data. After considerable thought, and with the opportunity for a visit looming, we decided to return these materials to the community in what we thought of as their "raw" form, as a bound set of kinship diagrams. We had gathered the information from a very wide range of the elders living on Nanumea in 1973–1975 and added more information to the sheets in 1984. The connections we charted emphasized the consanguineal and affinal linkages between families, coalescing information we had obtained from our many sources into as cohesive a whole as we could manage. Needless to say, this type of presentation resulted from our research interests and did not match the Nanumean orientation to genealogy, which is mainly concerned with linking a family branch to a line of ancestors and is usually bound up with pragmatic issues such as access to land or to sociopolitical status.

Our decision to return this genealogical information to the community stemmed from letters we had received from time to time while we were away from Nanumea, asking us for particular genealogical information. With the information apparently useful in daily life and valuable enough to write overseas to obtain, we felt an obligation to make our records available to everyone in the community. Since this information could be used to bolster political or land claims, equality of access seemed important to us. We reminded people, of course, that the information contained in the sheets was only provisionally accurate and that we ourselves had pooled knowledge from many family groups and interviews to create the more general genealogical connections depicted.

While the genealogies were raw data in one sense, the compilation and connection of the material from a wide range of oral sources had, in effect, created something processed and quite new. Our charting obscured or blended, to some extent, the sources of information. Like the theses and the report before it, the genealogical information had been synthesized in ways that reflected our interests as anthropologists and outsiders. The return of these genealogical sheets is probably more problematic than that of other materials because of complicated questions of "ownership" that are discussed below.

Overall, however, Nanumeans seem to have responded positively regarding our offering of ethnographic matters thus far, in part because some people have begun to see their "traditions" as in danger of being lost.[2] Especially concerned are those who have worked overseas for a long time or who currently live in the capital, where they contend with an impersonal economy and the distractions of bright-lights bustle. Many people in this now sizable group feel that they themselves do not have the grasp of tradition that their parents had, and they are disappointed that their children show little interest in Nanumean culture. Certainly, the pace of change has continued to accelerate since the 1990s, with the cash economy encroaching markedly into subsistence domains. Opportunities for work and education overseas have increased as well. In response, Nanumeans living in Funafuti began a project in the early 1990s aimed at compiling what they term a *fakavae* (cultural constitution), a summary of the unique traditions and customs that differentiate Nanumeans from other Tuvaluans. This constitution is also intended to provide specific information about key economic and political institutions (such as the chieftainship) so that differing interpretations can be resolved authoritatively and potential disputes avoided. Nanumeans see this compendium offering an authoritative reference on their social, political, and economic traditions.

Viewing the Nanumean elders at home as closer to the authentic source of tradition than themselves, the capital community drafted a list of questions that it hoped would provide the information needed to frame this constitution. The questionnaire that was finally sent back to Nanumea in

1993 focused on twenty-three topics, most of which listed several subques-
tions. Topics ranged from the selection and installation of the chief, to use of
communal resources, to customs surrounding birth and death. When the
list was received in Nanumea, a committee of elders began meeting twice
weekly to answer the questions, with the idea that its version of the answers
would be discussed with younger members of the community before the
responses were returned to the capital. Both the goal of creating a "cultural
constitution" and the process through which it was to develop appeared to
be premised on a view of history and cultural "truth" as enduring and
definitive entities, rather than as cultural constructions that shifted through
time and comprised situated versions.

On Nanumea the elders' meetings generated debate and contention.
"Family stories battled each other" we were told. The section on the chieftainship (*pulefenua*) became particularly difficult to deal with because the
community had become locked in a contentious dispute, part of which
involved one of the very issues on which "constitutional" clarification was
being sought. Questions such as "What if the reigning chief does not follow
or breaks the rules pertaining to his position?" or "What types of character
and behavior are appropriate and inappropriate for a reigning chief?" no
longer had a simple answer, whether one ever did exist in the past. By 1996,
three years later, we found that urban Nanumeans were still awaiting the
draft of answers from Nanumea. The reply from the home community had
been delayed because the elders could not agree on a definitive response to
some of the questions, many of which had direct implications for the dispute. However, we were told that our 1975 report, viewed as authoritative
knowledge gathered from the generation of elders now gone, had been
consulted on several occasions by the committee of elders as it grappled
with writing out answers to the cultural questionnaire.

The role that we have played, relatively unwittingly, in the selective
preservation of "tradition" and in the process of information transmission
from a prior generation of elders is sobering. Overall, we believe that this
role (helping to preserve "traditional" information useful to developing the
community's identity in the national context) has been largely consistent
with the tenor of our fieldwork relationship and has provided Nanumeans
with information they value. Nonetheless, we cannot help but realize that
some of our writings systematize information in ways that Nanumeans
themselves might not have been drawn to do and, inevitably, have not
preserved the full range of local viewpoints. As ethnographers, we know
that we have inevitably helped to create the culture we report as a logical

bounded entity. Our creative influence, as subtle "makers" of ethnographic tradition, seems to us to have had particular significance in regard to the following three issues.

Competing Versions—The Danger of Oversystematization

The ethnographic and theoretical literature provides many cautionary tales about the need for sensitivity to competing versions of "traditional" material and the danger of homogenizing or oversystematizing it. The issue of cultural variability and the extent to which shared understandings can be assumed was quintessentially captured as early as 1884 in J. O. Dorsey's innocent remark "Two Crows denies this," referring to a disagreement between two of his Omaha informants, an incident then insightfully probed for its theoretical significance some fifty years later by Edward Sapir (Dorsey 1884, discussed in Sapir 1949, 569 and following). In Nanumea, traditional knowledge, particularly accounts of the island's founding and the establishment of the chiefly lineages, is locally contested and has provided a focal point for our analysis of local political processes. Most of the key elders with whom we originally worked in the 1970s were active in island affairs and vocal about the "truth" of their accounts of the past. From the outset, we have been interested in the extent of variability and tape-recorded as many narratives as we could.

It is also clear that most community members share a general outline of Nanumean history: a founding by the godlike hero named Tefolaha, a political structure based on the roles allocated to his children, and a series of attempts at conquest by outsiders. But beyond a general framework, particular genealogical connections to the founding lineages determined the emphasis of each family's stories. One family, for example, stressed the founder's allocation of a key leadership role to his youngest son, who was, not surprisingly, a founding ancestor for them. Another family's story, focusing several generations lower down in the same family tree, emphasized the role one descendant of that youngest son had played in outsmarting and killing invading outsiders while other leaders fled for safety to a neighboring island. This event legitimated the family's current political claims. Genealogical connections linked all these families, yet the unique potentialities inherent in particular historical events (rather than in their shared kinship) were highlighted in the stories. Clearly, the political fortunes of extended families wax and wane at least partly in response to the persuasiveness with which their members wield their versions of historical-mythical narratives.

We have not yet been able to publish the full texts of our collected narrative materials, though we hope to do so in the future. The few narratives that have appeared, therefore, may have assumed a centrality not intended by us. "Why did you use so-and-so's tale and not so-and-so's," people have asked (in almost the same breath that they express appreciation that something *is* published). Since the narratives in question are still used in ongoing jockeying over political position and leadership, we are unsettled to realize that our publication of some of them has undoubtedly privileged some versions over others. For example, the dissertation that we shared with the community in 1996 focuses on the way traditional history creates and supports the community's sociopolitical system. Space considerations meant that only narratives most central to that analysis were included and much material was provided in summary. As this book is read and, perhaps, comes to be used in ongoing discussions and disputes, we are concerned that the texts included in greatest detail may gain authority at the expense of those less featured. This selectivity raises questions for which there are no easy answers, either from the island's point of view or our own. We wonder whether it would have been fairer to have included texts of all versions or, if that were impossible, perhaps none. Not returning this information at all would have prevented these problems—but would also impede our returning information to the community, a responsibility that we take seriously and want to honor.

"Freezing" of Tradition

A related issue might be called the "freezing" of tradition, a process wherein the very act of selecting or publishing formerly oral materials affects their nature, giving them a solidity or a reified quality they did not previously have. The myth-history of Nanumea's founding is an oral tale, fluid and in process. It is told as many "versions," depending on narrator and performative skill, family tradition, individual memory, and many other contextual variables. Yet our published accounts can be seen to have created specimens of several of these, in effect pinning our cultural "butterflies" in the "display case" of our published work.[3] The risk is that these selected accounts, caught in full motion but pinned down through publication, may come to exemplify Nanumean tradition as "official" versions, to the exclusion of other equally significant or authoritative accounts.

Where tradition is mutable and oral, caught up with the ongoing creation and negotiation of political structure, there is no edifice of past constructions to dismantle. Outmoded versions simply fall into disuse and are

Venu carving a canoe prow, 1974 (Keith S. Chambers and Anne Chambers)

forgotten. People remember the events that support today's reality and "authenticity" remains a fluid, creative process. When we began to collect oral traditions in Nanumea in the 1970s, the island's mythical founder, Tefolaha, was widely described as a Samoan who had fought in the Tongan wars. His background in either place was not specifiable by any of the elders, though most people did agree that he had brought a Tongan woman to Nanumea as his wife. Just as we were ending our first period of fieldwork in 1975, we heard of an elderly Nanumean living in the capital who maintained a uniquely different version of the founder's origins. In his narrative, Tefolaha had a Tongan genealogy, which placed him as a descendant of the Tongan kings. The Nanumeans who told us about this version regarded it as fabricated and said that the old man kept his family ledger books hidden from public scrutiny. We visited this elder in 1975, listened to his account, and noted down an outline of his version. But because this man was so isolated from the ongoing political maneuvering, which we had observed, and his version was discounted by elders residing in Nanumea, it was not discussed in the dissertation.

As may always happen in fieldwork, this decision returned to haunt us when we presented copies of the dissertation to Nanumeans in 1996. The old man's son had become a prominent leader of the Nanumean capital community and was insisting on the legitimacy of his father's version of the founder's Tongan genealogy. In the fluid dynamics of oral tradition, his version seems currently to be in the process of becoming more widely known and accepted, and may perhaps even transform some aspects of the charter account in the future. However, because this version was not considered in the study, its authenticity was implicitly questioned. (From the point of view of this community leader and his family, of course, the authenticity of the thesis can be challenged as well!) We were disappointed to see that our work had tacitly prejudged an important debate that was still developing.

Accessibility and Ownership

We have consistently tried to provide copies of our ethnographic writings to Tuvalu and to individual Nanumeans, hoping to make some small return for the major investments of time, concern, and effort that people have made in our work. Having been written for a variety of audiences and purposes, these writings are something of a "mixed bag," and some are of only limited interest to many Tuvalu readers. Nevertheless, now that Tuvalu has a National Archives building in the capital and people are increasingly able to read English, copies of our publications are potentially of greater interest and need to be easily and widely available. This raises some important issues regarding accessibility, ownership, and gatekeeping.

These issues are implicit in all our ethnographic writing, but they became especially important when we returned two sets of genealogical data sheets to the community in 1996.[4] Since Nanumean interest in genealogy and descent continue unabated into the present, and kinship relations are important for land claims and political authenticity, these materials were eagerly received. But "received by whom?" we soon found was the important question. Finding an appropriate answer involved clarifying the responsibility we felt toward our host community as well as ascertaining the community's own ability to manage access to these materials in a way that was consistent with its ideology and current political realities.

We ourselves and the Nanumean community alike found it hard to pinpoint the rightful caretakers of this information. Should it be the capital residents? Only those living in Nanumea itself? Should the genealogy sheets be deposited in the National Archives, where anyone could consult them? Was there any suitable repository for them at all in Nanumea? Though the Island Council and Land Court were "of the government," might not this information be useful to the members of these bodies? All of these questions assume that the corpus of genealogies could legitimately be compiled and returned (as we had tried to do) to the community as a whole. The question remains, of course, whether this was an entirely appropriate thing to do, given the fact that genealogical information has traditionally been the province of each particular family group. As Rosemary Coombe (1997, 25) has pointed out in regard to cultural information control in global-era policy making, assumptions about access and the way that "information" is understood are implicit and culturally constituted. Western understandings and assumptions are not shared everywhere. Perhaps returning the genealogical compilation to the Nanumean community as a whole resonated with our ethnographic obligations more than it did with Nanumean expectations.

In any case, even defining the Nanumean community is becoming difficult. Nanumeans in the capital now number close to 500 people, more than half that of the current resident population of Nanumea atoll, and the influence of the capital's Nanumeans has grown with its numbers. Now calling themselves "Nanufuti" (from the combination of Nanumea and Funafuti, the capital), this group has its own elected leadership and organization, which works closely with leaders residing on the home island to achieve mutual goals. Nanufuti increasingly plays a key role in articulating and protecting Nanumean interests at the national level. Understandably, Nanufuti leaders wanted a set of the genealogies. However, they have no official storage for records other than the homes of the community's leaders. If we gave a copy to the current leaders, was it likely that the genealogies would disappear from public access and become someone's personal property, thereby calling into question any public benefits that might result from our sharing the information? We were not the only ones to have this concern. Some of the capital dwellers not currently holding public office said that this would be inevitable.

The National Archives, newly refurbished, is also located in the capital. Should a set of the genealogies be placed there? While some of the people we consulted felt this was a good solution, others were concerned that the sheets might disappear into the possession of an influential politician or other individual. Checkout procedures at the archives can be somewhat informal, with politically important people having greater access to materials than ordinary members of the public. There was also a general reluctance to give the genealogies over to the control of a government institution, since Nanumeans dichotomize between community affairs and associated "traditional" issues in contrast to aspects under central government control, a topic we discuss more fully below.

Nanumeans on the home island had little interest in which of these suggestions was followed, since any materials located hundreds of miles away were unlikely to be usable by them, in the short-term at least. But where (and with whom) would materials repose on Nanumea itself? The elected Island Council office has a small library, but materials there are easily lost or damaged. In any case, using this office as a repository was complicated by the political dualism that differentiates the true "affairs of the community" (*fai faiga o te fenua*) from the "affairs of the government" (*fai faiga o te maaloo*). Giving jurisdiction over the genealogies to the council, even though the council is made up exclusively of members of the Nanumean community, would be placing them with the "government," not with the "island." Alternatively, since the island now vests traditional authority in its recently reestablished council of chiefs, should the set be given to this group? Many people thought this would be the best idea, but the pragmatic difficulty of *place* arose: a tidal wave had destroyed the island's office building in the late 1980s, and the community still lacked any secure place to store official documents. The genealogy sheets, if given to the chiefs, would end up in the house of the reigning chief or his speaker. While this was not deemed ideal by those we spoke with (since the office rotates every few years), it was the solution that most appeared to favor, and we opted to do this.

Simply "giving back to the community" that which is rightfully its property proved more difficult than we had assumed. In this small, face-to-face society, individuals speak for differing constituencies and levels of representation. Safe and accessible repositories are still being developed, and the means for protecting and preserving paper in Tuvalu's humid climate are still rudimentary. There is justifiable concern that valuable items can easily disappear into private hands. In the end, we decided to leave one set of genealogies with Nanumea's reigning high chief and another with the senior of Nanumea's two elected members of parliament. The parliamentarian, a member of the national cabinet and thus a resident in the capital, took the set with him to the capital about the time we left the island in July 1996. He agreed to try to get it laminated for protection from the elements and then to deposit it in the National Archives.

These plans did not fully eventuate. While we left the genealogies several years ago with the island's reigning chief, it is not clear whether local people still have access to them. Even more problematically, the chieftainship has become embroiled in a factional dispute, perhaps making it less likely that the genealogies will be passed along to the next incumbent as a community resource. The set left with the island's senior representative to the national parliament was passed to the leader of the Nanufuti (capital) Nanumean community. It had not been possible, we were told, to have it laminated, nor had it been deposited in the National Archives. Several people asked Keith when he visited in 1998 about what our intent in returning the genealogies had been, indicating to us indirectly that the materials were inaccessible. Some people apparently had heard that we had instructed that a charge should be levied for access or that use of the genealogies was to be restricted. Either of these possibilities was, of course, the direct opposite of what we had intended.

Looking Forward, Looking Back

The issues we have described here are, to a large extent, specific to our relationship with the Nanumean community and the particular choices we made during fieldwork. Limitations on our time and resources imposed some constraints, just as the community's political situation and the histori-cal period of our research influenced our perception of options, effects, and possibilities. These variables are the necessary starting points, as Alan How-ard suggests in chapter 2, in creating a repatriation equation appropriate to a given ethnographic situation. Here we would like to look back to assess the contexts framing our repatriation decisions, but also ahead to comment on some possible future outcomes.

One conclusion is clear: the best repatriation equations are constructed with reference to a historical perspective. Ethnographic materials are de-fined as valuable (or problematic) only in regard to particular social, politi-cal, and economic contexts, and these, inevitably, change through time. While our decision to return the compiled genealogies now seems some-what naive, we thought that it resonated appropriately with the commu-nity's political situation in the 1970s, the time of our first fieldwork. This period now stands out as an era of remarkable social cohesion, one in which dissonant voices and contrasting interpretations were downplayed and the rate of change was relatively slow. Such times come and go in any society's history. The community's situation today is more polarized, and differing interests are accentuated. Change, both within the Tuvalu communities themselves and in their wider relationships with the world, has accelerated.

How can significant contextual changes such as these be anticipated in the repatriation equation? Should decisions be geared to some hypothesized "worst of times" rather than to existing conditions? Or would framing the equation in that way be unnecessarily pessimistic? Knowing that we had compiled a resource that the community prized, should we have withheld it? Should we perhaps have continued to make the knowledge available bit by bit, only to those people who directly asked us for it? Clearly, the best context for answering these questions encompasses a broader sweep of time

Nanumea's newly renovated church, 1996 (Keith S. Chambers and Anne Chambers)

than just the conditions that frame one epoch. After all, repatriation choices will be judged from the perspective of the future and must endure the test of time. Unlike the cases involving institutionalized access to materials, described in part 2 of this volume, our ethnographic relationships with Nanumea are ongoing and will hopefully continue to unfold in the future, providing a context for working out some of the issues raised here.

Alan Howard (chapter 2) has suggested that communities go through developmental stages in their approach to and use of ethnographic information. This likelihood suggests that the repatriation equation need not be completely idiosyncratic and that some general guidelines might underlie many fieldwork situations. Taking our experience in Nanumea as a test case, what sorts of materials seem to stand the best chance of being appropriate returns in the long term? Clearly, one such category involves materials that circulate to the wider world. Usually written to address issues important to a Western academic audience, these are sometimes dismissed as not relevant to the community they have been written about. While the local interest they arouse can be marginal, these items must be returned home. As examples in this volume show, local interest in these materials tends to be related to each community's internal issues and its connections to wider institutions. These situational factors change through time and vary by community. See, for example, Mokil assessments of earlier ethnographic work as reported by Bryan Oles (chapter 10) and Amy Stillman's discussion of Hawaiian use of archived hula material (chapter 8). Also compare the relatively disinterested reception that Howard (chapter 2) reports his compendium of published materials received among Rotumans with the interest displayed in some of our writing by Nanumeans. Although the content of these processed materials (and, as the Counts assert in chapter 1, the style of their presentation too) constrains local usefulness, any of these assessments may be reversed in time.

The second type of material that clearly should come home includes original texts that can be ascribed to specific individuals. Such materials may support the cultural vitality of the community since they can be interpreted in authentic ways and are not likely to be inappropriately reified to "freeze" tradition. They are, in Howard's terminology, "heteroglossic." Fieldwork goals that include returning a wide variety of these materials to individuals and perhaps to the community as a whole would lead an ethnographer to document as many disparate voices as possible, creating a rich compendium from which community members can draw in the future in much the same way that people selectively use their cultural repertoire at any point in time. Insofar as these materials are "taken" rather than "made" by the ethnographer, their return to community members is natural and relatively un-problematic, even though they may have a more static and enduring form than is traditional.

But what of the "made" materials? Especially for such items, we agree with Howard's assertion that rules for repatriation cannot be made in the abstract. Not only are the materials too widely variable in themselves, but their cultural meanings, the contexts from which they were produced, and their repatriation effects are too complex and idiosyncratic to support simple generalization. Rather than rules, however, what is needed is heightened awareness among ethnographers that repatriation issues will inevitably arise. Discussing repatriation decisions with the community, and with as many of its individual members as possible, is critically important and man-dated in American Anthropological Association ethical guidelines (AAA 1971, 1998). Especially in long-term ethnographic relationships, such discussions have the potential to offer important insights. Not only can they clarify the community's hopes for benefiting from the ethnographic endeavor, but they can also illuminate local values and sociopolitical organization to the benefit of the fieldworker. Ideally, this would be an ongoing collaboration central to the ethnographic process, rather than simply a study of the consequences of repatriation decisions made by the ethnographer (the "impact analysis," which Sjoerd Jaarsma recognizes as problematic; see chapter 3).

Given these considerations, how would the return of our compiled genealogical materials pencil out in a "repatriation equation?" In Nanumea, as elsewhere in the Pacific, genealogical knowledge is the valuable intellectual property of families, preserved and manipulated by elders for the long-term benefit of the kin group as a whole. Our initial decision to return our genealogical compendium to the community assumed this value and was a response to the direct requests we were receiving for this information. Unlike our other ethnographic materials, which people were often delighted to have but rarely requested, people actually wrote to ask us for genealogical information. Given the demise of an entire generation of elders since the onset of our fieldwork, these requests seemed logical to us. They seemed to embody the community's systematic need for this knowledge and made us want to give it back in some way that would make it available to everyone. Perhaps we were partly led by the value that academia (or Western culture as a whole?) places on systematized, interrelated information, but we also hoped that once the resource was publicly available, people could independently draw out whatever was important to their own interests. We envisioned the materials being used for much the same purposes that elders had previously dug deep for into their memories and family notebooks.

Perhaps this decision was naive. Perhaps it will prove to be impractical, even problematic, should access to the compendium become restricted and no longer available to the whole community. Had our initial fieldwork occurred in the less solidary context of contemporary Nanumea, we doubt we would have thought it as appropriate to repatriate genealogical information in a compiled format. The contested nature of community life would probably have led us to return transcribed and individually attributed versions instead. We may well have felt it necessary to restrict some information, perhaps to direct descendants of each source, raising issues similar to those described by Jaarsma, as well as by David Akin and Kathryn Creely (chapter 5). Perhaps the wisest course now would be to explicitly disallow the use of the genealogical compendium in regard to political or land-related disputes, as Robert Borofsky (1987, 157) did in publishing some Pukapuka materials. Perhaps we could add a written caveat to that effect on each page of our materials when we next return to Tuvalu. Would that help to bring the equation into better balance? But since the eventual use of information can never be entirely knowable in advance (Mary McCutcheon provides a good example; see chapter 4), would such a statement have any binding power or practical effect?

Clearly, there are no easy solutions to the dilemmas we have encountered and that others in this volume have struggled with. Ethnography is a dangerous enterprise, by definition. It affects the lives of people, including the ethnographer, in ways unforeseen and unforeseeable. Its risks are not fully calculable. Just as in other domains of our lives, each of us must assess the situation and then move ahead. As the many case studies in this volume attest, repatriation decisions must be made deliberately, but potentially negative effects can result both from action and inaction, unfortunately, and people have to deal with dissonance and with disparity. Between the poles of danger and purity, we seldom have the luxury of waiting for purity—of intent, act, or outcome. In any case, purity is likely to be illusory, given the vagaries of time.

In conclusion, we want to turn briefly to the changes looming in the medium of ethnographic representation and particularly to consider how the future shape these media may take will affect repatriation options. Like other ethnographers of the mid to late twentieth century, our work made major use of pen and paper, typewriter, photographic images, and magnetic tape. These are the physical forms of "materials" we collected, synthesized, produced, and have grappled with returning. Increasingly, however, data and the products of ethnographic work will exist primarily in electronic form as the Gutenberg revolution gives way to the pixel revolution. The implications this has for representation and especially for the "return" issues as they have been discussed in this volume are enormous and have not yet become fully clear to any of us. Consider these examples, however. Pacific Island Web pages (including those produced by Alan Howard and Jan Rensel for Rotuma, the Counts for West New Britain, and by nonanthropologists for Tuvalu) span the world's electronic network and make available to anyone with interest a vast information and communications resource.[5] As access to entry points and computer terminals increases, it seems inevitable that much "return" will take an electronic form. Increasingly, our ethnographic work and materials (words, sounds, images, three-dimensional, rotatable renderings of objects, perhaps even fragrances) will be stored and manipulated for our own ethnographic and analytical use in this manner. Making such materials available to our host societies might entail devising methods to permit differential access. This might be conceived of as nested levels of "penetration" to the material—ranging from limited access to the general public, to deeper and deeper levels for those with the proper "key." Publishing of polished texts will be but one portion of this electronic hypermedia spectrum, which can accommodate raw notes, recordings, genealogical data, images, and more. Could levels of access to these complex information hives be handled in some coded manner, similar to the way ATM technology is evolving away from PIN numbers to other personal identifiers?

Without moving further into this brave new realm, it seems obvious that this type of scenario is one of numerous possible outcomes and that it may profoundly affect the way we think of these "materials" and the various modes of return and sharing we envision. The possibilities are just slightly over the horizon for many of us, but that horizon is closer than it seems. What new dimensions must we be ready to add to the return "equations" we have grappled with in this volume? It is time to begin working them out, now.

Bryan P. Oles

10

Dangerous Data from Mokil Atoll

Between 1947 and 1948 participants in the Coordinated Investigation of Micronesian Anthropology (CIMA) conducted anthropological studies on Mokil Atoll under the auspices of the Pacific Science Board and the Office of Naval Research.[1] The three participants, Joseph Weckler, Conrad Bentzen, and Raymond Murphy, each submitted final reports of their findings to the Naval Administration in the late 1940s. Data contained in the final reports has since made its way back to the people of Mokil. My recent fieldwork experience on Mokil brought into relief many of the theoretical, practical, ethical, and methodological dilemmas generated by the repatriation of those studies. In this chapter I will illustrate some of these dilemmas by focusing on two issues. First, I will examine the Mokilese attitudes toward the anthropological objectifications of their culture. Second, I will consider how Mokilese perceptions of past and present social relationships affect the perceived value of ethnography. This analysis will contribute to the theoretical dimension of repatriation by considering the way in which the objectified ethnographic record constitutes a threat to the flexibility and fluidity embedded in Mokilese social relations and epistemology. In response to the inherent danger of the monolithic cultural history that is inscribed in CIMA reports, the Mokilese have largely chosen to ignore the repatriated data. The chapter concludes by discussing the divide between the anthropologist's goal in repatriating data and the ultimate fate of repatriated data determined by local agency in accordance with epistemological and social demands.

Throughout the chapter I will provide examples of the researcher's role in the repatriation process and the effects of repatriation on the community and the researcher's rapport with the community, thereby highlighting some of the ethical considerations of the repatriation process.

Anthropological Objects

Before embarking on the trip to Mokil Atoll I equipped myself with certain items that I felt would be needed while doing fieldwork on a tropical island. In addition to copious quantities of sunscreen and peanut butter, a motley assortment of trolling lures, decks of cards, and reams of Ziploc bags, I brought copies of the ethnographic reports and papers written by two anthropologists and one geographer who conducted research on Mokil in 1947, as well as a videotaped copy of the movie *Mokil* (Bentzen 1949, 1950; Murphy 1948, 1949, 1950; Weckler 1949, 1953). Originally, I simply intended to keep the ethnographic reports for my own reference, but the intended use of these and many other sundries in my possession was challenged by a series of questions that many, if not all, anthropologists must confront: What shall I keep? What must I keep? What shall I give away? What must I give away?

Although I entertained the possibility of sharing the reports with residents of Mokil, I originally balked at the idea in light of the data's form and content. Joseph Weckler and Conrad Bentzen collaborated throughout their fieldwork on two objectives, including an evaluation of Mokil's socio-economic organization and the production of a documentary film (Bentzen 1949, 1). Their work was funded by the United States Naval Administration as part of the Coordinated Investigation of Micronesian Anthropology, one of three projects designed to amass information about the newly acquired Micronesian islands (see Suzanne Falgout, chapter 6). Joseph Weckler and Conrad Bentzen divided the fieldwork between themselves according to their respective areas of interest. Weckler focused on social structure, history, and land tenure, while Bentzen examined the relationship between economics and the status system. Weckler compiled extensive genealogical data and land transfer histories, while Bentzen mapped individual land holdings and amassed information on production, cooperation, and exchange. As Bentzen indicates in his introduction, the film production focused on what the two researchers deemed the resident's most dire problem—population pressure on limited land resources (Bentzen 1949, 2). Raymond Murphy, who conducted seven weeks of fieldwork on Mokil, also investigated land tenure. He produced a separate set of maps and compiled a modest number of land histories.[2]

All three CIMA reports include the names of individuals who lived in the community at the time of the research. Furthermore, the reports submitted by Conrad Bentzen and Joseph Weckler describe in detail scurrilous exploits of named individuals, exemplifying the strife and discontent that characterized social relations during a period of increasing population pressure on the atoll's resources. Weckler inscribes detailed accounts of land alienation, cheating land dealers, physical fights involving "old ladies . . . tearing each other's hair," and a man biting off part of an antagonist's ear, while making numerous references to incidents of illegitimacy resulting in disputed land titles. He even reveals intimate details of family histories to account for the depauperate state of certain households. Included is the story of a man driven to poverty by his domineering elder brother who repeatedly took the younger brother's wife for his own sexual pleasure (Weckler 1949, 123). Early in his ethnographic overview, Weckler delineates the names and offenses of no fewer than twenty-four individuals who were fined by the local chief between 1946 and 1947 (1949, 31–33). Among the crimes cited are detailed cases of adultery, sexual assault, fighting, theft, and illegitimate birth.

Bentzen's CIMA report also pins the dirty laundry of Mokil on the public clothesline. In the third chapter, somewhat dubiously entitled "Cooperation and Exchange," Bentzen categorizes household organization and then proceeds to sketch portraits of each household's structure and internal relations. Included in the accounts are references to domestic abuse, intrafamilial strife, and corrupt authority. Of greatest potential embarrassment is his analysis of "Religion and the Moral Order" (1949, 142–60), which draws attention to the dissolute attitude of the congregation toward religious prohibitions. In this chapter he records one of the most scandalous events of the 1940s, featuring a complicated love affair between high-ranking secular and church officials, furious beatings, and the implementation of a form of "Japanese torture" to boot (1949, 154–55).

Besides the written ethnographic reports, Bentzen and Weckler produced *Mokil* (Bentzen 1950), a documentary film focusing on the island's economic dilemmas generated by an increasing population, land fragmentation, and the growing influence of market forces. This fifty-year-old film does not occupy a dusty shelf in a dimly lit, basement archive. It is considered a classic ethnographic portrait of Pacific island culture, and has recently been remastered. It is still widely used to depict Pacific atoll social relations in introductory anthropology courses. Its content, therefore, must be queried not only in reference to Mokilese perceptions, but also in light of its current use as an educational medium.

An American actor hired by Bentzen narrates the color film in the first person. His resolute voice proudly describes the vivid scenes of subsistence activities. Later in the film, the voice critiques with a steely bitterness the interminable changes fomented by Christianity and the copra trade. The grave voice of the narrator also criticizes the competitive feasting and exchange relations that strain household resources in the context of increasingly fragmented land holdings. The film's images are as unforgettable as the dignified, yet doleful words of the narrator. The memorable sight of insouciant children playfully leaping into the cerulean sea is later extinguished by the stark image of Meliton and his adopted son, slowly returning to his paddling canoe with the meager items received in exchange for copra. The narrator's voice ruefully describes the scene: "So, there goes Meliton with his adopted boy. He didn't get much. He hasn't much copra left; no wife; only half a man." Following this scene the film briefly describes the history of land tenure on Mokil and the transition from communal to private ownership that purportedly resulted from the copra trade. Attention is then drawn to the feverish boundary vigilance, fears of land alienation, and disruptive feuds that plague the community. Steven, a man who owns very little land, is shown flailing his arms in frustration over an accusation that he slashed the bark from his neighbor's breadfruit tree that was shading his taro. As Steven argues his case in front of the camera, the narrator translates his words: "Schwab has plenty of land. Why does he crowd on mine? I slashed the tree! How are we to live?" The camera pans over and frames the profile of an old man with a bloody ear. The narrator continues to translate Steven's words: "Look at Harry. Jorim bit his ear in a quarrel over land! Can we go on like this?" The film certainly does, depicting indigent Jimion who sits all day making cord—"women's work," we are told; poor Joaj, whose penury is the result of his landlessness; and who could forget the three pretty, dowryless, and unmarried daughters of impoverished Jorim?

Anthropological Objects, the Anthropologist, and Mokilese Reactions

These examples of the material found in the CIMA reports should help explain my reluctance to share them with the people of Mokil. Unaware of the extent to which the members of the community were familiar with the

ethnographic reports produced by past researchers, I decided that dissemination could only lead to embarrassment—not simply the residents' embarrassment, but my own. I selfishly feared that were the contents known, I
would become guilty by association with the unsavory discipline of colonial-
ist anthropology. I quickly discovered that guilt had been hanging over my
head since the moment I set foot on Mokil's soil.

The people were well aware of the film and the ethnographic reports
submitted by Bentzen and Weckler. After a time, I learned about the various
ways in which the information from those early reports made its way back
to the community. For the most part, the ethnographies were brought to
Mokil by Peace Corps volunteers (PCV) and shared with certain individuals.
The film was also brought to Mokil by a PCV who, according to reports,
held an islandwide screening. Additionally, the ethnographies are available
at the Community College of Micronesia's (CCM) Micronesian-Pacific Collection in Pohnpei and other university libraries in the United States. Therefore, it is likely that Mokilese students enrolled in CCM and universities
abroad have discovered the reports on their own. I did not seek to determine
the breadth of access and the extent to which all members of the community
were informed, but most adults certainly knew enough about what was
written to exercise extreme caution when first dealing with me as an anthropologist. Although the ability to read and comprehend English texts is quite
high among residents of the atoll, I doubt that many adults have actually
read the reports. More likely, the majority of Mokilese have simply been told
the most unseemly parts of the ethnographies by others. With a high degree
of confidence, one could say that the gossip about what was written is at
least as damning as what was actually recorded, if not worse, considering
the hyperbolic aspect of gossip on Mokil.

The local awareness of the salacious stories inscribed in the CIMA reports had immediate consequences for my work. Virtually everyone with
whom I spoke was aware of the fact that no pseudonyms were used in the
reports, and they naturally believed that my research would be reported in a
similar fashion. This belief persisted despite my insistence upon confidentiality and my delivery of numerous public dissertations on the transformation
of the anthropological discipline since 1947. This was a difficult hurdle to
surmount. I was introduced as "Bryan, an anthropologist. You know—like
Bentzen." A first-time fieldworker might quickly jump to the conclusion
that the repatriation of field material, especially in raw form, creates an
insuperable obstacle for future research and researchers. Insuperable—no,
but formidable to be sure.

Skepticism, paranoia, and wariness characterized the overall reaction toward my research and me in the early days of my fieldwork. I intended to study maritime exploitation, a relatively benign topic that did not require the pursuit of sensitive questions. So benign was the subject of my study, in fact, that certain members of the community were incredulous, unable to fathom an anthropologist's interest in a phenomenon so dry as fishing. One day Levon,[3] a well-educated man of forty-eight, asked me why I came to Mokil. I replied that I came to learn about how their fishing practices relate to the economy. "Fishing?" he queried, "Anthropologists don't study fishing!" Levon was perhaps the most wary of all the Mokilese that I met. He ultimately proved to be an extremely knowledgeable and generous informant despite his initial misgivings, but he was ever doubtful of my motives. I was pigeonholed as an anthropologist from the start, which is a none-too-prestigious hole to occupy considering the track record of anthropologists on Mokil. Bentzen is remembered for abandoning Ruth, the sixteen-year-old star of his film, whom he married during his stay on Mokil. Levon described to me the strange behaviors exhibited by Anthony Lord, the only other anthropologist who conducted extensive fieldwork on Mokil since Bentzen and Weckler. During his stay in the late 1960s Lord allegedly spent time collecting exotic shells, embalming turtles, and drying shark jaws. These activities truly perplexed Levon, who asked bluntly, "Do you think he sold these things in America?" The answer to this question as well as many others concerning Anthony Lord are unknown. He had promised to send to Gordon, his primary informant, the fruits of his arduous assistance, but these fruits, like Lord's shell and bone curios, were simply plucked from Mokil and never returned.[4]

The appropriation and exploitation of Lord's anthropology, coupled with the lurid inscriptions and depictions found in the products of Weckler and Bentzen's fieldwork, undeniably resulted in the creation of a scarlet letter A for Anthropology on Mokil. Imagine my fear when three months into my study on maritime exploitation I realized that fishing could not be the topic of my dissertation. I denied what my intuition screamed—that land is the issue on Mokil, just as it had been in 1947. What was I to say in order to justify my shift in inquiry? Perhaps no one will realize, I thought. Maybe they won't care if I begin investigating genealogies and land histories. Levon, that protective bastion of doubt and curiosity, called my hand one day soon after I had begun my investigation of land tenure. "Why are you asking people about land? What does it have to do with fishing?" I stumbled through a silly explanation regarding the integrated nature of culture and something about holism, but I could tell he did not buy it.

And so it went for the next few months, battling their fears and my own, stanching the flow of bile from old wounds reopened, cursing the past and ever trying to forge ahead. Difficulties were exacerbated by my own methodology. Although I had a stable core of generous, informative friends who assisted me throughout my fieldwork, I sought assistance from every family on the atoll rather than rely on the words of a few sagacious culture carriers or marginal cultural critics. I thought that this strategy would provide members of the community with a channel through which their stories could be told, thereby encouraging an awareness of the "heteroglossic" nature of ethnography.[5] Many reasons for the reticence of others to assist me were articulated to me through the grapevine. A prosperous, well-educated islander who worked as a schoolteacher studiously avoided me on the grounds that I was living and associating with "crazy" people. Unable to understand why I did not choose to live with one of the teachers who, he claimed, knew everything about Mokil, he refused his assistance with subtle yet steadfast determination. Others withheld knowledge that they thought I would publish in a book for which, it was rumored, I would make a million dollars. These reasons relate directly to the perceived exploitative nature of anthropology, but the primary reason for people's reticence was the fear born of their knowledge of the repatriated CIMA reports. People were simply afraid of what I might write about them.

These fears were exacerbated by my investigations into genealogies and land histories. Other contributors to this volume (Keith and Anne Chambers, chapter 9; David Akin and Kathryn Creely, chapter 5) illustrate the sensitive nature of genealogical information and its use in competing land claims and political title contestation. On Mokil there is a strong connection between illegitimacy and land alienation. This makes the repatriation of genealogies especially difficult. An anthropologist's indelible record of kinship relations is much less capable of accommodating the principles of flexibility inherent in orally transmitted genealogies.[6]

In light of the obstacles to my own anthropological inquiries into land tenure and kinship, it is not surprising that during my entire stay on Mokil, only one person asked to see the CIMA reports that I brought along. Despite the ubiquity of generators, video recorders, and television sets coupled with the high demand for videotapes, only one man asked to borrow my tape of Mokil. Initially I thought it was strange that so few would be interested in seeing the film and reports. I reasoned that since people felt no compunction about borrowing my other possessions, the disinterest in these items could not be attributed to respect for my "personal" property. So, when the initial requests were made, I feared that acquiescing would start an avalanche of petitions. Even still, I did not withhold them in spite of the desire to protect identities and my less altruistic fear that my rapport would be threatened. Only later did I put the puzzle together and understand why the people of Mokil Atoll seemed to care so little about the work of the CIMA researchers.

Toby, the young man who borrowed the CIMA ethnographies, returned them within a few days and offered to me his opinion of what he read. He said he was disappointed to see the raw and unseemly printed stories about his relatives and asserted that they were false. Arguing that his English-speaking informants deceived the anthropologist, Toby requested that I not show the reports to anyone else. Others with whom I spoke about the CIMA reports shared his sentiments, claiming that Bentzen and Weckler were duped by dissembling informants.

This attitude was not restricted to atoll dwellers. Even longtime Moki-lese residents of Pohnpei expressed a negative perception of the CIMA data, despite demonstrating a much more open and accepting disposition toward me and my work. Sid, a gracious and obliging man of fifty, endeavored to answer my questions with candor and honesty, yet he clearly articulated his people's disdain for the CIMA work.

In this passage, transcribed from a taped interview conducted in English, Sid speaks about the film *Mokil*.

> The people of Mokil have a hard time watching that movie. They are now so Americanized that they get embarrassed when they see themselves and their grandparents walking around naked. I don't think this kind of movie should be available to the people unless they want to go and watch it. There should be a place to watch it. I don't know what those men thought they were doing; the impact of the movie on the people. Bentzen had no formal marriage to Ruth and when I was young I never knew any better. But when I grew up and looked back I see that they were like guinea pigs. The children of Ruth were very upset to watch this. I don't want to see my mother with her breasts hanging out running around like some kind of a savage.

Sid has lived away from his home island for over thirty-five years in an environment marked by a much greater Western social, economic, and political presence than what is experienced on Mokil. It may be the case that acculturation assuages indigenous angst generated by the collision of past behaviors and changing values, but according to this man's rationalization, the very process of "Americanization" has widened the chasm separating the past and the present.

Alan Howard states that a people's interest in its collective history grows as group consciousness emerges through acculturative processes that include migration and formal education (chapter 2). People at the first stage in the development of historical consciousness are said to have little concern for their culture's collective history, while those at the second stage are becoming more aware of it through contact with others. In the third and final stage, historical consciousness of collective culture is well developed and evidenced by a strong interest in documentation of the past. This model seems to suggest that those people who do not cherish historical documentation of their past have not reached the final stage of development. It also predicts that all cultures will inevitably come to value the documented past.

According to the model, Sid may be expected to exhibit a more pronounced interest in the ethnographic reports of his people's past due to his spatiotemporal experience of separation from his cultural roots. Since he does not, must we conclude that he has not reached the final stage in the development of a historical consciousness? I would argue that the development of a culture's interest in the past does not necessarily entail an acceptance of documented history, regardless of its form and content. Further, the generation of a historical consciousness may not follow a linear trajectory. We must maintain a distinction between a culture's understanding of the past and the social uses of historical documentation. Sid, like many Mokilese on and off the atoll, most definitely conveyed to me an interest in a pan-Mokilese past, despite his disapproval of the film *Mokil*. This supports Alan Howard's idea that various acculturative processes, including migration and Western education, contribute to the development of a peoples' interest in a shared historical identity. At issue, however, is the extent to which ethnographic portraits are accepted as accurate and valued representations of the past given present social needs. As I argue in the following pages, the value assigned to ethnographic representations of the past, and the uses to which they are put, depends on an entire constellation of social relations and practices and cannot be predicted by a culture's degree of historical consciousness.[7]

There is some evidence to suggest that Bentzen understood that the product of his fieldwork would not be assigned great value among the Mokilese. Kordell, another middle-aged Mokil man living in Pohnpei, asserted during an interview that Bentzen knew his film would be an embarrassment to the people and therefore sought to keep it from them. He learned this from Anthony Lord in the late 1960s. "When Tony Lord met with Bentzen, Bentzen did not want to release the film to him because there are disputes and fighting and he didn't want people to see themselves in those disputes over land. He didn't want other family members to be embarrassed that they had no land. That is what Tony said." Avoidance of shame and embarrassment constitutes the conscious rationale for the present distaste for the original CIMA reports, but there are at least two epistemological reasons why repatriated data are not well received on Mokil. To begin with, the ethnographies report on a period of history that, in the Mokil perception, was a time of harmony and cooperation. Older Mokilese remember the post-World War II period with relish, entertaining what Berman calls a "pastoral vision" (1982; cited in Keesing 1989, 30). Concerning this period of history, informants speak of the cooperative labor undertaken, the maintenance of reciprocal ties, the respectfulness of the youth, the cleanliness of the atoll, the solidarity among and between families, and the industriousness that atoll living required. These features of an idealized past are juxtaposed to the negative influences of modernization—market forces that encourage laziness, a lack of consistent authority, corrupt leaders, financial woes, the degradation of cooperation, and an increasing individual rapaciousness. Mokilese rely on this particular lens of their view to the past for generating discourse on and critiquing current social relations. The ethnographic objectification of this past blatantly challenges the Mokilese version of this historical period by describing antagonistic social relations and conflicts.[8]

A Question of Representation? Mokilese History and Identity

The question is: If the ethnographies glorified the Mokilese culture or sought to depict the social relations without naming individuals and employing ugly examples of conflict, would the Mokilese embrace the repatriated data as reinforcement for their version of the postwar period? In my opinion the answer is no. The Mokilese view of history is not static or monolithic in any sense, and the point to be made is that any written objectification of the Mokilese past, or present, is a challenge to the flexibility inherent in the Mokilese concept of history and the maintenance of social relations, broadly speaking.

For example, despite the idealized image of post-World War II life on Mokil, the same time period played host to well-remembered social ills, including chiefly displays of despotic power that, during my stay, were often compared to the present chief magistrate's abuses. Of utmost importance, therefore, is the renegotiability and multifaceted nature of Mokilese history. Mokilese routinely generate temporary oral objectifications of the past that are designed to critique present behavior. Due to the oral nature of these objectifications, their creation does not sacrifice the inherent dynamism of history.

A closer examination of Mokilese identity will illuminate the continuing necessity of a fluid historical construct. In the following pages I will discuss three different planes upon which Mokilese constructions of identity and historical formulations intersect.[9] First, I contend that the Mokilese face no current crises of legitimization spawned by colonial domination that would require or encourage the genesis of a shared, "politicized" culture. Second, I assert that the threat to the maintenance of flexible social identities and relationships entailed by the generation of politicized culture outweighs the possible benefits that might flow from it. Finally, and perhaps most significantly, I demonstrate that "politicization" can take place within a microcosm of social relations without necessitating the objectification of a frozen, monolithic past dependent on recorded portraits that lend legitimacy. I will argue that Mokilese identity is, indeed, politicized through essentialized representations of the past. However, the objectified past is not a rigid, immutable standard that all Mokilese carry into battle against the external foe. It is primarily compelled by complex internal contests, one of which involves competing land claims in a context of absenteeism and alienation.

To begin with, there are no present-day pressures to reify an idealized past for the creation of an ethnic identity in response to decolonization. As a whole, the Mokilese people face no unified crisis of legitimization, no previously alienated land to reclaim from colonial powers. The people of Mokil are much like the Kapinga as described by Lieber (1990), in that they have embraced the dependency fostered by colonialism, thus inhibiting the formulation of an ethnic identity in opposition to Western structures of domination (compare Hanson 1989; Hobsbawm and Ranger 1983; Keesing 1989). There is no pressure for the Mokilese to reclaim the past in order to legitimize the present or to recast the distant days of darkness and ignorance, locally referred to as rosros, in the light of cultural revitalization.[10]

This does not mean, however, that ambivalence created by disjunctures between newly incorporated Western goals and the inability to attain them does not compel a critical comparison of past and present. Indeed, individuals may glorify the subsistence diet of the past in fiery denunciations of their own insatiable hunger for imports, but they are just as likely to embrace the present market system in opposition to the past. In one such instance, certain residents lauded plans to raze one of the islets for the development of a Japanese tourist resort, while criticizing the financial ignorance of their forebears. Lin Poyer's work among the Sapwuahfik people reveals that "visions of the past present an ideology in which certain arenas of behavior become key symbols in contemporary statements about identity" (Poyer 1993, 152). In a similar vein, Mokilese reconstructions of the past are employed as social commentaries on present behavior and social relationships among and between members of the community. These commentaries facilitate the construction and maintenance of a flexible Mokilese identity. The Mokilese, therefore, maintain a malleable view of history that admits a wide range of possible critiques of social action. In this regard Mokilese are similar to the islanders of Pulap where "people interpret their history to serve a contemporary purpose, and they interpret events in light of their beliefs about these histories" (Flinn 1992, 55). The Mokilese depiction of their own island's social history, as an evolution from past ignorance to present enlightenment, coexists with images of an idealized past constituted by harmony and cooperation. Each representation adds a dynamic dimension to the Mokilese historical perspective.[11]

A pan-Mokilese political consciousness generated in opposition to Western structures of dominance is antithetical to the dynamic principles embedded in the epistemological bedrock of Mokilese history and identity. This does not mean that Mokilese culture is not "politicized." In fact, it is politicized for identity maintenance purposes, but this process is conducted in a way that does not eliminate the conditional nature of history. In a sense, every use of a historical reference objectifies some oppositional reality, but among Mokilese there is no consistent contest between external Western values and commonly internalized indigenous "custom." The contest takes place within and between factions of the Mokilese population itself. Forces compelling this "micropoliticization" of Mokilese identity spring not only from external threats, but also foment in the crucible of relations among Mokilese. In fact, reified cultural behaviors and stereotyped identities (past and present) are most consistently employed within the context of the tenuous and at times contentious relationship between absentees and atoll residents.

One such objectification of Mokilese traits and behaviors occurs within the context of competing land claims, the maintenance of which are important for enhancing both resident and absentee sense of attachment to the atoll (see also Schneider 1998).[12] Although the commercial and subsistence value of the atoll's land has diminished since the middle of the twentieth century, the land remains an important touchstone of identity. The atoll is also a place to which longtime absentees and circular migrants may return, of necessity or in retirement. The land on the atoll is valued for its inalienability.

However, certain principles of the Mokilese land tenure system militate against both resident and absentee senses of security and attachment to the land. For absentees, physical separation from the land can lead to an attenuation of their ownership claims due to the importance assigned to use.[13] As elsewhere in the Pacific, use of the land validates ownership claims to the land (Crocombe 1971, 1994a, 7; Rodman 1984, 64; Walter 1978, 94). Because use is important for validating ownership claims, physical separation and long-term absence from the land can enfeeble ownership claims to the land. Adverse possession is a common result of absenteeism throughout the Pacific and on Mokil (Bonnemaison 1984; Carroll 1975; Crocombe 1971, 1994a; Firth 1968; Larcom 1990; Lundsgaarde 1974; Schwimmer 1977). Absentees, therefore, experience a greater sense of marginalization, despite their need to maintain attachment to the atoll for identity affirmation and for potential economic need.

Atoll residents' sense of security is also threatened by a principle embedded in the system of land tenure. In the past, individual ownership of land was the norm. Typically, when a man died his oldest son would divide the property among the male siblings, taking the lion's share for himself. Younger siblings could be disenfranchised entirely by forceful elder siblings who usurped the majority of the land. Today, over half of all household heads on Mokil could theoretically be the subordinates of older male siblings who live abroad. The probability that an elder sibling will return and take over the land is not great, but the possibility of such an event remains an ever present threat to a resident's sense of attachment to the land.

Due to the necessity of maintaining access to the land of Mokil and the principles of land tenure that erode both absentee and resident land claims, oppositional identities based on objectifications of Mokilese behavior are created. The longer absentees remain on Pohnpei, the more Pohnpeian they will become in the eyes of atoll residents. By creating and imposing an oppositional identity on absentees, residents enhance their own sense of security as inhabitants on land, the claims to which are held by many. Unfortunately, the use of opposition, in concert with the importance assigned to use in determining ownership claims, results in the attenuation of an absentee's sense of connection to the land and its community. This forces absentees to resist their marginality by sustaining a cultural critique of residents, thus perpetuating the battle between opposing constructions of identity.

Pete, for example, lived on Pohnpei for most of his adult life. When he returned to Mokil in 1992 he felt alienated by the residents. "They didn't like me. They said, 'Oh, he is Pohnpeian,' because I had been away so long." As this statement reveals, the maintenance of a Mokilese identity is critical for absentees who face the possibility that one day they might want, or need, to return. This is why absentees create and depend upon an idealistic portraiture of Mokil: to substantiate their claim to the atoll by adducing their identity as Mokilese and to bolster that claim by excoriating residents for their un-Mokilese behavior.

Sid is a well-educated absentee with whom I had many long conversations concerning his feelings about Mokil and life on Pohnpei. He articulates the ambivalence at the heart of an absentee's relationship with his home—the shining memories that guide proper conduct and identity formation and the alienation that may result from long absence, unrealistic expectations, and the incongruity between reality as it is lived on Mokil and the mythical childhood image: "One guy asked me one time, what do I really miss about Mokil, and I said, 'my spear,' and on the other half of my mind, 'my boyhood talent.' He said, 'Aren't you satisfied with all these modern conveniences?' I said, 'Of course I am satisfied, but you know something else, I have headaches all the time with this. I never heard of bills, bills, bills, coming in and worries, worries; people's problems coming in.' But when we decided to step off the island and go to a different environment, we blame ourselves not anyone." Here, Sid remembers the easy life of spearing the plentiful fish of Mokil's reefs as a boy, a life free from his present financial burdens on Pohnpei. His "modern conveniences" are portrayed as being of little comfort compared to the stress of life outside of his home island. Later in the interview, this idyllic vision rotted as Sid recalled the creeping malignancy of culture loss witnessed during his last trip to Mokil. "When I returned to Mokil in the early 1990s I went and joked and laughed with the people, but left feeling sick. I saw how there was no curfew, no respect by the noisy kids, how the wharves were falling apart and the *pwel* [taro garden] uncared-for. The people who could build have all left the island—not just builders of houses, but builders of character. People now sell their fresh fish to each other or exchange it for other things. They no longer know how to make *oaj* [pandanus thatch roofing] and never help one another to build houses. I know I am being hard on Mokilese but I am one of them. Of course they sometimes make me feel like an outsider when I visit."

By contrasting his ideals and behavior with the real-life wants and needs of Mokil residents, Sid is attempting to contest his marginal relationship to the atoll, its people, and his land. The process requires an instantiation of his intimacy with, and the reification of residents' moral remoteness from,

Mokilese culture. In this way, absentees envision themselves as the guides, teaching residents how to behave as Mokilese by setting an example and expressing a commitment to the maintenance of "traditional values."

Behavior such as this represents a "hyper-Mokilization" of absentee identity designed to combat the alienation entailed by living abroad and to reinforce attenuated claims to the atoll's land (see also Underwood 1985). Confronted by the challenges of their multicultural environment, the absentees rely on touchstones of identity, such as industriousness, which define Mokil in opposition to other cultures and ethnicities. As many others have pointed out, opposition brings greater resolution to one's values and ideals, especially in the context of diaspora and population movement (Fernandez 1988; Gupta and Ferguson 1992; Malkki 1992; Pinney 1995). Therefore, behavior exhibited by Mokilese that does not conform to the projected, archetypal Mokilese character is deprecated because it threatens the foundation on which absentee identity is built. These objectifications of Mokilese culture are employed within the struggle between residents and absentees and do not represent a pan-Mokilese political movement in opposition to an external force.

To what end are such essentialized representations directed? Unlike Sapwuahfik emigrants who are generating a shared identity in opposition to others on Pohnpei for the acquisition of supralocal power and status (Linnekin and Poyer 1990, 144), the Mokilese use of oppositional identity pertains to internal power relations. As I have argued on the previous pages, these objectifications serve primarily as corrective commentary on internal social relations and as shields against the threat of alienation that results from long-term absence from the atoll. Supralocal political power can be obtained without recourse to a pan-Mokilese ethnicity. In fact, absentees who create essentialized portraits of Mokilese identity and critique the behavior of atoll residents are guilty in the eyes of atoll dwellers of abandoning their legal status as Mokilese voters in favor of their new municipality of residence. Pete explained to me the reason why Mokilese on the atoll have little influence in political decision making at the state and federal level: "Pingalapese are smart, no matter where they move, they stay registered with Pingelap so they have a voice. Mokilese do not care when they move away." Mokilese do appear to have less interest in generating a consolidated voting alliance.[14] Once again, "micropoliticization" involving internal processes of identity negotiation appears to compel the use of essentialized representations rather than a contest between strictly defined ethnic or ethnopolitical constituencies.

Static Data and the Demand for a Dynamic Reality

So, if Mokilese culture is "politicized" after all in the struggle between various factions and individuals seeking to bolster land claims, why do not Mokilese demand the repatriation of the detailed land histories recorded by CIMA investigators and embrace the recorded past? The reason is due to the necessity of maintaining a land tenure system that must be as flexible and negotiable as is history. In fact, my research has revealed a fascinating shift from individual to corporate ownership of land that is part of a vast transformation in the nature of people's relationship to land. As emigration opportunities have drawn more and more islanders abroad, the number of absentees confronted by the possible need to return and reclaim rights to land has burgeoned.

All three CIMA researchers claim that land on Mokil was owned and transferred by individuals at the time of their fieldwork. According to Bentzen, individual ownership of dry land on Mokil grew in importance as the copra trade infiltrated local production and exchange during the late nineteenth century (1949, 23). The CIMA research demonstrates that individual owners of dry land and taro land were allowed to restrict access to their land, alienate and assign use rights, and transfer ownership of their land, often without the consent of extended kin.[15]

In the past fifty years a host of dramatic socioeconomic changes has compelled the transformation in the nature of landownership on Mokil. Massive out-migration coupled with a decline in the commercial importance of land-based production regimes on Mokil has reduced the pressure on land resources and encouraged a change in the perception of land tenure. According to my research on Mokil's economy, copra production accounts for a mere 6 percent of local cash income. With the ubiquity of government-funded projects and employment, wage labor, remittances, and social security, an individual's access to cash is no longer dependent upon his or her individual ownership of land. Furthermore, the value of local foods such as taro and breadfruit has declined for both subsistence and feast production as a result of increasing dependence on imported goods, including rice, flour, and sugar. Individual ownership of dry land and taro plots, therefore, is no longer crucial in determining a person's status and ability to participate in local exchange. While these forces have undermined the importance of owning and transferring land individually, the growing number of Mokilese living abroad is compelling the trend toward corporate ownership. The identity and potential economic security of absentees depends on the maintenance of use rights to land on Mokil, to which they may someday need to return. The threat of alienation and adverse possession that existed under the system of individual ownership is ameliorated under a system in which no one individual in a land-owning kin group has the authority to transfer land to another individual. In short, land is increasingly being conceptualized as the property of corporate ramages, or nonunilineal descent groups, members of which share usufruct claims to the land.

This trend in the system of land tenure, which reveals the importance of maintaining flexible and negotiable ties to land, helps explain why inscribed histories of landownership are presently unwelcome among those who are claiming corporate, usufruct rights to land. The ethnographic record no longer accords with the lived reality of the majority of Mokilese. The record's emphasis on individual ownership conflicts with the current movement toward corporate ownership, which is why many Mokilese have simply chosen to ignore it. The two paradigms of landownership, individual and corporate, are not mutually exclusive, nor do they represent a linear historical shift. Elements of both paradigms constitute present, competing understandings of land tenure for residents and absentees alike, which is a primary reason why Mokilese identity is contested.

It is doubtful that Bentzen's maps of land holdings would ever be accepted as the final word on Mokilese landownership. For example, a survey and registration of Mokilese land holdings proposed to the people in a general meeting in 1996 by representatives of the Pohnpei Public Land Office was met with consternation and disapproval. Although the titling process would allow titleholders to obtain secured loans of higher value through the Pohnpei State Housing Authority, many feared that it would lead to alienation and protracted disputes. Inscribing the name of an owner on a legally binding document could empower an individual to alienate those with a usufruct claim to corporately owned land. This further illustrates the need to maintain flexible, negotiable ties to the land and to the past.

Anthropological Ends and Indigenous Means

So, what does all of this have to do with the repatriation of anthropological data? To the Mokilese, the written word is indelible. I remember inquiring at the municipal office about the local ordinances. I was told that many of the ordinances have disappeared, physically. On further questioning I learned that, through the years, various chief magistrates, unhappy with certain laws in the books, have simply discarded those laws by "putting them under the foot" (*kihdi pehn pwalik*). The physical removal of an ordinance provides a rationale for disregarding the written word of the law. The products of anthropology are similar to written ordinances on Mokil. In short, ethnography is a method for "culture collecting" that objectifies specific elements of much larger social realities (see Clifford 1988, 230–51). Once these elements are removed from their original contexts and inscribed, they become rigid and inflexible in certain aspects. Renegotiating perceptions of the past becomes more difficult when the written history is experienced as presenting a monolithic portrait. On Mokil, it is no surprise that people turn a blind eye to the ethnographies written by Bentzen, Weckler, and Murphy. Not only is their portrait one of conflict and discontent, but its very existence threatens to arrest the ability of community members to utilize the flexibility of their system in renegotiating the past for present social needs.

The Mokilese are much like the Malekula as Joan Larcom (1982) found them in the early days of her fieldwork before the grip of *kastom* took hold— generally unconcerned with employing anthropological objectifications of their past in the construction of a pan-cultural identity. I, too, was dismayed when I first arrived on Mokil and found that community members seemed unreflective about their culture. I wondered if fieldwork would have been easier to conduct in a society struggling to assert their "culture" or "*kastom*" in the legitimization of a national or ethnic identity. It wasn't just a question of pulling teeth and the travails of fieldwork with which I was concerned. The question occurred to me whether my work would even be appreciated or wanted by the very subjects of my study.

This question returns us to the issue of repatriation. The endeavor appears to be an appropriate, even morally correct, mission to undertake. Certainly "we" would appreciate having data written about us or gathered through our help returned to us. According to Tuzin, the ethnographic record is a gift, a memorial to humanity: "Ethnography and the act of writing it . . . is a gift in kind to the people who made it possible. Never mind that they may never be able to read it; their literate children or grandchildren will appreciate it as a record—often the only record—of a way of life now lost to them. . . . Never mind, either, if no member or descendant of the group in question ever reads the account; the gift is made by way of memorializing to others, remote in space or time, the instance of cultural humanity" (1995, 23). This conceptualization of the anthropological record is in danger of transforming culture into an ethnographic collectible, a rigid, objectified curio. The assumptions inherent in this approach toward ethnography and its value as a "gift" are based on Western values. Fowler observes that "it is perhaps the Western concept of property more than any other that guides individual decisions as to what to do with the records that have accumulated from a research project or a lifetime—it also seems to be this Western view that is at the roots of the present debates about who owns data" (1995, 64). There is no denying that anthropological data are highly valued by indigenous peoples throughout the world who are in the throes of politicized identity crises. For example, certain scholars contend that one of the primary purposes of efforts to record Melanesian *kastom* is to aid the preservation of culture on the cusp of the yawning maw of modernization (Bolton 1994, 148; Gegeo 1994, 47; Keesing 1994). The ironic result of such struggles is that, while anthropologists are repatriating data for the noble purpose of preserving indigenous pasts, indigenous peoples are incorporating the data in structures of hegemony derived from the very Western ideologies from which they are trying to be free (see Keesing 1982, 1989).

Furthermore, it is clear that the "gifts" offered to the future generations will not simply be valued as a record of bygone days. These gifts will be reinterpreted, invested with new meanings, and employed in local contests between those with competing interests. One of the most common issues embedded within the contributions to this volume is the divide separating the anthropological goal of repatriation from the local interpretation, understanding, and use of repatriated data. Amy Stillman (chapter 8) sees this as a difference between anthropological "description" and indigenous "prescription." The anthropologist's goal to foster knowledge through repatriation (see Dorothy and David Counts, chapter 1; Howard, chapter 2) inevitably collides with the cultural realities of the contexts within which the data is returned. For example, Akin and Creely (chapter 5) discuss the competing claimants to Roger Keesing's data and the various sociopolitical ends to which use of this knowledge will be directed. Repatriated genealogies are not simply understood as memorials to deceased ancestors. They may become powerful chips in a high-stakes game of competing land claims or contested political titles (see the Chambers, chapter 9).

The very integrity of cultural artifacts may become threatened by repatriation as they become subject to current social contingencies and needs (Nancy Guy, chapter 11; Stillman, chapter 8). This is to be expected. It is rather unrealistic to believe that repatriation is solely a means of preserving culture for posterity. If the goal of repatriation is to preserve an immutable past as understood by anthropologists, then repatriation must fail. Such a goal ignores the agency and creativity of those among whom we are seeking to foster knowledge. In the end, anthropologists must recognize that all repatriated data are subject to local agency and the demands of its epistemological foundation.

Dangerous Data: Repatriation in Context

This chapter began by describing the content of several anthropological studies of Mokil that were later repatriated to island residents. The reports' unseemly stories of conflict, told in lurid detail, including islander names, evince shame and disgust and partially constitute the reason for my difficulty in establishing fieldwork rapport. Not only are the reports embarrassing, they challenge the "pastoral vision" of post–World War II life that many older Mokilese embrace. The question was posed whether the ethnographic reports would be accepted and incorporated into local constructions of the past if they contained less sensitive information. In my opinion they would not. Mokilese identity is "Lamarckian" in that its construction is based on acquired characteristics that are continually demonstrated and reaffirmed through contextualized action. Oral objectifications of the past provide situationally appropriate critiques of social behavior, but because they are created in response to ever-changing contexts, they allow Mokilese history to maintain its malleable character. The Mokilese representations of the past are indeed components in a process of "politicized" identity formation, but the contested ground lies not between the Western hegemonic structures or external agencies and the Mokilese as a unified ethnopolitical unit. The contest is held in internal arenas of power. In one such arena on which this chapter focused, Mokilese residents and absentees contest each other's land claims by employing ideal portraitures of the past and archetypal identities in critiques of present behavior. A mutable history is necessitated by the inherent fluidity of identity formation among Mokilese to which it must be capable of responding. The past is recast not only in light of present social relations, but in anticipation of the future and what it might bring (Larcom 1982). Because ethnographic inscriptions are static and non-negotiable, they constitute a threat to the dynamic nature of Mokilese epistemology. For this reason, Mokilese have chosen to marginalize the ethnographic record simply by ignoring the reports, thereby minimizing the inherent danger of an inscribed, monolithic cultural history.

In conclusion, this chapter suggests that a thorough assessment of indigenous epistemology is a prerequisite for the proper management and distribution of anthropological data. It must not be assumed that anthropological products have the same value across cultures, or that by returning data we are fostering knowledge and preserving an authentic past. We must recognize that our intentions for repatriation may differ from the local meanings assigned to, and uses of, repatriated data. The lessons to be learned from Mokil are that repatriated data are not necessarily welcome, and that the proper meaning and place of the data will be assigned in light of the local epistemological and social demands, regardless of the anthropologist's intentions. Therefore, I suggest that we view repatriated data not as a "gift" based upon a Western moral imperative, but as an offering to the societies we study to be used, discarded, hallowed, or decried in accordance with local understandings and needs.

Nancy Guy

11

Trafficking in Taiwan Aboriginal Voices

Everyone in the world knows my voice, but no one knows it's mine.

KUO YING-NAN

Of the varieties of primary materials generated by anthropologists and ethnomusicologists during fieldwork, recordings of music making carry perhaps the greatest potential for attracting the interest of parties who have no tie to the research population, the collector, or the academy. With the growing popular interest in world music and world beat, First World recording artists increasingly comb the world's sound archives in search of "fresh" and "exotic" materials to incorporate into their own musical compositions. Whether deposited in archives or sold commercially, field recordings created with the purposes of cultural preservation, research and analysis, or dissemination make music vulnerable to unauthorized use.

When we record musical sounds in the field and bring them into "our" world, we introduce our informants' cultural products to an author-centered regime that privileges the single, "creative genius" and disparages (and, in fact, makes invisible) custodians of traditional knowledge, carriers of oral traditions, and practitioners of communal creativity. The dominant paradigm of a transformative individual who creates original works in solitude is, as James Boyle observes, "neither natural nor inevitable. . . . It arose at a specific time and place—eighteenth-century Europe—in connection with a particular information technology—print" (1996, 195). The notion of the single author stands firmly at the base of contemporary intellectual property laws and is, for all intents and purposes, applied indiscriminately and universally. The concept of "authorship" acts as "a gate through which one must pass in order to be given property rights, a gate that shuts out a disproportionate number of non-Western, traditional, collaborative, or folkloric modes of production" (Boyle 1996, 195).[1]

While there are international copyright treaties and conventions, "there is no such thing as an 'international copyright.' "[2] United States copyright laws—which are among the most powerful in the world, since about 50 percent of all sales of prerecorded music worldwide are made in this country—offer indigenous musicians little protection against the hunting and gathering activities of elite recording artists and multinational corporations. In her overview of these copyright laws pertaining to music, lawyer Sherylle Mills noted that a musical piece must meet three criteria in order for someone to be able to claim its copyright (1996, 63): (1) it must have a specific "author;" an author is defined as "the originator" or "he to whom anything owes its origin"; (2) it must have a tangible form; its "physical rendering" may include a piece of notation, a tape recording, or some other tangible form; (3) it must be "original." Any work failing to possess one of these qualities is deemed to be in the "public domain"; in other words, anyone can use it for free.

Since indigenous musicians often pass their art from generation to generation through oral rather than written means, they frequently possess no tangible representation of the music, and they frequently cannot name the "composer" of a piece. A field recording may be the only tangible rendering of a piece; therefore, the ethnomusicologist-anthropologist may own the copyright by virtue of having created the recording. How do we as fieldworkers handle the responsibility that this entails? What do we do with the materials shared with us by our informants, recordings to which—due to the Western nature of the current intellectual property regime—we may claim copyright while the singers and musicians may not?

Central to the question of repatriation of field materials are issues of ownership and control of cultural property.[3] Returning to the musicians the right to control and to profit from uses of their music is obviously a desirable goal. Doing so, however, may prove to be highly complex legally and logistically. In this chapter, I report on a tangled web involving a Han-Chinese ethnomusicologist and his field recordings, several aboriginal singers from Taiwan's Amis tribe, and a wealthy First World recording artist.

The focus of this case is the song "Return to Innocence," released in 1993 by Michael Cretu, who works under the name "Enigma." The Amis singers recently sued Cretu and the multinational corporation EMI / Capitol Records, among others, in an attempt to gain recognition for their artistic contribution and to gain some profit for the use of their voices in a song that has earned a small fortune for Cretu.

This case stands as a cautionary tale that illustrates the degree to which our informants may be made powerless to control or profit from uses of their own music. The case also documents the extremes that they may be forced to go to and the expense they may be forced to incur in an effort to regain some measure of recognition and ownership.

While the number of pieces produced by First World elite artists involving digitally sampled excerpts of traditional music are probably too numerous to count, this particular case stands out for several reasons. First, it is among the most egregious cases, due to Cretu's complete failure to recognize the aboriginal singers' musical contribution. Over two minutes of Cretu's four-minute-and-fifteen-second song feature the voices of Kuo Ying-nan and his wife, Kuo Shin-chu.[4]

Cretu, however, gave no indication of the source of his materials. The CD liner does not give the names of the aboriginal singers, it does not indicate where the music originated, nor does it name the recorded source from which the sample was taken. Printed boldly on the last page of notes are the words "All songs written by Curly M.C." (also known as Michael Cretu). At the bottom of this page, in small print, is a list of sampled sources. Absent from this list, however, is any reference to the materials heard in "Return to Innocence."

The second reason that this case is exceptional is that, with the financial backing of a Taiwan-owned record company, the Kuos have sued Michael Cretu, EMI / Capitol, and Virgin Records, among others. This case could have important implications for copyright laws and for the legal enforcement of musical cultural ownership. The third factor making the investigation of this affair valuable is that the "victims" are alive and relatively accessible. This means that it is possible to seek an understanding of how they feel about the situation and to observe the ways in which their lives have been impacted as a result of the unauthorized use of their voices. During the summer of 1998 I traveled to Taiwan and spoke with the Kuos for several hours. I also met with their lawyer in Taipei and a number of other people on the periphery of the case. Upon my return, I contacted the San Jose law office representing the Kuos in their U.S. lawsuit, and I eventually became an expert witness in the case.

Amis singer Kuo Ying-nan (a.k.a. Difang) in his home in Taidong, Taiwan, 22 June 1998 (Nancy Guy)

In view of the current popular interest in world music and world beat, it is likely that field researchers will increasingly find themselves positioned between the people who allow them to record their music and the people in the music business who hunt their way through these recordings in search of new sounds. After investigating the particulars of this case, one conclusion that can be drawn is that one of the greatest calamities that may befall a fieldworker is to have someone, particularly a famous, well-marketed musician such as Michael Cretu, discover and choose to use her or his field recordings. Indeed, the "Enigma affair" has cast an unfortunate shadow over the career of the ethnomusicologist, Hsu Tsang-houei (died, January 2000), who was near retirement at the end of the affair. As Anthony Seeger (an ethnomusicologist trained in anthropology) has pointed out, field recordings can be both a gold mine and a minefield for all those involved, including performers, collectors, archives, and commercial companies (1996, 97).

Another well-publicized instance involving the unethical use of ethno-

Amis singer Kuo Shin-chu (a.k.a. Ignay) in her home in Taidong, Taiwan, 22 June 1998 (Nancy Guy)

musicological field recordings is the "Deep Forest" affair. Prominent French ethnomusicologist Hugo Zemp retold his story in an article that he wrote for the *Yearbook for Traditional Music* in the hopes that it might "encourage others to reconsider their own experiences and clarify their roles and objectives in dealing with the international music business" (1996, 36). With the entry of field recordings into the "web of the world market," Zemp warns, "It will not help to seek refuge in the ivory tower of pure, disinterested knowledge" (53).

Zemp recalls that he was initially approached by the chief of the Intangible Cultural Heritage Section of UNESCO who informed him of Michel Sanchez and Eric Mouquet's (that is, the two musicians of Deep Forest) intention to use several samples of traditional African music that Zemp had recorded decades earlier and that had been previously released on UNESCO records on their own CD honoring an international Day of the Earth. Initially, Zemp refused to allow the Deep Forest musicians to use his field recordings; however, after they applied heavy-handed tactics of persuasion, Zemp finally granted his guarded approval. Zemp later learned that the Deep Forest CD was produced first and foremost as a commercial release, and not in support of an environmental cause, as had been promised. Most disturbing, however, was the discovery that the CD's most successful hit, "Sweet Lullaby," made extensive use of samples of music from the 'Are'are people of the Solomon Islands. Nowhere on the CD or liner notes was this original source acknowledged. The Deep Forest CD, like Enigma's, has sold millions of copies and has earned the two Europe-based musicians, Michel Sanchez and Eric Mouquet, very sizable profits.[5]

Zemp wrote to Sanchez and Mouquet saying that he did not personally seek financial compensation for their use of his field recordings. However, he said that as an ethnomusicologist he was obligated to defend the interest of the people of the Solomon Islands who had allowed him to record their musical inheritance with the aim of its preservation and study. He requested that they pay back part of the profits to the *real owners of this music*. Not surprisingly, no compensation or recognition of the music's origin has been forthcoming. Unlike in the Enigma case, there has been no sustained support for the launching of a lawsuit against Deep Forest.

The "Return to Innocence" Story

The events that culminated in the Kuos filing a lawsuit began in 1978 when the Kuos were recorded as part of an islandwide project to tape-record representative examples of Taiwan's folk music. The Folk Song Collection Movement (*minge caiji yundong*) was initially launched in 1966 by the composer Shi Weiliang. Ethnomusicologist and composer Hsu Tsang-houei quickly joined the movement, and the two of them together acted as the project's conceptual leaders (Fan 1994, 44).[6] A systematic coverage of the island's folk music involved the efforts of numerous fieldworkers and was conducted in several waves, with the last one taking place in the summer of 1978. The purpose of this project was twofold: first, it was hoped that the recordings would aid in the preservation of folk music; second, Shi Weiliang, Hsu Tsang-houei, and other composers saw the island's folk music as a possible source of material and inspiration for their own compositions. Shi Weiliang mentioned that Bela Bartok's collection and use of Hungarian folk music served as inspiration for the project (Fan 1994, 45).

As the Kuos tell the story, Hsu Tsang-houei arrived in their village of Malan in southeast Taiwan in August of 1978 in a search of traditional Amis singing. The Amis people, who are well-known in Taiwan for their polyphonic singing, are one of nine distinct tribes of aborigines. Taiwan aborigines are a Malayo-Polynesian people who are Austronesian speaking. On the basis of linguistic evidence, it is believed that they have occupied the island for at least 3,500 years (Hsu 1991, 10). They remained Taiwan's majority population until the nineteenth century. Currently, however, the aborigines make up less than 2 percent of the island's predominately Han-Chinese population.

Hsu was directed to the Kuos' home when he asked where to find the area's best singers. He explained to the Kuos that his recordings would be used for research and teaching, and the couple agreed to sing free of charge. Some of the recordings made that day, along with the others collected as a part of the Folk Song Collection Movement, were initially released in a series of record albums by the Taipei-based Number One Record Company (*diyi changpian changyouxian gongsi*) in 1979.[7]

The next major development in this case occurred in 1988 when Hsu Tsang-houei, under the auspices of the Chinese Folk Arts Foundation, led a group of about thirty singers and dancers from four different Taiwan aboriginal tribes to Europe. The Kuos were among the small group that represented the Amis tribe. In France, they gave two performances as part of the Festival of the Pacific arranged by the Maison des Cultures du Monde—a semiofficial French cultural organization, partly subsidized by the French Ministry of Culture and the Ministry of Foreign Affairs.[8] In the interest of creating an archival record of festival events, the president of the Maison des Cultures arranged to record the concert and informed Hsu Tsang-houei of his plans to do so. The aboriginal performers knew nothing of these arrangements.

The Maison des Cultures decided to release a CD of these recordings. However, the conditions during the performance had not been ideal and some of the selections were unusable. The recording of the performance of the "Song of Joy," which is the piece that was later used by Enigma,[9] was among those that was too poor to reproduce.[10] Determined to release the CD, the French contacted Hsu Tsang-houei and asked if he might have field recordings that could stand in place of the unusable selections. Hsu sent his recordings including his 1978 recording of the "Song of Joy." Of the five Amis selections to appear on the Maison des Cultures CD, *Polyphonies vocales des aborigenes de Taiwan: Ami, Bunun, Païwan et Rukaï*, only one was actually recorded during the performance in France. It is still not clear as to whether the Maison des Cultures paid Hsu or the Number One Record Company for their use.[11]

It was the *Polyphonies vocales des aborigenes de Taiwan* CD that presumably provided Michael Cretu with his first exposure to Taiwan aboriginal singing. Once he had decided to make the "Song of Joy" part of one of his own compositions, Cretu authorized his manager, Jürgen Thürnau of Mambo Musik in Munich, to pay the Maison des Cultures du Monde 30,000 French francs (about 6,000 dollars U.S.) for its purchase (Chen 1997a, 51). Writing in response to questions posed by a Taiwanese reporter, a production manager in Virgin's Munich office described the transaction as follows: "Substantial amounts of money were paid to Maison des Cultures du Monde by Michael Cretu for the world-wide exploitation as to time unlimited regarding: a) the use of these samples in a movie soundtrack; b) the use of these samples in a record production and all other possibilities of exploitation. In point 7 of the contract between Michael Cretu . . . and Maison des Cultures du Monde, Maison des Cultures du Monde explicitly state that all claims to them as well as the artists concerned have been transferred."[12] In a letter written to the same reporter, Jürgen Thürnau gave further details of the arrangement between his client and Maison des Cultures du Monde. According to the contract signed on 19 April 1993, the French organization guaranteed that it had ownership of the master tape and that it was entitled to license. Thürnau cited a portion of the contract, which incidentally reiterated a point made in the letter from the Munich office, " 'Maison des Cultures du Monde' declares that herewith all claims to them as well as the artists concerned have been transferred." In closing, Thürnau wrote that "We are in this business for more than 20 years and we know that we have to clear rights per contract before using musical parts. So we did with all used parts before the recording, otherwise we never would use them." And finally, he added, "By the way, the payment was higher than what we normally have to pay in Europe."[13]

Later, the Maison des Culture transferred half of the 30,000 French francs paid by Cretu to Hsu Tsang-houei. Hsu placed the sum in an account that is maintained by the Chinese Folks Arts Foundation where it has remained (Chen 1997a, 51). It is important to recall that when they were led on their performance tour to Europe " 'no one ever solicited the view of the aborigines' with regard to recording and public release" (Huang Hsiu-lan quoted in Chen 1997a, 51). Furthermore, the sale of the rights to use their voices was made by the Maison des Cultures du Monde without consulting, informing, or financially compensating the aboriginal singers.

Cretu's song "Return to Innocence" enjoyed enormous popularity. It rose to the top of song charts in Europe and in the United States. The album, *Cross of Changes*, which includes the hit song, remained on Billboard's Top 100 for thirty-two consecutive weeks and sold between five and seven million copies. In addition to profit earned from CD sales and royalties, the song earned further income through its licensing for use in a number of films and several television shows, including "The Outer Limits" and "My So-Called Life." The song has also found its way onto several compilation CDs such as *Dance Mix USA* (vol. 3), *Do Something*, which was distributed at Taco Bell outlets as part of a fund-raising campaign for the "Do Something Foundation," and the New Age extravaganza *Pure Moods*. A Tower Record web page describes "Return to Innocence" as adding "exotic world-music flavor" to the *Pure Moods* compilation.[14] It is extremely difficult to estimate precisely how much profit "Return to Innocence" has earned for Cretu and EMI / Capitol. The dollar figures were revealed as part of the lawsuit's discovery procedure; however, every document that included such information was marked "confidential." It is unlikely that such information will ever be made public.

One of the most ironic uses of "Return to Innocence" was its selection by the International Olympic Committee in its promotional video for the 1996 Atlanta Games. Gill Blake, an assistant producer in the British firm that produced the video, explained that the production team listened to several pieces, which they "felt had something spiritual and timeless about them. It was then purely a matter of making a subjective choice . . . 'Return to Innocence' seemed to work in conjunction with the ideas expressed in the video of fair play, peace, [and] unity" (Chen 1997a, 49).[15] The International Olympic Committee is one of the many parties that were sued as part of the Kuos' lawsuit.

It is fair to speculate that if the song had not been used for a high-profile event, such as the Olympics, Kuo and his wife might never have pursued this legal case. It is beyond the scope of this chapter to discuss the role that advocacy for aboriginal rights plays in contemporary Taiwanese politics. Let it suffice to say, however, that politicians increasingly call upon aborigines and their culture to stand as a symbol of Taiwan. This symbol, which is most often invoked by politicians who advocate Taiwan's independence from China, contrasts sharply, and in opposition, to past symbols that aimed to tie the island's identity to China and mainland Chinese culture. Therefore, when the Olympic story broke in Taiwan, and it became clear that the Amis singers had not been recognized for their musical contribution, nor financially compensated, the conditions were perfect for the Kuos to gain the media attention and support that led to the launching of a lawsuit.

This is by no means the first time that the marketing of the Kuos' music has directly benefited others and not themselves. In fact, before the Enigma song was released, the Kuos had called upon their relative, Li Taikang, a professor of music at Taiwan's National Institute of the Arts, to help them seek justice in another situation involving a different ethnomusicologist and the sale of his field recordings.

In 1992 Wu Rung-shun, who had earned his masters' degree in ethnomusicology under the tutelage of Hsu Tsang-houei at the National Taiwan Normal University, came to the Kuos' village and made a request not unlike the one Hsu had made in 1978. He asked the Kuos to sing for him and assured them that the recording would only be used for research and teaching.[16] In 1993 Wu released a CD of Amis Music, which included several songs sung by the Kuos.[17] This CD is one of a series of CDs produced by Wu, each of which features the music of a different aboriginal tribe. Several of the CDs, including the one of Amis music, have won prestigious national awards for Wu.[18]

The Kuos felt that Wu had taken advantage of them because he told them that the recordings were only for study and because he did not pay them for singing. In violation of local custom Wu, who earned his Ph.D. from the Université de Paris X in Nanterre and is now an assistant professor at the National Institute of the Arts, did not even treat them to a meal after they sang for him. In the words of Kuos' daughter, Wu "didn't even buy one bottle of mineral water." Meanwhile, Wu has profited handsomely (both financially and professionally) from the marketing of their music. When I met the Kuos they said that they are now very careful when someone says that they want to record for teaching purposes.[19] In fact when I visited them at their home, they offered to sing for me, but only if I turned off my tape recorder. Incidentally, Wu has sold the rights to use samples from his series to local Taiwan pop artists as well as to international groups, including Deep Forest.[20]

Seeking a Legal Solution

When Enigma released its "Return to Innocence," Li Taikang quickly saw that while Wu and Cretu had both profited from the use of Taiwan aboriginal voices, the collection of damages from Cretu would certainly surpass any amount that could be extracted from Professor Wu.[21] Therefore, Li focused his attention on Michael Cretu. Ultimately, Li was unable to help the Kuos strike a deal or even gain the attention of Cretu. In the words of an employee at the record company that hired Kuo a lawyer: "Kuo Ying-nan tried to communicate with other parties, like France, like EMI, like Michael Cretu, but he didn't make it because he is a tiny spot in their eyes."[22]

In early 1996 Kuo turned to Magic Stone, a division of the Taiwan-owned Rock Records, for help. Through a number of previous involvements with aboriginal musicians, Magic Stone's head, Landy Chang (Chang Pei-jen), had gained a reputation for being helpful and fair. The first step that Landy took was to sign Kuo Ying-nan as a Magic Stone artist. Incidentally, the Kuos' first CD on the Magic Stone label was released in October 1998 in Taiwan and had a second release in late 1999.[23] Magic Stone agreed to cover Kuos' legal cost if the case was not successful. Before the case was filed, the company had hoped that the matter could be settled through some form of mutual agreement, and it approached Cretu about the possibility of his working directly with the Kuos on a recording project. Cretu showed no sign of interest in their overtures. Next Magic Stone hired a lawyer who spent five months in negotiation with EMI's lawyers, but to no avail. It was reported back to the Kuos that the EMI lawyers refused to settle because they knew that the Kuos were poor and could not afford the cost of a lawsuit, estimated to run to about one million U.S. dollars.[24]

Determined to proceed with the case, Kuos' Taiwan lawyer then hired a lawyer from the Oppenheimer, Wolff, and Donnely firm in San Jose, California, to represent the Kuos in the United States courts.[25] Because Enigma's CD sold the most copies in the United States, the amount of potential damages would be greater if won in the U.S. than elsewhere.[26]

"Squarish" Pegs in Round Holes

For many reasons it is impossible to give a complete overview of the evidence and arguments presented by all of the parties involved in this case. First, I am not a lawyer and am not prepared to offer an analysis of specific laws and legal procedures. Second, and more to the point, while serving as an expert witness I was privileged to read the written statements by many of the key witnesses in the case and to view critical documents containing sales figures and other pertinent information. Before being permitted access to these materials, however, I had to sign a *declaration re "confidential information"* form. I thereby agreed not use any confidential information for purposes outside of the litigation and not to reveal any confidential information to anyone not involved in the case. Therefore, my discussion of the case is limited: first, to what I learned before I signed the statement; second, to information that can be gained through avenues other than those related to the trial evidence; and third, to my own personal thoughts and opinions.

It is no secret that lawyers working for EMI / Capitol's side based their case on several key points. First, they argued that Hsu Tsang-houei, the ethnomusicologist, owned the rights to the recording, and he willingly gave them to the French. They asserted that since the French transferred the rights to Cretu, they belonged to him. Second, they claimed that the piece is in the public domain. "Public domain music may be freely used by anyone, without legal limitations or royalty payments" (Mills 1996, 61); therefore, they charged that the Kuos had no claim to copyright.

In constructing their case, Kuos' lawyers chose not to introduce the notions of cultural ownership or indigenous intellectual property rights into the case. When I asked one of the lawyers why they were not pursuing this avenue, he explained that they must work within the current legal framework. The job of courts at this level, he explained, is to interpret existing laws, not to create new ones. In order for this case to break new legal ground, they would have had to lose at this level and then appeal upward. He noted, "it is a huge battle if you want to take it up this way."[27] Clearly, for an individual case to bring change to current laws would require enormous financial resources and could take years. Major record companies have virtually unlimited financial resources and no pressing time constraints. The Kuos' financial resources were limited. Both in rather poor health at ages seventy-eight and seventy-five—in fact, both of the Kuos were hospitalized at least once during the litigation period—time was of significant concern.

One of the primary grounds upon which Kuos' lawyers established their case was the notion that Kuo Ying-nan's performance of the "Song of Joy" was unique. Following this line of argument, Kuo Ying-nan—as the creator of a unique piece—was, therefore, entitled to claim its ownership. The use of this approach clearly illustrates the legal team's decision to steer clear of the much broader, and potentially more contentious, arena of cultural ownership and indigenous intellectual property rights. Fortunately for the Kuos, their performance of the song was, in fact, unlike all other commercially released versions of the song.[28]

In some musical cultures, like that of the Amis, singers and musicians traditionally draw upon a body of preexisting musical materials out of which they shape their own unique performance. There are a large number of basic melodic formulae available to the Amis singer.[29] These formulae, or musical building blocks, may be viewed as belonging to the Amis musical

Kuos' lead counsel, E. Patrick Ellisen, holding the Kuos' copy of their and Enigma's platinum album, *Cross of Changes* (Photo courtesy of E. Patrick Ellisen and Oppenheimer, Wolff, and Donnelly)

culture as a whole. However, the way in which a singer assembles these building blocks typically varies from performance to performance and from singer to singer. Much of the individual composition, or creativity, happens at the moment of performance.

Due to the nature of the Amis creative process, it was not inappropriate for the Kuos' lawyers to argue their case within the confines of the "author-centered regime" (that is, to argue within the boundaries of existing copyright laws). Kuos' lawyers gambled that they could get Kuo and his song through the "authorship gate," so to speak, and won.[30] On 16 June 1999, just a month before the case was scheduled to be heard in a Los Angeles district court, lawyers representing the two sides reached a settlement. Details of the settlement, especially those regarding finances, are confidential. However, it appears that one of the most significant gains for the Kuos is that they will, at long last, be given recognition for their artistic contribution to the "Return to Innocence." As their lawyer informed me, the Kuos' names will be listed on the liner notes of all future releases of the song. They will also be given platinum albums for their "hit" song.[31] In addition, the settlement makes it possible for the Kuos to establish a scholarship foundation for perpetuation of Amis culture.[32] Taiwanese newspapers have reported that the Kuos are very satisfied with the settlement; one article even noted that Mr. Kuo said that he was grateful to have lived long enough to see the matter settled.[33]

When I was told of the terms of the settlement, I recalled a conversation I had had with the Kuos' daughter back in the summer of 1998 when she said "if Enigma had only written 'Taiwan, Taidong county, Amis tribe, Mr. and Mrs. Kuo Ying-nan' on the CD cover then there would never have been a legal case."[34] As Kuo Ying-nan further explained, what made him angry the most about the Enigma affair was that everyone in the world knew his voice, but no one knew that it was his.[35]

A Tangled Web We Weave

At the center of the tangled web described in this article is a well-meaning ethnomusicologist who did not understand copyright law. He did not imagine that his actions would eventually place his informants in a position where they have virtually no rights to control the use of their own music; nor did he imagine that nearly two decades after making a field recording he would be at the center of a legal investigation.

It is essential that we educate our graduate students and ourselves about copyright laws in order to protect our informants and ourselves. Anthony

Seeger has written that some graduate students and many of his colleagues still "appear to be insufficiently aware of the ethical issues their apparently simple recordings may raise" (1992, 356). A review of copyright law and the practice of preparing contracts should be a standard part of the training of young fieldworkers who may potentially record music sound. As lawyer Emil Chang has stated, the infringement of the Kuos' rights began as soon as the recording moved into the commercial sector because this went beyond the original intent of the recording as expressed to the Kuos by Hsu Tsang-houei.[36] Our contracts must state clearly what the intended purposes for the recording are, and they should also state who owns the copyright to the recording. This in itself is no simple matter, since every fieldwork situation is different and the preparation of each contract must take into consideration a multitude of factors.

We are at a critical point and have both an ethical obligation and a practical need to act. We cannot afford to ignore this topic, and we cannot afford to let our students continue in ignorance of the legal and moral implications of their work.

Anne Chambers, Keith S. Chambers,
David R. Counts, Dorothy A. Counts,
Suzanne Falgout, Nancy Guy, Alan Howard,
Sjoerd R. Jaarsma, Mary McCutcheon,
Bryan P. Oles, Karen M. Peacock, and
Amy Ku'uleialoha Stillman

Epilogue

Returning Ethnographic Materials

Looking around, Leslie immediately noticed the book, her thesis, sitting by itself on a shelf. She chuckled softly and said to herself: "Well, well, that's one for the books, the first public library on the island." Despite the humor of it, her second reaction was one of slight dismay. The entire scene looked like something out of an exhibit, out of place here. It might be likened to a public library, but the joke was on her. Had she really wanted this to happen? Sending her thesis back was one thing, but having it the sole attraction for the local readership was quite another.

Repatriation implies a paradigm shift in the way that the anthropological community thinks of the products of ethnographic research. Field notes, recordings, genealogies, journals, interviews—systematically collected data, descriptions, analytical writings—all are complex ethnographic artifacts. We now understand that they have been produced through an interplay between numerous actors and interests and that the information they contain is more an interpretation of social reality than simple "fact." While our ethnographic work becomes a historiographic rendering of community life, it remains a personal mapping of our own intellectual development as well. Correspondingly, questions of ownership, access, and control multiply too. In the long term, who is to have possession of ethnographic materials? And equally important, who should control access to them?

Clearly, decision making on the return of ethnographic materials must be governed by a twofold imperative: to foster knowledge, but equally to do no harm. Considering the often divergent needs of hosts and researchers, their conflicting concerns and interests, and differences in their levels of conscious engagement with repatriation issues, making decisions that will serve the interests of everyone—equally—will be extremely difficult. Knowledge beneficial to some may harm others.

Ideally, repatriation allows for a handing over of control, engaging the local community in defining access. Knowledge can be translated directly into power, we know. Thus, a continuum of access will often be essential, with decision making regarding ethnographic products and fieldwork situations based directly in the particularities of each situation. But communities change through time, and national community interests may not always parallel those of the local community. This further complicates decision making. In the face of this reality, can any general guidelines be devised to accommodate the varied products of ethnographic research? What compromises, and conflicts too, may result from opening up this issue for public discussion and resolution?

Such issues and ambiguities have woven their way through each of the case studies in this book. While a list of repatriation prescriptions would be overly simplistic, recurrent themes are apparent in the chapters in this volume, just as they have been in the contributors' discussions over the last three years. From these we have distilled the following suggestions, which we offer here for consideration.

Thoughts on Repatriation

• Repatriation issues should be considered at the start of fieldwork rather than being postponed to the end of a researcher's career. Access to ethnographic information and the eventual disposition of fieldwork materials are best incorporated into the initial planning preceding any research enterprise.

• Active engagement with the community regarding future repatriation is essential. Collaborative decision making is the best insurance against inappropriate use (or loss of) valuable information. Collaboration will also make culturally appropriate decisions possible and bring the perspectives of all parties together.

• Decisions made about repatriation must be contextualized. The return of ethnographic information should be tailored to fit specific ethnographic relationships, settings, and stages of historical consciousness. Professional ethical codes, personal understandings, and community perspectives should all be considered and weighed against each other.

• Distinguishing the personal from the more purely ethnographic in a researcher's work should be basic for repatriation decision making. Some data may need to be destroyed. This is best done by the initial researcher who knows the context in which dangerous or personally sensitive materials were created or collected.

• Repatriating data in a "raw" form, as authored by particular persons and connected to known contexts, is often preferable to returning generalized accounts. Here, traditional ownership rights and responsibilities are preserved to some extent and may assist community members in interpreting the materials as connected to wider cultural information and social positioning.

• Making ethnographic materials publicly available or enshrining them in a public archive may be problematic for information that is essentially private or linked politically and socially to particular individuals, families, or other groups. Public access to these materials, stripping these of the limitations normally prevailing within the community, may problematize the return of this information to the community or even change the meanings of what is returned.

• Ethnographic information—now as before—is likely to have different meanings to different segments of the community. Consideration must be given to the content and manner of returning ethnographic information to the community. Has one view inadvertently been privileged over another? Could the return of information benefit some people at the expense of others? These questions have to be weighed in advance.

• The multivocality of ethnographic information may also change through time. Consideration of the timing of return is as essential as the content of the materials returned.

• An element of unpredictability is an inherent part of repatriation. The consequences of repatriation decisions can never be entirely known in advance. Despite everyone's best efforts, unfortunate outcomes may occur. Understandings and needs inevitably change through time.

• Yet, simple inaction is almost always the worst choice to make. "Doing nothing" is actually a choice too. The people who were once "written about" are now involved as coproducers and consumers of ethnographic knowledge. Thoughtful repatriation of ethnographic materials can assist not only in the decolonization of anthropology, but in empowering both communities and the people who comprise them by allowing easier access to a greater range of ethnographic information. But due care is required in making repatriation decisions so that the well-being of everyone concerned results.

Notes

Introduction

I thank Anne Chambers, Alan Howard, and Kathryn Creely for their critical and constructive comments on this introduction, and for their efforts to keep my tendency to ramble in check.

1. This conference was certainly not the first of its kind. Since the First International Congress of Ethnobiology in 1988 that produced the Declaration of Belém (see Posey and Dutfield 1996, 2), representatives from indigenous and traditional peoples have been meeting with scientists and environmentalists "to discuss a common strategy to stop the rapid decrease in the planet's biological and cultural diversity" (1). The timing of the Mataatua Conference to coincide with the United Nations International Year for the World's Indigenous Peoples, as well as the scale of the conference, made it a unique and—more important—an indigenous political forum.

2. Intellectual property rights (IPR) first developed as a legal concept in Europe and North America to protect individual and industrial inventions. Its application to the collective, often verbally transmitted knowledge that comprises indigenous culture was and still is considered problematic. However, with the increasingly commercial value placed on traditional lifestyles, knowledge, and biogenetic resources, it has become clear to indigenous peoples that IPR law has become indispensable to them and needs to be reconceptualized to suit their future needs (see Posey and Dutfield 1996, 1).

3. For a description of these and related concepts, see Posey and Dutfield 1996, 93–100.

4. One of the most progressive proposals in this respect is the "Draft Code of Ethics and Standards of Practice of the International Society of Ethnobiology," resulting from its 1996 Nairobi conference. This proposed code of conduct is based on fourteen fundamental assumptions that define a scientist's relation to indigenous peoples. These principles include the right of self-determination of indigenous peoples; their inalienable rights to land, territory, and resources; the right to an ensured minimum impact of any research; the right to full disclosure on the nature of research; the right to prior informed consent and veto; the right to confidentiality; the importance of active participation by the local community; the importance of active protection of the relation between community and environment; the right to good faith, compensation, restitution, reciprocity, and equitable sharing (International Society of Ethnobiology 1996, 3–5).

5. Despite the role of audiovisual media, written text is the basic tool for documentation in our culture, and as anthropologists we document other cultures and societies. Talking throughout in terms of ethnographic writing—published or unpublished—

might falsely suggest that the role of such a basically anthropological instrument as participant observation is reduced to marginality. The difference between notes rendering our personal observations or our informants' information into writing is not in their nature as text, but in the ease with which we will let others access or share them (cf. Jackson 1990, 8–9). As Alan Howard (chapter 2) notes, dubbing a term used by Roger Sanjek (1990, 93), "Portions of our field notes are often nothing more than mnemonic devices . . . 'headnotes' that guide our research."

6. For some museum anthropologists, and applied anthropologists in particular, making decisions on these matters may be more difficult, as both the questions why and for whom they gathered materials influence the extent to which they can decide to dispose at will of field materials. The essential questions concerning the disposition of research materials and researchers' responsibilities vis-à-vis the research population are the same, but legal requirements toward the third parties that sponsor research or analysis may create complex ownership claims toward the results (see chapter 11). The contributions in the second part of this volume, dealing with repatriation by museums and archives, will deal more extensively with these issues.

7. Keith and Anne Chambers (chapter 9) point out that there is more at stake here. The "pixel revolution" may well make it inevitable that an increasing volume of ethnographic material will be returned or made accessible through the Internet. As they point out, this extremely public medium may present additional problems in securing and controlling access to information.

8. Pels notes that "European development showed a diversity of reactions that presented different attitudes to codes than those prevalent in the US" (1999, 30). Nevertheless, it is well accepted in Europe as elsewhere that anthropology benefits by living up to an ethical code and by ongoing discussion of professional ethical standards.

9. Maureen Fitzgerald (personal communication) was kind enough to point me toward an interesting report by Stephen McNabb. Involved in the impact study following the Exxon Valdez oil spill in Prince William Sound, Alaska, McNabb was subpoenaed in the court case held to determine the culpability of Exxon. He points out: "A strict reading of the subpoena would require me to turn over syllabi, course materials, and even grades and student evaluations from courses I taught that were unrelated to the oil spill and that were dated earlier than the spill. I thought that these materials would not be subject to what I saw as a 'fishing expedition.' Not so. Such records could show that I recommended research techniques that I did not employ in my Exxon Valdez research, that I advocated or supported premises or empirical findings at odds with my Exxon Valdez research, or that I evaluated student work in a way that I did not evaluate the work of junior colleagues working under me. As such, those records could provide a means to discredit me" (1995, 332). The quote from the subpoena text concerning the nature of the evidence sought (333–35) provides an interesting (and somewhat daunting) view on what can be legally considered relevant in research materials.

10. As McCutcheon shows in relation to the developments in the Freedom of Information Act (chapter 4), this may be less obvious than it seems.

11. A recent exchange in the correspondence columns of the *Anthropology Newsletter* should remind us that even "simple" returns that allow members of the community access to published ethnographies may provoke unexpected reactions, challenging

to even the wary. In an open letter to the newsletter's readers, Gilbert Herdt was accused of breach of contract: "We the people of 'Sambia,' Marawaka District, Eastern Highlands Province, Papua New Guinea, wish to deny the writings of Gilbert Herdt who lived in the area and studied our people in the 1970s and 1980s, and then wrote books describing our custom in quite erroneous terms. He has breached our intellectual property rights to our custom and has also breached contracts he made with us not to publish materials without our approval. He admits as much in his published works. . . . In his books he publishes his erroneous statements under pseudonymous names. . . . His data is thus completely unauthenticated and impossible to check. . . . Although we write this letter as representatives of 11 clans of the 'Sambia' people, we are supported by all 'Sambia' clans in our categorical rejection of all Herdt's writings" (Dariawo et al. 1999). An important problem here is "who is representing whose interests?" Herdt is very clear in his response: "I long ago promised the individuals and village communities with whom I worked that I would never reveal their true names or identities. I explained this decision in relation to the secret homoerotic content of ritual practices in my doctoral dissertation and subsequent books. My agreement resulted from conversations with numerous Sambia with whom I originally worked between 1974–76. . . . At my request, the AN has thus removed the true name of the culture from the letter. . . . By forcing me to respond directly to their allegations in the same context that they use the true name of the people, they would cause me to violate my agreement with the Sambia. . . . All this leads me to conclude that the accusers are desperate to determine the true identity of my Sambia informants. I believe that they would like to extract compensation from them either directly through the courts or, more likely, through blackmail or extortion" (Herdt 1999). In his final lines Herdt points to the wider implications of this interchange: "We are all vulnerable to accusations of this kind, especially misrepresentations in the media or on the Internet. It is unpleasant to deal with them without being defensive or overly cynical, and even more dreadful to think that they might bring real harm to the people whom we care about in other cultures. These issues merit renewed discussion about ethical agreements made decades ago in good faith and the protection—not only of our informants—but of the rights of anthropologists too."

Chapter 1

1. This comment came in e-mail correspondence between Dorothy and a member of the staff of the Secretariat of Pacific Communities in Noumea, New Caledonia.

2. This quote comes from a letter we received from an RVer who had ordered four copies of our book.

3. The address is ⟨http://arts.uwaterloo.ca/anthro/wnb/WestNewBritain.html⟩.

4. Our thanks to Roy Wagner for this unforgettable phrase coined by him in a conversation many years ago.

Chapter 2

1. I have long been intrigued with implications of hypermedia for anthropology and published an article on the topic in 1988. My initial proposals were based on visions of CD-ROM disks (Howard 1988); the Internet opened horizons even further.

2. The dictionary is based on an 11,000 plus word list in a Filemaker database. The basis for the wordlist is C. M. Churchward's Rotuman / English dictionary, initially published in 1940. We typed his entries into a database and converted it to an English / Rotuman word list. The dictionary and word list have been corrected and updated by Hans Schmidt in collaboration with Elizabeth Inia and Sofie Arnsten, two knowledgeable Rotuman women. The results were published in 1998 by the Institute for Pacific Studies, University of the South Pacific, in Suva, Fiji (Inia et al. 1998).

3. The address of the Rotuma website is ⟨http://www.hawaii.edu/oceanic/rotuma/os/hanua.html⟩.

4. The account by Keith and Anne Chambers (chapter 9) raises some interesting questions regarding the repatriation of genealogies provided by oral accounts. Synthesized genealogies may pose special problems because they do not allow people to assess them the way they do in real life. In the context of social life, genealogies are assessed on the basis of who presents them and where their assumed political and material interests lie. It may therefore be important to provide with each genealogy the source, and to avoid combining them into what may become a disembodied, authoritative source. In the act of synthesizing, the anthropologist creates a new kind of information, one that has all the pitfalls detailed so well by the Chambers.

5. A few years back we made a compendium of my publications, printed about fifty copies, and distributed them to schools, libraries, and interested Rotumans with the same purpose in mind. In contrast to the experience of Keith and Anne Chambers (see chapter 9), we received very little specific feedback on these writings, positive or negative. The general response we have gotten from Rotumans concerning our work is one of encouragement—that we are performing a valuable service—but we are not naive enough to take this as an accurate assessment of general opinion. After all, we are loyal to our friends, and they reciprocate the loyalty, and most of the people we communicate with regularly with have become close friends.

6. A means of reproducing documents approximating their original format is the PDF format produced by the software program Acrobat, by Adobe.

7. The term "headnotes" is attributed by Roger Sanjek (1990) to Simon Ottenberg. In Sanjek's words, "We come back from the field with fieldnotes and headnotes. The fieldnotes stay the same, written down on paper, but the headnotes continue to evolve and change as they did during the time in the field. Ethnography, Ottenberg explains, is a product of the two sets of notes. The headnotes are more important. Only after the anthropologist is dead are the fieldnotes primary" (Sanjek 1990, 93).

8. I am referring here to the process of bringing to consciousness that which was previously unconscious, or taken for granted. When aspects of culture are brought to conscious awareness, they become conceptual objects about which people can make explicit judgments and choices. Notions such as "Rotuman culture" and "Rotuman history" were not indigenous conceptualizations, but developed only after extensive exposure to other ethnic groups (see Howard 1977).

Chapter 3

I am grateful to Kathryn Creely and Mary McCutcheon for their comprehensive comments on a previous version of this chapter.

1. As Dorothy and David Counts indicate (chapter 1), the required level of sophistication can actually be very high due to the role of jargon in most anthropological work.

2. While I speak of anthropologists as an identifiable and homogenous group, I realize that this is in many respects an oversimplification.

3. Concepts such as "knowledge" and "data" are inherently vague. When speaking of "data" or "ethnographic data," I am referring to the raw notes or audiovisual registrations researchers made during their fieldwork. While these never will be without categorization, the level of analysis done on this material may be considered minimal. (In many respects analysis may not even be consciously performed.) Once we start manipulating data to inform others, we are dealing in terms of knowledge. There is nothing absolute about knowledge; it always exists relative to an audience or discourse. An elder telling an initiate what he needs to know to attain the next stage in his social life is imparting knowledge, yet to us as outsiders and researchers, this indigenous knowledge is a set of data, as we do not belong to the audience addressed. The thesis written on the basis of fieldwork is considered to be anthropological knowledge. To the community studied, however, it is a set of data it can manipulate. In that respect all audiences, whether we address this or not, can take our "knowledge" and manipulate it as data to further their own ends. It is only the audience we specifically address that may feel itself bound by the ethics implicit in the discourse.

4. There are, of course, degrees of sensitivity that will be of influence if we decide to repatriate knowledge and data. An example that is dealt with by different authors in this volume is the knowledge of land rights. How and why this becomes, at some stage, sensitive material depends on (1) the nature of the indigenous expectations concerning the repatriated data. (The very fact that land rights have been reified on paper can be important, as can the trust placed in the ethnographer who noted them down; see also Keith and Anne Chambers, chapter 9); (2) the extent to which the issue of land rights relates to local political discourse (see Alan Howard, chapter 2; Bryan Oles, chapter 10); (3) the background against which repatriation takes place; for instance, those people who have migrated away from the village where they were born and live as expatriates will have different priorities than those living locally (see Oles, chapter 10; the Chambers, chapter 9); (4) and finally, the medium through which repatriation takes place will also play a role (e.g., the Internet, but also material that is made accessible in archives and museum collections).

5. In a Western legal sense, a copyright has a limited lifespan, after which what is copyrighted is relegated to the public domain (cf. Brown 1998, 196). While Nancy Guy (chapter 11) addresses copyright in this restrictive sense, my intention here is to let it convey a sense of limited (or privileged) access to the knowledge covered by the copyright. Most cultures will not put a time limit to such limitations or privileges, though there usually is an awareness that the knowledge can become part of the public domain at some stage if specific circumstances change. What the specifics of these changes are is very much situation bound. In this respect we speak of copyright more in moral than in legal terms.

6. We are not the only ones spreading information this way, infringing upon otherwise presumably secret (or privately owned) knowledge. In essence, any outsider al-

lowed generalized access can do the same. For instance, in the not-so-distant past mobile bachelors in the Tor and Sarmi areas of West Papua routinely introduced new cultural elements in the ritual repertoire of their communities (Oosterwal 1959; Oosterwal 1961; van der Leeden 1956).

7. Both fragments are as cited by Susanne Kuehling (1998, 16), who was kind enough to bring them to my attention.

8. Certain types of data (especially quantitative material), like information on land rights and land use, may very well be collected on a short-term basis. However, it is unlikely that the depth and multivocality that may characterize debates on land issues can be assessed based solely on such research (see the Chambers, chapter 9; Oles, chapter 10).

9. Lamont Lindstrom and Geoffrey White, for instance, point to the adoption by the American Anthropological Association of a professional code of ethics to ensure that the anthropologists' research efforts benefit more than just their own disciplinary discourse. "This code demands that the interests of the people (and their cultures and languages) come first, before any academic or professional advantage" (1994a, 12). While admittedly such codes are only effective if and when professional self-control is applied, they are an important pointer to the ethical development of the discipline.

10. As the Counts point out, the tenure process at present favors a production of often highly esoteric and inaccessible (and hence private) texts. However, increased pressure from outside audiences, certainly when they are able to sponsor research and education, may very well turn the tables in the future. The potential spin off of the repatriation process as sponsored by the indigenous people themselves is but one possible example.

11. This is, of course, not only true of those ethnic minorities indigenous to areas such as Hawai'i and New Zealand, but also of those groups that have migrated from all over the Pacific to find work and are forced to maintain their ethnic and cultural identity in an expatriate context.

12. This point of view has changed considerably over the last few decades. Anthropologists working before and even shortly after World War II would not have wasted much thought on the ownership of the data they gathered (except in an analytical sense). They would have considered themselves to be caretakers, albeit in a very paternalistic sense. The cultures they studied were deemed to be disappearing quickly. The role of the ethnographer was to preserve and prevent loss of cultural heritage (perhaps not for the sake of culture, but for academic interest). This, too, relates to contemporary perceptions of ethnographic authority (Jaarsma 1998).

13. In a sense we might note that anthropologists are "copyrighting" the fields in which they work, claiming exclusive rights on the production of knowledge and transfer of information. While this is often jocularly referred to in terms of anthropologists and "their people," the claim to exclusivity can have more serious connotations with respect to free access to the research field and data (see for instance Anthony Lord's protectiveness of Joseph Weckler's field notes, as described by Oles, chapter 10. Where research data are shielded not because of their sensitive content, but because they are the results of individual research (i.e., they have become academic capital), this can only be seen as a negative development. A complicating factor here is the ascription of au-

thority. Ethnographers implicitly or explicitly claim authority over the knowledge they produce. This authority—and on occasion some counterclaims—will be part and parcel of what will be repatriated. The effects of repatriation of such texts will in part be dependent on the measure to which the ethnographer's authority is locally acknowledged or, on the contrary, challenged. Whatever its reception, it will not necessarily mirror the multivocality of the anthropological discourse it was taken from.

14. While we have mostly studied and analyzed orally transmitted knowledge (adding and comparing this to our own observations), we have turned these data into notes, published material, audiotapes, films, and videos. These materials all need to be stored properly; otherwise, they will deteriorate and eventually be lost. To prevent this, we will most probably be repatriating to some kind of local educational center or museum. Even there, however, arrangements will have to be made for proper storage.

15. Tikopian use of previous ethnographic descriptions made Judith Macdonald's own activities in the field almost into a parody: "I was told one of the nurses at the local hospital was a Tikopia and that he was an expert on traditional childbirth practices. I contacted him, and he agreed to tell me all he knew about childbirth in Tikopia. After giving me an hour of organized information, which I taped, he finished by saying, 'at least, that's what Raymond said'" (2000, 107). And this had disconcerting effects as Macdonald indicates: "My thesis supervisor was well versed in the Tikopia corpus. Several times while reading drafts of my thesis she marked passages and said that I should acknowledge the quotation from Firth. With irritation, I replied that they had said it to me, too" (2000, 123 n. 9).

16. The Institute of Papua New Guinea Studies as it was originally conceived would probably have served this function given adequate financing. As Voi indicates in his analysis of PNG cultural policies and politics, however, the shifts in policy whereby culture and tourism became combined purposes have created confusion and resentment, defeating the original purpose (1994).

17. Though phrased like this it seems an unlikely scenario, we should not readily dismiss it. The combination of politics and culture is a powerful mix, as Crocombe points out. Similar points can be made with respect to the debate on the reinvention of tradition (Keesing 1989, 1991; Trask 1991). There is no reason to suspect that repatriated material or the process of repatriation itself will be exempt.

18. As I indicate in the introduction to this volume, this argument may differ in detail for the ethical codes and practices in other countries, but will mirror the spirit.

19. Basically, Howard's considerations on the extent of historical consciousness (developmental trajectory) needed for successful repatriation run along the same lines (chapter 2).

Chapter 4

1. Kathryn Creely, Melanesian Archive at University of California, San Diego, personal communication, 1998.

2. Richard Emerick, personal communication, 1999.

3. Unpublished terms of donation are available from the National Anthropological Archives, National Museum of Natural History, Smithsonian Institution, Washington, D.C.

4. Karen Peacock, Pacific Collection at the University of Hawai'i's Hamilton Library, personal communication, 1998.

5. Richard Marksbury, Tulane University, personal communication, 1998.

6. Pam Wintle, Human Studies Film Archives, Smithsonian Institution, personal communication, 1999.

7. Edward Halealoha Ayau, personal communication, 1999.

8. Ronald Vanderwal, Victoria Museum, Melbourne (Australia), personal communication, 1998.

9. Pam Wintle, personal communication, 1999.

10. Robert Leopold, National Anthropological Archives, National Museum of Natural History, Smithsonian Institution, Washington, D.C., personal communication, 1998.

11. See Price 1997 for a discussion of the use of FOIA in anthropological research.

12. Joe McDermott, Office of Territorial and Insular Affairs, Department of the Interior, Washington, D.C., personal communication, 1999.

13. Monique Storie and Francis Hezel, personal communication, 1998.

14. Bruce Alberts, in a 1999 letter from the National Academy of Sciences to James Charney, Office of Management and Budget, in regards to revised Circular A-110.

15. Peggy Overbey, American Anthropological Association, personal communication, 1999.

Chapter 5

The authors thank Christine Jourdan, Shelly Schreiner, Donald Tuzin, Terre Fisher, Sjoerd Jaarsma, and Jennifer Care for assistance with this project, as well as Lynda Claassen, Steve Coy, Lynette Stoudt, Richard Lindemann, and Brad Westbrook at the Mandeville Special Collections Library at UCSD, and The Friends of the UCSD Libraries. Akin thanks the following sources of funding for fieldwork drawn upon here: National Endowment for the Humanities (grant FB-32097–95), National Science Foundation (INT-9504555), and Wenner-Gren (5800).

1. Documents such as the American Anthropological Association's "Principles of Professional Responsibility" (AAA 1971) can clarify some of the basic ethical issues involved, as can other more recent writings (e.g. Fowler 1995; Brown 1998). Several international conferences on cultural and intellectual property rights have been held in the Pacific in the last decade. In 1992 the conference Developing Cultural Policy in Melanesia took place in the Solomon Islands (Lindstrom and White 1994b). In 1993 the First International Conference on the Cultural and Intellectual Property Rights of Indigenous Peoples (1993) was convened in Aotearoa, New Zealand, by the Nine Tribes of Mataatua, with support from the United Nations. In 1995 the United Nations Development Program sponsored the Indigenous Peoples' Knowledge and Intellectual Property Rights Consultation in Fiji (UNDP 1995). In 1999 the symposium Protection of Traditional Knowledge and Expressions of Indigenous Cultures in the Pacific Islands was held in New Caledonia, under the auspices of the Secretariat of the Pacific Community and the United Nations Educational, Scientific, and Cultural Organization (UNESCO), in response to a request from the Pacific Council of Arts (Secretariat of the Pacific Community 1999a, 1999b). Much work has been done in Australia in the last

few years. Milestones include the 1998 publication of a major report written by Terri Janke, an indigenous legal consultant, commissioned by the Aboriginal and Torres Strait Islander Commission and the Australian Institute of Aboriginal and Torres Strait Islander Studies (Janke 1998). In early 1999 came the establishment of the Indigenous Cultural and Intellectual Property Task Force (Aboriginal and Torres Strait Islander Commission 1999, 74–75). The task force is under the wing of the Aboriginal and Torres Strait Islander Commission's Native Title and Land Rights Branch. To date its efforts have been focused on achieving legal reforms to implement the recommendations of the 1998 report, on both the national and international levels.

2. A large collection of material collected by Akin is also being gradually deposited in the Melanesian Archive and copied for the Kwaio collection in the National Museum, but for simplicity we focus here only on Keesing's materials. From 1963 to 1970 the late Honorable Jonathan Fifi'i, a Kwaio leader and research collaborator with both Keesing and Akin (e.g., Fifi'i 1988; 1989), authored a record of community events and detailed ethnography totaling over 3,000 pages, a work that raises singular repatriation issues. Fifi'i's papers, also held at UCSD (written in Kwaio language), will be the subject of a separate publication.

3. In the late 1970s Keesing deposited published papers, his dissertation, genealogies, and a small number of recorded interviews with a cultural center in the Kwaio mountains. Cyclone Namu destroyed the center's archive in 1986 (see Akin 1994; Keesing 1994).

4. Ideally, when a collection is deposited with an archive, it has already been organized and labeled by the anthropologist who compiled it. Basic inventories, subject indexes, and other finding aids are also best created prior to deposit. In recognition of this, the Wenner-Gren Foundation for Anthropological Research has set up a special grants program to assist with this type of processing, *before* a collection is transferred to an archive (Wenner-Gren 1998). A discussion of the recommended techniques is beyond the scope of this paper, but several guides specific to anthropological records exist (see Kenworthy et al. 1985; Silverman and Parezo 1995).

5. This is especially problematic for anthropologists in the Pacific who, more often than most researchers, work in field languages spoken by few if any outsiders.

6. A host of issues relating to genealogical records are too complex to pursue here, particularly as they relate to Malaitan land ownership (see for instance Burt 2001). Briefly, the primary basis upon which land rights are recognized in both government and local Kwaio courts is claimants' knowledge of their own links to the ancestors who founded the land in dispute. Thus genealogies recorded by Keesing (and by Akin or his Kwaio students) may become sensitive material in the future. Indeed, in one 1980s land court case a Christian man won by reading from one of Keesing's genealogies. The loser tried, unsuccessfully, to bar the use of written evidence. In most parts of Malaita land disputes are chronic and protracted, but there are currently few in Kwaio. This is largely because Kwaio have not engaged in cash cropping or logging, and so most land has not become commoditized (see Akin 1999). Many Malaitans have lost their land for want of genealogical knowledge, and Kwaio may soon face similar difficulties. Even now Kwaio Christians, who have been forced to drastically underfallow their coastal gardens, are beginning to assert their ancestral links to mountain land. Moreover,

Kwaio possess valuable timber that has only been protected to date by landowners denying access to logging companies. As elsewhere, companies seek land owners willing to buck their communities, allow cutting, and, they hope, inaugurate a rush of wholesale competitive logging (see Frazer 1997; Schieffelin 1995). Mining reportedly may also loom in Kwaio's future, and land disputes may then contest huge sums of money. Genealogies will likely be key weapons in these battles. The recent ethnic violence on Guadalcanal and the resulting mass exodus of thousands of Malaitans back to their homes is likely to exacerbate pressures on land.

7. See Burt 1998 for a discussion of the continuing interplay of oral and written history and ethnography in Kwara'ae and in the Solomons more generally.

Chapter 6

1. See Brown (1998) for a recent overview of this debate.

2. Greenfield (1995) shows that the term "cultural property" lends itself to various interpretations, differing from country to country and even from one international convention to another. Within Western understandings of this concept, there are two approaches: one internationalist and one nationalist. The internationalist approach, expressed in the 1954 Hague Convention, refers to the common heritage of all mankind and thus contradicts the notion of return. The nationalist approach, seen in the very influential 1970 and 1980 UNESCO conventions, refers to a particular culture's heritage and includes the notion of return to the country of origin. This, however, leads to another thorny question: what is the country of origin? Is it the place of origin, the place of manufacture, the nationality of the maker, the country for whom the item was made, or the country that last held the item? Even the attempt to determine the strongest historic link is an endeavor filled with ambiguities and complexities (see Greenfield 1995).

3. In *Beyond Intellectual Property*, Posey and Dutfield (1996) discuss the extension of intellectual property rights (IPR), first developed in European and American law, to indigenous and traditional peoples. In 1990 the Working Group on Intellectual Property Rights was formed by the Global Coalition for Bio-Cultural Diversity. This group has worked toward the protection of traditional resource rights (TRR), a concept designed to be both more inclusive and culturally relevant. Their book serves as a useful handbook to guide both indigenous communities and those who seek their traditional resources in the collection and use of those resources. Yet, the authors readily admit that their "book is only a broad and, therefore, relatively superficial treatment of the complex range of subjects it claims to cover" (1996, 3).

4. And, for some of these tangible items, another question emerges: what is cultural versus natural?

5. But see American Folklife Center (1983) and UNESCO (1989).

6. The Northern Marianas Islands opted to become a commonwealth of the United States.

7. The Republic of the Marshall Islands and the Republic of Belau (Palau) have negotiated separate compacts of free association with the United States.

8. The U.S. Navy governed from 1945 to 1947; the area was declared a United States Trust Territory in 1947, but continued to be administered by the navy until 1951; in 1951 the administration shifted to the Department of the Interior.

9. A few anthropologists worked on more than one project (see Kiste and Falgout 1999).

10. The U.S. Commercial Company, directed by Douglas Oliver, involved twenty-four researchers (including four anthropologists) who conducted assessments of postwar economic conditions in Micronesia. Their reports also included substantial ethnographic data. The Coordinated Investigation of Micronesia was undertaken by the Pacific Science Board, as a newly established committee of the National Research Council. It included forty-one researchers, mostly anthropologists, from twenty universities and museums who conducted research on a wide variety of topics throughout the region. The Scientific Investigation of Micronesia that followed was a program of studies in physical, biological, and life sciences; a major focus of this project was atoll research. It included thirty-one researchers from a wide variety of academic backgrounds.

11. A total of five anthropologists served as staff anthropologist; a few had served on earlier postwar Micronesian projects (see Kiste and Falgout 1999).

12. A total of eleven anthropologists worked as district anthropologists; four had worked on earlier postwar Micronesian projects (see Kiste and Falgout 1999).

13. The "Report on Anthropological Conference Held in Koror September 4–12, 1952" states that one purpose of the meeting was to improve communication between the district anthropologists and to allow them to develop an awareness of conditions in other parts of the USTT. However, the main agenda of the meeting was to assess anthropological interests and aims. The meeting concluded with the complaints that most of the anthropologists' working days had been consumed by routine administrative duties; special projects had been initiated at the high commissioner versus district level; working relations with other departments had been confined to either Education or Public Works, and occasionally the Judiciary; and research on local problems was given little attention, usually conducted during off-hours (USTT Archives 1950–1960).

14. The goals of the 1957 conference were similar. The conference also included an "Evening with Judge Ferber," in which an attempt was made to further clarify the role of the anthropologist in giving court testimony (USTT Archives 1950–1960).

15. In Executive Order No. 48, dated 24 January 1955, the deputy high commissioner of the USTT promulgated effective immediately the following addition to the code: "Section 342. *Certain Conversations with Anthropologists Privileged.* Subject to the limitations provided in this section, conversation held with an anthropologist in confidence in his professional character shall be privileged. No statement made in such a conversation nor the substance thereof, shall be divulged without the consent of the person making it, nor shall the identity of any person making such a statement on any particular subject be divulged without his consent, except as provided below. The privilege, however, shall not extend to the professional opinions or conclusions of an anthropologist even though they may be based in whole or in part on such conversations, nor shall it or the prohibition against divulging such statements or the identity of persons making them apply to admissions or confessions indicating that the person making them has committed murder in the first or second degree or voluntary manslaughter or is threatening to commit a crime in the future" (USTT Archives 1950–1960).

16. Ann Fischer is formally acknowledged as having provided assistance to her husband in the publication of *The Eastern Carolines* (1957).

17. Ten of the eleven district anthropologists who served were graduate students; six of them eventually received their Ph.D.s; only four went on to academic careers (see Kiste and Falgout 1999).

18. I am not aware if Fischer knew about or responded to this criticism before his death.

19. *Senator Ismael*: Mr. Speaker, Section 2 of Title 7 of the Trust Territory Code, provides for privileged conversations with anthropologists. The only other statutory privilege in the Code concerns the husband and wife not being compelled to testify against one another. Privileged . . . rules of evidence promulgated by the High Court are those of dependent(s) in a criminal case, lawyer-client, physician-patient, confidential marital communications, priest-penitent, etc. Your Committee does not believe the relationship between an anthropologist and an informant should be enshrined and promoted by statute, while privileged communications of benefit to Micronesians are not so recognized. Section 2 of Title 7 is pre-1955. It originated in a time when the anthropologist-informant relationship was deemed to be more important by the Administering Authority than relations between lawyer and client, and physician and patient. Your Committee finds its exclusive presence in the Code embarrassing and obsolete. For this reason, Mr. Speaker, your Committee recommends passage of this measure.

Senator Akapito: Mr. Speaker, I would like to say that we have come a long way in numerals, articles, books, and what have you. We Micronesians or FSM people for that matter have been classified one way or another. I hope we pass this legislation wholeheartedly in order to erase from the dirt of the earth the previous notion or concept that Micronesia was, and I hope not, would be a zoo any more. (First Congress of the Federated States of Micronesia 1979, 111)

Chapter 7

1. These provisions were specified in the 1982 "Agreement Pertaining to Preservation and Use of the Records of the Trust Territory of the Pacific Islands through the University of Hawai'i at Manoa Libraries" between the University of Hawai'i and Trust Territory of the Pacific Islands Government. The agreement was signed by representatives of both sides in Saipan and Honolulu on 1 March 1982. A copy of the agreement is on file in the Pacific Collection, University of Hawai'i, Honolulu.

2. The National Archives of Australia has purchased a full set of the Trust Territory Archives microfilm from the University of Hawai'i, making the full record of the Trust Territory government available to Australian scholars.

3. The Information Retrieval System was a project done by the Publications and Printing Division of the Trust Territory government on Saipan, in which material was filmed as either microfilm or microfiche and made available to offices throughout Micronesia and to interested parties from outside the region who could purchase sets. Materials covered in the project included the translations of Japanese land documents, education scholarship records, Ponape Land Commission records, College of Micronesia student transcripts, Micronesian News Services releases, judiciary general files, and clerk of court records, among others. The project was an attempt to increase ac-

cess, save space, and preserve records. A two-volume index was published to assist the user (see Trust Territory of The Pacific Islands Information Retrieval System 1979).

4. The printed index consisted of sixteen volumes arranged by subject, and within each subject arranged geographically. Within the geographic subsections, the material was organized chronologically from earliest to latest entry. The printed index had the advantage of assembling all material by topic, according to the subject headings used in the *TTPI Files System Manual* (Trust Territory Government 1968). As McPhetres has noted, there are many misspellings in data entries, and these complicate computer index keyword searching (1992a, 4).

5. Details on the nature of the transfer of the index from one format to another can be obtained from the author.

6. In the library's online index to the archives, a unique subset available on the menu of choices in the online catalog, searching is most productive when done by keyword. A search for the keyword "Woleai," for example, would yield all documents and other material specifically related to that island (36 entries). For larger geographic areas, such as Yap, it is necessary to add keywords, such as "schools" (139 entries), "transportation" (282 entries), or "land claims" (54 entries). The results from a broad search would yield overwhelming numbers (2421 entries for Yap). The first-time user is best served by consulting Pacific Collection staff regarding structure of the index, either in person or by letter or e-mail. Understanding the subject indexing used for the index, which is markedly different from Library of Congress subject headings, increases a user's success with keyword searching. Recent changes in programming of the library version of the index (summer 1999) now allow a user to employ subject browse capability. This means that one may go directly to a subject heading assigned by the original archives staff (e.g., "Marshalls Education Federal Aid") and examine all the citations filed under this heading. The University of Hawai'i Library is moving to a new web based catalog (fall 2000), and in the new setup the index will remain a separate database.

Another crucial factor in searching the index is the need to be aware of spellings used: Ponape rather than Pohnpei; Palau rather than Belau; Truk rather than Chuuk; Marshalls for Marshall Islands. One should also note that various spellings exist (both in the archives and in general literature, e.g., Enewetak once given as Enewetok). The safest measure in most cases is to search under all variants known for a given place name.

7. The construction of the index and the nature of the library's current online catalog (as of May 2000) does allow for modifying a search by date. For example, one can stipulate that the search retrieve only documents related to Peleliu that appeared after 1970. The system used in preparing the original data entry often gives a span of years covered by a file or set of files (1958–1975). The index recognizes the first year cited in the category of "year of publication," which would eliminate some pertinent records from the search results. Because of this difficulty, caution is necessary when utilizing modified searches.

8. Elbert D. Thomas was the first civilian high commissioner of the Trust Territory of the Pacific Islands. He served as a United States senator for eighteen years (Democrat, Utah) and in 1951 was appointed to the position of high commissioner by Presi-

dent Truman. He took up the post at Trust Territory headquarters in Honolulu. A former Mormon missionary to Japan, Thomas earned a Ph.D. from the University of California and taught political science at the University of Utah. Thomas died suddenly in 1953 at age sixty-nine.

9. For technical details of the scanning project, see Chantiny 1993.

10. The article "Online Access to the Trust Territory Archives Photograph Collection" was published both in *Contemporary Pacific* (1995) and *PARBICA Panorama* (1995), addressing different audiences.

11. The Trust Territory Archives was a major source for David Hanlon's recent work, *Remaking Micronesia: Discourses on Development in a Pacific Territory, 1944–1982* (1998). Trust Territory photographs have appeared in locally produced histories of the Northern Mariana Islands and Palau, as well as in Father Francis X. Hezel's *Strangers in Their Own Land: A Century of Colonial Rule in the Caroline and Marshall Islands* (1995) and Kiste and Marshall's *American Anthropology in Micronesia* (1999).

12. In the publication "Report on Fact Finding Advisory Mission South Pacific" (1989), Lindsay Cleland provides a detailed description of conditions as of 1987 in the various Micronesian archives. Various updates on the status of archives in Micronesia can be found in subsequent issues of *Pacific Archives Journal* and the *PARBICA Panorama* (newsletter).

13. McPhetres also indicates that this category was by far the largest in the project.

14. See note 1 for details on the agreement.

15. The documents that record the activities of the archives project are included as part of the microfilm records of the former Trust Territory Government.

16. In fact, the Republic of Palau's educational program has an extremely innovative curriculum development program that involves elementary school students gathering folklore, history, and photographs to create their own websites for use in local schools.

17. As discussed earlier, the index to the Trust Territory Archives has seen several incarnations, and the version currently being used by archives in the Micronesian nations is also the one at use at the library itself. Unfortunately, computer problems, equipment breakdowns, and other difficulties have prevented some of the archives from offering consistent availability of the index to local users. This is clear to our Pacific Collection staff, who have fielded numerous requests for assistance from government officials and private individuals. Using the web access is a possible solution, but the Internet costs may prohibit extensive searching for Micronesian users. This is an area where a more collaborative approach between the library and the individual archives could be extremely productive.

18. David Akin and Kathryn Creely (chapter 5) discuss the resource sharing through dissemination of microfiche of primary source materials from the Melanesian Archive at the University of California, San Diego.

19. It might be noted here that Yap State has been organizing its government archives, having had assistance from archivist John Wright of Honolulu, and more recently having secured the services of archivist Richard Overy, former national archivist of Kiribati. John Wright has also assisted with planning and developing the national archives of Palau.

20. The governments of the Micronesian nations and the University of Hawai'i formalized this relationship in the 1990 "Memorandum of Agreement between University of Hawai'i and Northern Marianas College Concerning the Index for the Trust Territory Archives" (identical agreements were signed between the University of Hawai'i and the Federated States of Micronesia, Marshall Islands, and Palau). A copy of these agreements is on file at the Pacific Collection, University of Hawai'i, Honolulu.

21. The set of microfilm was originally in the main facilities of the National Archives in Washington, D.C. It has recently moved to the College Park, Maryland, branch of the National Archives.

22. I learned that the National Archives staff receives one thousand inquiries per week, and that a six-to-eight-week time lag is common before one receives assistance. I was told that my query was referred to the military reference section, but over three months passed with no response to the original question as to the location of the Micronesian War Claims Records on film or paper. I hasten to add that once I was in touch with an archivist the assistance that I received was prompt, collegial and most helpful.

23. The library now has War Claims reels 241 and 244–76. According to the National Archives, reels 242–43 could not be reproduced (copied) because of poor quality film.

Chapter 8

1. The Native American Graves Protection and Repatriation Act (NAGPRA) of 1990 grew out of attempts by Native American peoples—including Native Hawaiians—to repatriate human remains for reburial. While the legislation establishes procedures for the return of human remains and funerary objects associated with those remains, it also extends repatriation to objects of cultural patrimony in general. For an excellent sketch of the genesis of NAGPRA and a discussion of issues surrounding its implementation, see Monroe 1997. The full text of NAGPRA is available at ArchNet, ⟨http://archnet.uconn.edu/archnet/topical/crm/usdocs/nagpra14.htm⟩.

2. Session report on the informal session held at the 1997 annual meeting of the Association for Social Anthropology in Oceania, Pensacola, Florida.

3. As of October 2001 the Bishop Museum Library databases can only be accessed through the University of Hawai'i's Online Public Access Catalog via telnet to ⟨telnet://uhcarl.lib.hawaii.edu⟩. A telnet connection can also be made from Hawai'i Voyager (University of Hawai'i Library's new gateway) at ⟨http://uhmanoa.lib.hawaii.edu⟩ or through the Bishop Museum's gateway at ⟨http://www.bishopmuseum.org/bishop/library/cat.html⟩.

4. Personal communication, 20 April 1999.

Chapter 9

1. *Kaualiki*, "council of chiefs," was a phrase we commonly heard used for the then-disbanded chiefly council during our work in the 1970s and 1980s. By the mid 1990s, this group had been reestablished and relegitimized with seven members and was referred to obliquely as *te toko fitu*, literally "the seven." The reigning chief himself is currently known as *pulefenua*, "leader of the community." The terms used to describe

the traditional leadership roles have evolved in deference to the Tuvalu church's view that *aliki* (chief) is a word best reserved today for the Lord Jesus, God, as it has been used in the recently translated Tuvalu Bible. In 1996, the seven members of the chiefly group included representatives of the seven existing chiefly lineages plus an eighth individual selected to serve as "speaker" for the member chosen as reigning chief. More detail on the traditional system is provided in K. Chambers 1984. Contemporary developments are described in Chambers and Chambers 2001.

2. We have found it difficult to avoid the word "tradition" in this chapter, though we are aware of its semantic burden and reified quality. The Nanumean phrase is *tuu Nanumea* (Nanumean customs) or *tuu mo aganuu* (customs and traditions, the latter phrase a probable Samoan borrowing).

3. Leach (1961, 2) also inveighed against "butterfly collecting," a pejorative term he applied to cultural comparisons that were used to produce typological classifications rather than the analytical generalizations that he believed were necessary to move anthropological understandings productively forward. Our use of the metaphor here is slightly different from his.

4. Because each set, consisting of thirty-two 24" by 36" sheets, cost over 100 dollars U.S. to reproduce and was heavy and bulky to transport, we were only able to bring three copies with us, one as a working set for our use and two as sets for presentation to the community.

5. Tuvalu established its own local internet service provider late in 1999, allowing residents of Funafuti access to the world's digital electronic media. Several Tuvalu-focused web pages function as information and "chat room" services for the growing Tuvaluan population resident abroad, some of them publishing edited versions of scholarly and popular work by Tuvaluans and expatriates. Of note are *Tuvalu Online*, maintained by an expatriate–Tuvaluan couple living overseas ⟨http:// members.nbci.com / tuvaluonline⟩; *Jane's Tuvalu Home Page* maintained by Jane Resture, a Tuvaluan living overseas, at ⟨http:// members.nbci.com / __XMCM / janeresture / tuvalu2 / tuvalu__home__page.htm /⟩; and *Tuvalu.tv*, the Tuvalu government's site at ⟨http://www.tuvalu.tv⟩.

Chapter 10

1. Suzanne Falgout's chapter in this volume contextualizes the presence of American anthropologists in Micronesia during the post–World War II period.

2. According to Weckler, Raymond Murphy, a geographer from Clark University who spent seven weeks on Mokil as part of his fieldwork for the CIMA project, preferred to work alone rather than collaborate with Weckler and Bentzen. I am not aware of any instance in which his published work or unpublished CIMA report was repatriated to the atoll. His original report is, however, located in the Micronesian-Pacific Collection of the Community College of Micronesia, Palikir, Pohnpei. Hence Mokilese seeking higher education at this institution do indeed have access to his work.

3. In keeping my promise of confidentiality to the Mokilese people, all names that I use in this chapter are pseudonyms. The names quoted from the CIMA reports and film *Mokil* are real names that belong to living and deceased members of the Mokilese community.

4. Anthony Lord was a graduate student in the Anthropology Department at California State College, Long Beach, when he conducted fieldwork on Mokil in the late 1960s and early 1970s. I corresponded with him while I was in the field and learned that he has in his possession the field notes produced by Joseph Weckler. Apparently, Weckler's wife gave her deceased husband's notes to Lord before he went to Mokil. My correspondence with Lord makes for an interesting subtext to the issue of repatriation. Anthony Lord terminated our correspondence after I made a series of attempts in writing to acquire the notes in his possession. My first requests were gentle and cautious, suggesting that the interests of scholarship (including my own) would be well served by archiving the notes and making them available. His cool response prompted increasingly firm requests that went unanswered. I have since sent letters to which no responses have been forthcoming. I have contacted the wife of Joseph Weckler, but she could offer no assistance in acquiring her husband's field notes. She does not recall giving them to Lord. Here the issue of repatriation takes a new guise, as one anthropologist attempts to obtain the data of another that is held hostage by a third party.

5. Alan Howard's chapter in this volume discusses the "heteroglossic" character of anthropologist Gordon Macgregor's field notes on Rotuma. These field notes contain information gathered from multiple consultants with a variety of viewpoints.

6. Mary McCutcheon (personal correspondence) asked if there were individuals who cooperated with my inquiries in the hope of gaining future leverage in disputes from documentation resulting from my work. Indeed, my friend and informant Toby told me that two men who were quite cooperative had lied about their land holdings. He pointed out that their willingness to cooperate was linked to their hope that my maps would feature their names on parcels of land owned by others, or land to which they have a usufruct claim through corporate ownership.

7. It is almost certain that Mokilese living in Pohnpei have employed the realization of a pan-Mokilese past, or heritage, in asserting their identity in opposition to other ethnic groups. This does not mean that such a "historical consciousness" is dependent on historical documentation for validation. Further, Mokilese representations of their collective past do not constitute a monolithic historical consciousness that only allows for a unified portrait of the past. Mokilese representations of the past are responses to present social needs and conditions varying greatly across time and place.

8. This chapter does not directly consider the reasons why the CIMA researchers emphasized interpersonal and interfamilial strife, nor does it question the accuracy of the reports. As aforementioned, land tenure was the focus of Bentzen and Weckler's collaborative effort. Land was an important topic of study among the postwar researchers in Micronesia who participated in projects funded by the U.S. Naval Department. The United States Trust Territory administration was concerned with establishing general guidelines for use in court decisions on land issues (Falgout 1995, 107). Bentzen describes how his initial fieldwork guided the decision to make land the focus of the film *Mokil*: "From the fieldwork already done it became apparent that the most serious problem of the people of Mokil was the pressure of population on the land. Using this as a central theme we wrote a script that developed the way of life of the people, their close dependence on the land, the high degree of cooperation and social integration found within their economy, and the conflicts and dissensions that de-

velop as a result of their limited resources" (Bentzen 1949, 2). The imbalance between the portrayal of cooperation and the portrayal of conflict is noticeable. The negative assessments of the film and the reports articulated by Mokilese with whom I spoke indicate that the stories of strife and community dissension outweigh the positive images of cooperation and assistance.

Had the reports glossed over the conflicts surrounding land tenure, their acceptance among Mokilese would be questionable, nonetheless, due to the necessity of maintaining a flexible and negotiable history of land transfers.

9. Linnekin and Poyer (1990) discuss the range of Pacific identity schemes, arguing that "Mendelian" identities (i.e., based on a model of biological inheritance) emerge during the creation of ethnicities in arenas of increasing politicization. Briefly put, the process, which is well documented in the ethnicity / nationalism, identity, and *"kastom"* literature, involves an inversion of the intrusive, ideological structures of colonialism in contexts of political contestation and the reification of "tradition," or a reclamation of a precolonial past (see Thomas 1992). This process necessitates both a deconstruction of Western ideology and an objectification of the past along Western epistemological lines in the reformulation of identity. Unfortunately, ethnicity that emerges from this process "may conflict with the contingent and situational character of indigenous cultural identity" (Linnekin and Poyer 1990, 13) and limit personal action. This way, Oceanic people's cultural identity "that privileges environment, behavior, and situational flexibility over descent, innate characteristics, and unchanging boundaries" (Linnekin and Poyer 1990, 6) is confined within a rigid, delimiting framework with precisely defined margins.

10. The word *rosros* is an intensive reduplication of the word *ros*, meaning "darkness." *Rosros* is literally translated in the *Mokilese-English Dictionary* as "pagan" (Harrison and Albert 1977, 79). It is used to describe the culture and people of Mokil during the pre-Christian past—the "dark" age of immorality and ignorance. This dichotomy between the dark, pagan past and the enlightened, Christian present is a common product of missionization in the region. In Sapwuahfik and Pohnpei, *rotorot* is the equivalent to *rosros*. For a similar use of this metaphor in Pohnpei State, FSM, see Poyer 1993, 224 (Sapwuahfik); Falgout 1984 (Pohnpei); Bernart 1977 (Pohnpei).

11. Elsewhere in the Pacific, "traditions" that erase indigenous diversity have been invoked to empower the disenfranchised and stem the overwhelming tide of colonial domination. Political movements in Hawai'i (Linnekin 1983, 1990, 1991, 1992), New Zealand (Dominy 1990; Hanson 1989; Sinclair 1990), Island Melanesia (Keesing and Tonkinson 1982), and Australia (Berndt 1977; Jones and Hill-Burnett 1982; Tonkinson 1990) employ models of a shared cultural past that legitimize present political unity among subordinate minorities. This process of politicizing identity requires the objectification of shared traditions and the validation of those traditions' authenticity. In the words of Nicholas Thomas, the genesis of shared tradition involves "reactive objectification" (1992), or the reification of models of behavior in opposition to externally imposed constraints. Validation of traditions that have been "invented," reconstituted, or resurrected may necessitate the use of anthropological data gathered by non-indigenous "authorities" (Feinberg 1995, 94; see also Adams 1995). Unfortunately, the codification of anthropological objectifications of past social relations can result in the

creation of a "museum culture," the boundaries of which are rigid, inflexible, and much less accommodating than identity based on social action (Larcom 1990, 188).

12. Mokil Atoll today is the usual residence of a very small number of Mokilese. According to the *1994 FSM Census of Population and Housing*, 209 people list Mokil as their "place of usual residence." All but one of the residents, a Pohnpeian, are Mokilese (Pohnpei State Government 1996, 7). It is difficult to determine what percentage of the total Mokilese "ethnic" population resides on Mokil because there are no reliable estimates of the number of Mokilese living abroad. Although the *1994 FSM Census of Population and Housing* does include tabulations based on "ethnicity," Mokil is lumped with Pingelap. According to the census, there are 2,745 people living in the FSM who identify themselves as Mokilese or Pingelapese, 2,428 of whom are five years of age or older. Among those in this category who are five years of age and older, 1,112 speak Mokilese as their first language (Pohnpei State Government 1996, 76). Language does not necessarily indicate ethnicity, but because this table cross-references ethnicity with language, it is probable that those who listed Mokilese as their first language also consider themselves to be of Mokilese ethnicity. Pingelapese is the only other ethnic group to which they could possibly assign themselves. The number of Mokilese living in the FSM may be even larger in light of the fact that of all FSM residents five years of age and older included in the census survey, 1,419 claim that the Mokilese language is their first language (Pohnpei State Government 1996, 59). The same census indicates that 1,565 people five years of age and older claim that Mokilese is the language "usually spoken at home" (Pohnpei State Government 1996, 59). Judging from these numbers, it should be apparent that Mokil Atoll is home to only a very small percent of the total Mokilese population, the majority of which live on Pohnpei.

13. An absentee is here defined as anyone who has a usufruct or ownership claim to land on Mokil, but whose primary residence is abroad. There is undoubtedly a great deal of circular migration to and from Mokil Atoll, but data from the "Pohnpei State Detailed Tables" of the *1994 FSM Census of Population and Housing* suggest that atoll residents have maintained residences on Mokil for relatively stable time periods. Of the 209 people who usually reside on Mokil, 35 percent, or 73 individuals, have previously resided elsewhere (Pohnpei State Government 1996, 38). Of the 73 individuals who previously resided elsewhere, 52 claimed to have been living on Mokil for over five years, 10 said they moved back to Mokil between two and five years prior to the census, 4 moved back between one and two years prior, 2 moved back between six months and one year prior, and 2 claimed that they returned within the six months preceding the administration of the census. So, despite the fact that 35 percent of the usual Mokil residents have lived elsewhere, the majority of these people (70 percent) have lived on Mokil for at least the past five years.

14. Data from the *1994 FSM Census of Population and Housing* provide indirect evidence in support of Pete's contention. There are 1,741 persons five years of age and older included in the census who cite Pingelapese as their usual language (Pohnpei State Government 1996, 76). Although language does not an ethnicity make, it gives an idea of the number of people who might consider themselves members of a particular language-speaking group. The tables also demonstrate that 1,043 people list Pingelap as their municipality of legal residence (Pohnpei State Government 1996, 111). Although

1,565 citizens of FSM five years of age and older included in the census are listed as usually speaking Mokilese at home, only 606 people are official residents of Mokil (Pohnpei State Government 1996, 111). Many more persons of Mokilese parentage have established legal residence in Sokehs, Kolonia, and other districts of Pohnpei where they vote not as Mokilese, but as constituents of their own district of residence.

15. Land tenure on Mokil was and is extremely complicated. The transfer history of each parcel, the status of a parcel's owner, and many other issues factor into the ability of owners to alienate land from others. After studying the CIMA reports and discussing the land plot histories with my informants, I am convinced that individuals had a much greater control over the use and disposal of land during the mid twentieth century than they do at present.

Chapter 11

1. This quote is taken from the "Bellagio Declaration," which was written during the Bellagio Conference on Cultural Agency / Cultural Authority. Organized by Peter Jaszi and Martha Woodmansee, the conference brought together an international group of academics, environmentalists, anthropologists, authors, publishers, and legal scholars, among others, to discuss the impact of intellectual property on their communities and professional fields. The entire "Bellagio Declaration" is published in James Boyle's book *Shamans, Software, and Spleens: Law and the Construction of the Information Society* (1996, 192–200).

2. Quoted from the U.S. Copyright Office, Library of Congress' web page, ⟨http:// lcweb.loc.gov / copyright / fls / fl100.htm⟩), accessed on 25 February 1999.

3. As pointed out by Falgout (chapter 6), the concept of "cultural property" is in itself a complicated and potentially contested issue.

4. The singer's Amis name is Difang, while Kuo Ying-nan is his Chinese name. I have used the Chinese name here because it is the one used for the legal proceedings. Likewise, his wife's Amis name is Ignay and Kuo Shin-chu is her Chinese name.

5. A recent article in *RhythmMusic* reported that the CD sold over two million copies (Keating 1998, 14). However, a website site operated by Sony, ⟨http:// www.sonymusic.fr / DeepForest / discography.html⟩, reported that it sold three million copies worldwide.

6. In romanizing Chinese personal names, I use the spelling that the parties involved used most often. For example, following his own personal preference, the ethnomusicologist's name appears as "Hsu Tsang-houei" rather than "Hsu Chang-hui" (following the Wade-Giles romanization system) or "Xu Changhui" (following the pinyin spelling). In cases where I am unfamiliar with an individual's preference, I use pinyin romanization.

7. Some of the materials, including the Kuos' recordings, were rereleased in CD format by Taiwan's Crystal Record company in 1994, but have since gone out of print.

8. E-mail from Pierre Bois of the Maison des Cultures du Monde to the author, dated 23 October 1998.

9. One of the song's titles in the Amis language is "Balafang." The song is sung in a number of different contexts, however, and its title changes accordingly. For example,

when accompanying drinking, it is called "The Drinking Song," and when friends re-unite, it is called "The Song of Reunion" (Chen 1997b, 65).

10. Interview with Huang Hsiu-lan, 15 June 1998, Taipei, Taiwan.

11. Ibid.

12. Li Taikang generously shared a photocopy of this letter with me. The letter, dated 6 July 1995, was written by Anja Schiegl to Renata Huang, a reporter for the *China Post*.

13. Li Taikang generously shared a photocopy of this letter with me. The letter, dated 18 July 1995, was written by Jürgen Thürnau to Renata Huang, a reporter for the *China Post*.

14. Retrieved from the Tower Records website on 9 June 1999, ⟨http://www.towerrecords.com/product.asp?pfid=1184738⟩.

15. The firm was Trans World International based in London.

16. Interview with Kuo Ying-nan, Kuo Shin-chu, and others, 22 June 1998, Taidong, Taiwan.

17. The CD is entitled *Taiwan yuanzhumin yinyue jishi, 2: Ameizude fuyin yinyue* [The Music of the Aborigines on Taiwan Island, Vol. 2: Polyphonic Music of the Amis Tribe] (Wind Records TCD-1502).

18. The CD *Polyphonic Music of the Amis Tribe* won the Best Album award in the 1993 Tri-Pod competition sponsored by the Government Information Office of the Republic of China on Taiwan.

19. Interview with Kuo Ying-nan, Kuo Shin-chu, and others, 22 June 1998, Taidong, Taiwan.

20. Local artists who have used samples of Wu's field recordings include Ju Toupi. A brief sample from Wu's CD of Yami music—*Taiwan yuanzhumin yinyue jishi, 3: Yameizu zhi ge* [The Music of the Aborigines on Taiwan Island, Vol. 3: The Songs of the Yami Tribe] (Wind Records TCD-1503)—is heard on track three of Deep Forest's second CD, *Boheme* (Columbia 478623.2).

21. Interview with Li Taikang, 13 June 1998, Taipei, Taiwan.

22. Interview with David Fan, 4 June 1998, Taipei, Taiwan.

23. The album, *Circle of Life* (Magic Stone MSD030), became popular in both Taiwan and Japan. According to an article in a Taiwanese newspaper, the CD has sold 50,000 to 60,000 copies in Japan alone (*Zhongguo Shibao*, 5 July 1999, p. 19).

24. Interview with Huang Hsiu-lan, 15 June 1998, Taipei, Taiwan.

25. The case—*Kuo Ying-nan, an individual, and Kuo Hsin-chu, an individual, Plaintiffs, v. Virgin Schallplatten GmbH, Mambo Music, Charisma Records of America, Capitol-EMI Music, Inc., Enigma, Michael Cretu, International Olympic Committee, Defendants*—was filed in the United States District Court for the Central District of California Western Division on 30 December 1997.

26. In her June 1998 interview with me in Taipei, lawyer Huang Hsiu-lan reported that her firm had hired a lawyer in France and planned to file a case there in the next several months.

27. Phone conversation with Emil Chang, 16 October 1998.

28. A detailed musical analysis shows the five or six commercial recordings of the

song are different enough to view them as unique. The recordings that are still available for purchase at the time of writing include (1) the Maison des Culture du Monde recording *Polyphonies vocales des aborigenes de Taiwan* (Inedit W 260011), 1989, track one; (2) a compilation of the field recordings of Wu Rung-Shun: *The Music of the Aborigines on Taiwan Island, vol 2: Polyphonic Music of the Amis Tribe* (Wind Records TCD-1502), 1993, track thirteen; (3) *Circle of Life* (Magic Stone MSD-030), 1998, track eleven; (4) *Pagcah kavalan* (Crystal Records CIRD 1026–2), 1994, tracks two and five. Of these, numbers 1 and 2 are readily available in the U.S. Number 3 can be ordered through the following website: ⟨www.imarnet.com / rockEN / album.asp?sku=0887⟩ (accessed 1 June 1999). Number 4 is only available in Taiwan.

29. Some of the most important early scholarship dedicated to the study of composition and creativity in nonliterate societies was conducted by Albert Lord (1960) and Milman Parry (1971) in their studies of oral epic traditions. Their scholarship demonstrated that artists operating in an oral tradition draw upon a large body of formulae from which they construct their unique compositions.

30. The legal newspaper, *The Recorder*, reported that "By settling out of court, the record company has snuffed out the prospect of a judicial finding damaging to the record industry" (Sandburg 1999, 11). In other words, this case did not make any changes to current laws. However, one of Kuos' lawyers, Huang Hsiu-lan, told me during an interview in Taipei in August 1999 that she believes that the recording industry will be more careful in their use of aboriginal music in the future as a result of the case.

31. Phone conversation with E. Patrick Ellisen, 17 June 1999.

32. "Guo Yingnan jiangshe jiangxuejin." *Zhongyang Ribao*, 8 July 1999, 13.

33. "Guo Yingnan manyi zai you shengzhinian kandao jieguo," *Zhongguo Shibao*, 8 July 1999, 19.

34. Interview with Kuo Ying-nan, Kuo Shin-chu, and others, 22 June 1998, Taidong, Taiwan.

35. Ibid.

36. Phone conversation with Emil Chang, 16 October 1998.

References

AAA (American Anthropological Association). 1971 (1986). "Statements on Ethics: Principles of Professional Responsibility." ⟨www.aaanet.org/stmts/ethstmnt .htm⟩, accessed 5 May 2000. Arlington, Va.: American Anthropological Association.
——. 1998. "Code of Ethics." ⟨www.aaanet.org/committees/ethics/ethcode.htm⟩, accessed 5 May 2000. Arlington, Va.: American Anthropological Association.
——. 1999. "American Anthropological Association Response to OMB Circular A-110." ⟨www.aaanet.org/gvt/ombresp.htm⟩, accessed on 24 May 2000. Arlington, Va.: American Anthropological Association.
Aboriginal and Torres Strait Islander Commission. 1999. "1998–99 Annual Report." ⟨www.atsic.gov.au⟩, accessed 18 May 2000. Woden ACT, Australia: Aboriginal and Torres Strait Islander Commission.
Adams, Kathleen M. 1995. "Making-up the Toraja? The Appropriation of Tourism, Anthropology, and Museums for Politics in Upland Sulawesi, Indonesia." *Ethnology* 34, no. 2:143–53.
Akin, David. 1994. "Cultural Education at the Kwaio Cultural Centre." In *Culture, Kastom, Tradition: Developing Cultural Policy in Melanesia,* edited by Lamont Lindstrom and Geoffrey White. Suva, Fiji: Institute of Pacific Studies, University of the South Pacific.
——. 1999. "Cash and Shell Money in Kwaio, Solomon Islands." In *Money and Modernity: State and Local Currencies in Melanesia,* edited by David Akin and Joel Robbins. Pittsburgh: University of Pittsburgh Press.
——. n.d. "Ancestral Vigilance and the Corrective Conscience in Kwaio, Solomon Islands."Manuscript in preparation.
Allardyce, W. L. 1885–1886. "Rotooma and the Rotoomans." In *Proceedings of Queensland Branch of the Geographical Society of Australia,* 1st sets. Brisbane: Watson, Ferguson and Company.
Allen, William. 1895. "Rotuma." In *Report of Australasian Association of the Advancement of Science.*
American Folklife Center. 1983. *Cultural Conservation: The Protection of Cultural Heritage in the United States: A Study.* Coordinated by O. H. Loomis. Publication of the American Folklife Center, no. 10. Washington, D.C.: Library of Congress.
Archaeological Resources Protection Act. 1979. *U.S. Code.* Vol. 16, sec. 470bb.
Ashkenazi, Michael. 1997. "Informant Networks and Their Anthropologists." *Human Organization* 56:471–78.
ATSILIRN (Aboriginal and Torres Strait Islander Library and Information Resource Network). 1995. "Aboriginal and Torres Strait Islander Protocols for Libraries,

Archives, and Information Services." Compiled by Alex Byrne, Alan Garwood, Heather Moorcroft, and Alan Barnes. ⟨www.ntu.edu.au / library / protocol.html⟩, accessed on 24 May 2000. Queen Victoria Terrace, Australia: Australian Library and Information Association.

Barnett, Homer G. 1956. *Anthropology in Administration*. Evanston, Ill.: Row, Peterson and Company.

Barrere, Dorothy B., Mary Kawena Pukui, and Marion Kelly, eds. 1980. *Hula: Historical Perspectives*. Pacific Anthropological Records, no. 30. Honolulu: Department of Anthropology, Bernice P. Bishop Museum.

Benét, Stephen V. 1928. *John Brown's Body*. New York: Doubleday.

Bennett, George. 1831. "A Recent Visit to Several of the Polynesian Islands." *United Services Journal* 33:198–202, 473–82.

Bentzen, Conrad. 1949. "Land and Livelihood on Mokil: An Atoll in the Eastern Carolines." Part 2 of Coordinated Investigation of Micronesian Anthropology. Final Report, no. 11. Unpublished manuscript. Los Angeles: University of Southern California.

——. 1950. *Mokil*, 16mm, 57 minutes. Directed and produced by Melvin Sloan. Los Angeles: Department of Cinema, University of Southern California. Rereleased in 1986 on videocassette. Aptos, Calif.: Special Purpose Films.

Berman, Marshall. 1982. *All That Is Solid Melts into Air: The Experience of Modernity*. New York: Sal and Schuster.

Bernart, Luelen. 1977. *The Book of Luelen: A Ponapean Manuscript*. Translated and edited by John L. Fischer, Saul H. Riesenberg, and Marjorie G. Whiting. Pacific History Series, no. 8. 2 vols. Canberra, Australia: Australian National University Press; Honolulu: University of Hawai'i Press.

Berndt, Ronald M. 1977. "Aboriginal Identity: Reality or Mirage?" In *Aborigines and Change: Australia in the 1970s*, edited by Ronald M. Berndt. Atlantic Highlands, N.J.: Humanities Press.

Beteille, André. 1998. "The Idea of Indigenous People." *Current Anthropology* 39, no. 2:187–91.

Bishop Museum Audio Recording Collections. 1997. *Na Leo Hawai'i Kahiko: The Master Chanters of Hawai'i / Songs of Old Hawai'i*. Directed by Elizabeth Tatar. MACD 2043. Honolulu: Mountain Apple Record Company. Originally published as *Na Leo Hawai'i Kahiko: Voices of Old Hawai'i*, 1981. 2 LPs, ARCS-1.

Boddam-Whetham, J. W. 1876. *Pearls of the Pacific*. London: Hurst and Blackett.

Bolton, Lissant. 1994. "Bifo Yumi Ting Se Samting Nating." In *Culture, Kastom, Tradition: Developing Cultural Policy in Melanesia*, edited by Lamont Linstrom and Geoffrey M. White. Suva, Fiji: Institute of Pacific Studies, University of the South Pacific.

Bonnemaison, Joel. 1984. "The Tree and the Canoe: Roots and Mobility in Vanuatu Societies." *Pacific Viewpoint* 25, no. 2:117–51.

Borofsky, Robert. 1987. *Making History: Pukapukan and Anthropopological Constructions of Knowledge*. Cambridge: Cambridge University Press.

Boyle, James. 1996. *Shamans, Software, and Spleens: Law and the Construction of the Information Society*. Cambridge: Harvard University Press.

Brown, Michael F. 1998. "Can Culture Be Copyrighted?" *Current Anthropology* 39, no. 2: 193–222.

Burt, Ben. 1998. "Writing Local History in Solomon Islands." In *Pacific Answers to Western Hegemony: Cultural Practices of Identity Construction*, edited by Jürg Wassmann. Oxford and New York: Berg.

——. 2001. Introduction to *A Solomon Islands Chronicle: As Told by Samuel Alasa'a, with Contributions from the Kwara'ae Chiefs*, edited by Ben Burt and Michael Kwa'ioloa. London: British Museum Press.

Campbell, Alan. 1996. "Tricky Tropes: Styles of the Popular and the Pompous." In *Popularizing Anthropology*, edited by Jeremy MacClancy and Chris McDonaugh. London: Routledge.

Carroll, Vern. 1975. "The Population of Nukuoro in Historical Perspective." In *Pacific Atoll Populations*, edited by Vern Carroll. ASAO Monograph Series, no. 3. Honolulu: University of Hawai'i Press.

Chambers, Anne. 1975. *Nanumea Report: A Socio-Economic Study of Nanumea Atoll, Tuvalu.* Rural Socio-Economic Survey of the Gilbert and Ellice Islands. Wellington, New Zealand: Victoria University, Department of Geography.

——. 1984. *Nanumea, Atoll Economy: Social Change in Kiribati and Tuvalu.* Rev. ed. Development Studies Centre series, report no. 6. Canberra, Australia: Australian National University Press.

Chambers, Keith S. 1984. "Heirs of Tefolaha: Tradition and Social Organization in Nanumea, Tuvalu." Ph.D. diss., University of California, Berkeley.

Chambers, Keith S., and Anne Chambers. 2001. *Unity of Heart: Culture and Change in a Polynesian Atoll Society.* Prospect Heights, Ill.: Waveland Press.

Chantiny, Martha. 1993. "Incorporating Digitized Images in the UHCARL PAC Online Catalog." *Library Software Review* 12, no. 1:22–26.

Chen Shumei. 1997a. "Ami Sounds Scale Olympian Heights." Vol. 3 of *The Struggle for Renaissance: Taiwan's Indigenous Culture.* Taipei: Sinorama Magazine.

——. 1997b. "True Feelings from the Bosom of Nature." Vol. 3 of *The Struggle for Renaissance: Taiwan's Indigenous Culture.* Taipei: Sinorama Magazine.

Churchward, C. Maxwell. 1940. *Rotuman Grammar and Dictionary.* Sydney: Australasian Medical Publishing.

Cleland, Lindsay. 1989. "Report on Fact Finding Mission South Pacific, Part 2, 13 March–16 April 1987." *Pacific Archives Journal* 8:25–60.

Clifford, James. 1983. "On Ethnographic Authority." *Representations* 1:118–46.

——. 1988. *The Predicament of Culture: Twentieth Century Ethnography, Literature, and Art.* Cambridge: Harvard University Press.

——. 1990. "Notes on (Field)Notes." In *Fieldnotes: The Making of Anthropology*, edited by Roger Sanjek. Ithaca, N.Y.: Cornell University Press.

Cohn, B. S. 1996. *Colonialism and Its Forms of Knowledge: The British in India.* Princeton: Princeton University Press.

Copyright Act. 1976. *U.S. Code.* Vol. 17, secs. 101–810.

Coombe, Rosemary. 1997. "Assertion of Rights in Cultural Environments." *Anthropology Newsletter* 37:25.

Counts, Dorothy A. 1982. *The Tales of Laupu: Stories from Kaliai, West New Britain.* Told by J. M. Laupu, B. S. Laupu, and M. Sapanga. Boroko, Papua New Guinea: Institute of Papua New Guinea Studies.

Counts, Dorothy A., and David R. Counts. 1992. "They're My Family Now." *Anthropologica* 34:153–82.

———. 1996. *Over the Next Hill: An Ethnography of RVing Seniors in North America.* Peterborough, Ontario: Broadview Press.

Creely, Kathryn. 1992. "Melanesian Studies at the University of California, San Diego." *The Contemporary Pacific: A Journal of Island Affairs* 4, no. 1:209–14.

Crocombe, Ron G. 1971. "The Cook, Niue, and Tokelau Islands: Fragmentation and Emigration." In *Land Tenure in the Pacific*, edited by Ron G. Crocombe. London: Oxford University Press.

———. 1994a. "Trends and Issues in Pacific Land Tenures." In *Land Issues in the Pacific*, edited by Ron G. Crocombe and M. Meleisea. Suva, Fiji: Institute of Pacific Studies, University of the South Pacific.

———. 1994b. "Cultural Policies in the Pacific Islands." In *Culture, Kastom, Tradition: Developing Cultural Policy in Melanesia*, edited by Lamont Lindstrom and Geoffrey M. White. Suva, Fiji: Institute of Pacific Studies, University of the South Pacific.

Danielson, E. 1989. "The Ethics of Access." *American Archivist* 52:52–62.

Dariawo, Ben, Titus Pameko, Daniel Meian, Mark Nawokre, Joseph Simbaisipta, Joel Amburi, Wevin Meyande, Kevin Kambarumo, and Narson Aguleko. 1999. "Breach of Contract?" *Anthropology Newsletter* 40, no. 7:4.

Dillon, Peter. 1829. *Voyage in the South Seas.* Vol. 1. London: Hurst Chance.

Dominy, Michele D. 1990. "Maori Sovereignty: A Feminist Invention of Tradition." In *Cultural Identity and Ethnicity in the Pacific*, edited by Jocelyn Linnekin and Lin Poyer. Honolulu: University of Hawai'i Press.

Dorsey, J. O. 1884. "Omaha Sociology." *Annual Report, Bureau of Ethnology, Smithsonian Institution* 3:211–370.

Elbert, S. H., and Mary Kawena Pukui. 1986. Hawaiian Dictionary. Rev. and enlarged ed. Honolulu: University of Hawai'i Press.

Emerson, Nathaniel B. 1909. *Unwritten Literature of Hawaii: The Sacred Songs of the Hula.* Bureau of American Ethnology Bulletin, no. 38. Washington, D.C.: GPO.

Falgout, Suzanne. 1984. "Persons and Knowledge in Ponape." Ph.D. diss., University of Oregon.

———. 1992. "Hierarchy versus Democracy: Two Strategies for the Management of Knowledge in Pohnpei." In *Transforming Knowledge: Western Schooling in the Pacific*, edited by Suzanne Falgout and Paula Levin. Theme issue of *Anthropology and Education Quarterly* 23, no. 1:30–43.

———. 1995. "Americans in Paradise: Custom, Democracy, and Anthropology in Postwar Micronesia." In *Politics of Culture in the Pacific*, edited by Richard Feinberg and Laura Zimmer-Tamakoshi. Special issue of *Ethnology* 34, no. 2:99–111.

Fan Yangkun. 1994. *Minge caiji yundong' zhongde yuanzhumin zhuzu yinyue diaocha* [An investigation of the music of various aboriginal tribes from the "The Folk Song Collection Movement"]. *Taiwande Shengyin* [The sound of Taiwan] 1, no. 2:38–48.

Feinberg, Richard. 1995. Introduction to *Politics of Culture in the Pacific*, edited by

Richard Feinberg and Laura Zimmer-Tamakoshi. Special issue of *Ethnology* 34, no. 2:91–98.

Fernandez, James W. 1988. "Andalusia on Our Minds: Two Contrasting Places in Spain as Seen in a Vernacular Poetic Duel of the Late Nineteenth Century." *Cultural Anthropology* 3, no. 1:21–35.

Fifi'i, Jonathan. 1988. "World War Two and the Origins of Maasina Rule: One Kwaio View," translated and edited by David Akin. In *The Big Death: Solomon Islanders Remember World War II,* edited by Geoffrey M. White, David W. Gegeo, David Akin, and Karen Ann Watson-Gegeo. Suva, Fiji: Institute of Pacific Studies, University of the South Pacific.

——. 1989. *From Pig Theft to Parliament: My Life between Two Worlds.* Translated and edited by Roger M. Keesing. Suva, Fiji: Institute of Pacific Studies, University of the South Pacific; Honiara, Solomon Islands: Solomon Islands College of Higher Education.

First Congress of the Federated States of Micronesia. 1979. *Journal of the Second Regular Session,* October 24. Kolonia, Pohnpei: Office of the Speaker.

First International Conference on the Cultural and Intellectual Property Rights of Indigenous Peoples. 1993. "The Mataatua Declaration on Cultural and Intellectual Property Rights of Indigenous Peoples." ⟨www.tpk.govt.nz / mataatua / mataengl. htm⟩, accessed on 23 May 2000. Whakatane, New Zealand.

Firth, Raymond. 1968. "A Note on Descent Groups in Polynesia." In *Peoples and Cultures of the Pacific: An Anthropological Reader,* edited by Andrew P. Vayda. New York: Natural History Press.

Fischer, John L. (Jack). 1957. *The Eastern Carolines.* With the assistance of Ann M. Fischer. HRAF Behavior Science Monograph. New Haven, Conn.: Human Relations Area Files Press.

——. n.d. *Fieldnotes of John L. Fischer.* 3 vols. Museum Archives, ref. no. PAC.Po.2. Honolulu: Bernice P. Bishop Museum.

Fischer, John L., Saul H. Riesenberg, and Marjorie G. Whiting, trans. and eds. 1977. *Annotations to the "Book of Luelen: A Ponapean Manuscript."* Pacific History Series, no. 8. 2 vols. Canberra, Australia: Australian National University Press; Honolulu: University of Hawai'i Press.

Flinn, Juliana. 1992. *Diplomas and Thatch Houses: Asserting Tradition in a Changing Micronesia.* Ann Arbor, Mich.: University of Michigan Press.

Forbes, Litton. 1875. *Two Years in Fiji.* London: Longmans, Green, and Company.

Fortune, Reo F. 1932. *Sorcerers of Dobu: The Social Anthropology of the Dobu Islanders of the Western Pacific.* London: Routledge.

Fowler, Catherine. 1995. "Ethical Considerations." In *Preserving the Anthropological Record,* edited by Sydel Silverman and Nancy J. Parezo. 2d ed. New York: Wenner-Gren Foundation for Anthropological Research.

Frazer, Ian. 1997. "The Struggle for Control of Solomon Island Forests." In *Logging the Southwestern Pacific: Perspectives from Papua New Guinea, Solomon Islands, and Vanuatu,* edited by Kathleen Barlow and Steven Winduo. Special issue of *The Contemporary Pacific: A Journal of Island Affairs* 9, no. 1:39–72.

Freedom of Information Act. 1966. *U.S. Code.* Vol. 5, sec. 552.

Friedman, Jonathan. 2000. "Ethnography as a Social System: Parts, Wholes, and Holes." In *Ethnographic Artifacts: Challenges to a Reflexive Anthropology*, edited by Sjoerd R. Jaarsma and Marta A. Rohatynskyj. Honolulu: University of Hawai'i Press.

Friesen, Steven J. 1996. "The Origins of Lei Day: Festivity and the Construction of Ethnicity in the Territory of Hawaii." *History and Anthropology* 10:1–36.

Gallimore, Ronald, and Alan Howard. 1968. *Studies in a Hawaiian Community: Na Makamaka O Nanakuli.* Pacific Anthropological Reports, no. 1. Honolulu: Bishop Museum Press.

Gardiner, J. Stanley. 1898. "The Natives of Rotuma." *Journal of the Royal Anthropological Institute* 27:396–435, 457–524.

Gegeo, David W. 1994. "Kastom Nao Stretem Iumi: Views from Kwara'ae on Cultural Policy in Melanesia." In *Culture, Kastom, Tradition: Developing Cultural Policy in Melanesia*, edited by Lamont Linstrom and Geoffrey M. White. Suva, Fiji: Institute of Pacific Studies, University of the South Pacific.

George, Jones S. 1990. "Federated States of Micronesia Country Report." *Pacific Archives Journal* 9:25–32.

Gewertz, Deborah B., and Frederick K. Errington. 1991. *Twisted Histories, Altered Contexts: Representing the Chambri in World System.* Cambridge: Cambridge University Press.

Greenfield, J. 1995. *The Return of Cultural Treasures.* 2d ed. Cambridge: Cambridge University Press.

Gupta, Akhil, and James Ferguson. 1992. "Beyond 'Culture': Space, Identity, and the Politics of Difference." *Cultural Anthropology* 7, no. 1:6–23.

Hambruch, Paul. 1932–1936. *Ponape: Ergebnisse der Südsee Expedition, 1908–1910.* Edited by Georg Thilenius. 3 vols. Hamburg: Friederichsen, de Gruyter.

Handy, E. S. C., and Mary Kawena Pukui. 1958. *The Polynesian Family System in Ka-u, Hawaii.* Wellington, New Zealand: Polynesian Society.

Hanlon, David. 1992. "The Path Back to Pohnsakar: Luelen Bernart, His Book, and the Practice of History on Pohnpei." *ISLA: A Journal of Micronesian Studies* 1, no. 1:13–36.

——. 1998. *Remaking Micronesia: Discourses on Development in a Pacific Territory, 1944–1982.* Honolulu: University of Hawai'i Press.

Hanson, F. Allan. 1989. "The Making of the Maori: Cultural Invention and Its Logic." *American Anthropologist* 91:890–902.

Harrison, Sheldon P., and Salich Albert. 1977. *Mokilese-English Dictionary.* Honolulu: University of Hawai'i Press.

Herdt, Gilbert H. 1999. "Response to Dariawo." *Anthropology Newsletter* 40, no. 7:4.

Hezel, Francis X. 1995. *Strangers in Their Own Land: A Century of Colonial Rule in the Caroline and Marshall Islands.* Pacific Islands Monographs Series, no. 13. Honolulu: University of Hawai'i Press.

Hobsbawm, Eric, and Terence Ranger, eds. 1983. *The Invention of Tradition.* Cambridge: Cambridge University Press.

Howard, Alan. 1977. "Rotumans in Fiji: The Genesis of an Ethnic Group." In *Exiles and*

Migrants in Oceania, edited by Michael D. Lieber. Honolulu: University of Hawai'i Press.

——. 1988. "Hypermedia and the Future of Ethnography." *Cultural Anthropology* 3:304–15.

——. 1994. "History in Polynesia: Changing Perspectives and Current Issues." In *Politics, Tradition and Change in the Pacific,* edited by Paul van der Grijp and Toon van Meijl. Special issue of *Bijdragen tot de Taal-, Land- en Volkenkunde* [Journal of the Royal Institute of Linguistics and Anthropology] 149:646–60.

Hsu Mutsu. 1991. *Culture, Self, and Adaptation: The Psychological Anthropology of Two Malayo-Polynesian Groups in Taiwan.* Taipei: Institute of Ethnology, Academia Sinica.

Ii, J. P. 1959. *Fragments of Hawaiian History.* Translated by Mary Kawena Pukui. Honolulu: Bishop Museum Press.

Inia, Elizabeth K. M. 1998. *Fäeag 'Es Füaga: Rotuman Proverbs.* Suva, Fiji: Institute of Pacific Studies, University of the South Pacific.

Inia, Elizabeth K. M., Sofie Arnsten, Hans Schmidt, Jan Rensel, and Alan Howard. 1998. *A New Rotuman Dictionary.* Suva, Fiji: Institute of Pacific Studies, University of the South Pacific.

International Society of Ethnobiology. 1996. *Draft Code of Ethics and Standards of Practice of the International Society of Ethnobiology.* Nairobi, Kenya: Fifth International Congress of Ethnobiology.

Jaarsma, Sjoerd R. 1998. "Ethnography: Authority and 'Voice': Some Thoughts on the Changing Nature of Ethnography." In *Anthropology of Difference: Essays in Honour of Professor Arie de Ruijter,* edited by Selma van Londen and Els van Dongen. Utrecht, the Netherlands: ISOR.

——. 2001. "Conceiving New Guinea: Ethnography as a Phenomenon of Contact." In *In Colonial New Guinea: Anthropological Perspectives,* edited by Naomi McPherson. In Press. ASAO Monograph Series, no. 19. Pittsburgh: University of Pittsburgh Press.

Jaarsma, Sjoerd R., and Marta A. Rohatynskyj, eds. 2000. *Ethnographic Artifacts: Challenges to a Reflexive Anthropology.* Honolulu: University of Hawaii Press.

Jackson, Jean E. 1990. " 'I Am a Fieldnote': Fieldnotes as a Symbol of Professional Identity." In *Fieldnotes: The Making of Anthropology,* edited by Roger Sanjek. Ithaca, N.Y.: Cornell University Press.

Janke, Terri. 1998. "Our Culture, Our Future: Report on Australian Indigenous Cultural and Intellectual Property Rights." ⟨www.icip.lawnet.com.au / culture.pdf⟩, accessed 24 May 2000. Surrey Hills, New South Wales, Australia: Frankel and Company; Canberra, Australia: Aboriginal and Torres Strait Islander Commission.

Jarman, Robert. 1832. *Journal of a Voyage to the South Seas, in the Japan, Employed in the Sperm Whale Fishery, under the Command of Captain John May.* London: Longman and Company, and Charles Tilt.

Jones, Delmos J., and Jacquetta Hill-Burnett. 1982. "The Political Context of Ethnogenesis: An Australian Example." In *Aboriginal Power in Australia,* edited by M. Howard. St. Lucia, Australia: University of Queensland Press.

Kaeppler, Adrienne L. 1993. *The Hula Pahu: Hawaiian Drum Dances.* Vol. 1 of *Ha'a and*

Hula: Sacred Movements. Bishop Museum Bulletin in Anthropology, no. 3. Honolulu: Bishop Museum Press.

———. 1996. "Paradise Regained: The Role of Pacific Museums in Forging National Identity." In *Museums and the Making of "Ourselves": The Role of Objects in National Identity*, edited by Flora E. S. Kaplan. London: Leicester University Press.

Kamakau, Samuel Manaiakalani. 1961. *Ruling Chiefs of Hawaii*. Honolulu: Kamehameha Schools.

———. 1964. *Ka Po'e Kahiko / The People of Old*. Translated by Mary Kawena Pukui, edited by Dorothy B. Barrere. Bernice P. Bishop Museum Special Publication, no. 51. Honolulu: Bishop Museum Press.

———. 1976. *The Works of the People of Old / Na Hana a Ka Po'e Kahiko*. Translated by Mary Kawena Pukui, edited by Dorothy B. Barrere. Bernice P. Bishop Museum Special Publication, no. 61. Honolulu: Bishop Museum Press.

———. 1991. *Tales and Traditions of the People of Old / Na Mo'olelo a ka Po'e Kahiko*. Translated by Mary Kawena Pukui, edited by Dorothy B. Barrere. Honolulu: Bishop Museum Press.

Keating, M. 1998. "Deep Forest." *RhythmMusic* 7, no. 5:14–17.

Keesing, Roger M. 1982. "Kastom in Melanesia: An Overview." *Mankind* 13, no. 4:297–301.

———. 1989. "Creating the Past: Custom and Identity in the Contemporary Pacific." *The Contemporary Pacific: A Journal of Island Affairs* 1, nos. 1–2:19–42.

———. 1991. "Reply to Trask." *The Contemporary Pacific: A Journal of Island Affairs* 3, no. 1:168–171.

———. 1992. *Custom and Confrontation: The Kwaio Struggle for Cultural Autonomy*. Chicago: University of Chicago Press.

———. 1994. "Responsibilities of Long-Term Research." In *Culture, Kastom, Tradition: Developing Cultural Policy in Melanesia*, edited by Lamont Lindstrom and Geoffrey M. White. Suva, Fiji: Institute of Pacific Studies, University of the South Pacific.

Keesing, Roger M., and Peter Corris. 1980. *Lightning Meets the West Wind: The Malaita Massacre*. New York: Oxford University Press.

Keesing, Roger M., and Robert Tonkinson, eds. 1982. *Reinventing Traditional Culture: The Politics of Kastom in Island Melanesia*. Special Issue of *Mankind* 13, no. 4.

Kenworthy, Mary A., Eleanor King, Mary E. Ruwell, and Trudy van Houten, eds. 1985. *Preserving Field Records: Archival Techniques for Archaeologists and Anthropologists*. Philadelphia: University Museum, University of Pennsylvania.

Kierkegaard, Søren. 1967. *Søren Kierkegaard's Journals and Papers*. Vol. 1. Bloomington, Ind.: Indiana University Press.

Kiste, Robert C., and Suzanne Falgout. 1999. "Anthropology and Micronesia: The Context." In *American Anthropology in Micronesia: An Assessment*, edited by Robert C. Kiste and Mac Marshall. Honolulu: University of Hawai'i Press.

Kiste, Robert C., and Mac Marshall, eds. 1999. *American Anthropology in Micronesia: An Assessment*. Honolulu: University of Hawai'i Press.

Kuehling, Susanne. 1998. "The Name of the Gift: Ethics of Exchange on Dobu Island." Ph.D. diss., Australian National University.

Larcom, Joan. 1982. "The Invention of Convention." *Mankind* 13, no. 4:330–37.

——. 1990. "Custom by Decree: Legitimation Crisis in Vanuatu." In *Cultural Identity and Ethnicity in the Pacific*, edited by Jocelyn Linnekin and Lin Poyer. Honolulu: University of Hawai'i Press.

Leach, Edmund. 1961. *Rethinking Anthropology*. Monographs on Social Anthropology, no. 22. London: Athlone Press.

Leibowitz, Arnold H. 1989. *Defining Status: A Comprehensive Analysis of United States Territorial Relations*. Dordrecht: Kluwer Academic Publications.

Lepowsky, Maria. 1994a. "Writing for Many Audiences." *Anthropology Newsletter* 35, no. 8:48.

——. 1994b. "An Anthropologist in Media Land." *Anthropology Newsletter* 35, no. 9:27.

——. 1995. "Getting the Word Out." *Anthropology Newsletter* 36, no. 1:37, 47.

Lesson, René P. 1838–1839. *Voyage autour du monde . . . sur "La Coquille."* Paris: Pourrat Freres.

Lieber, Michael D. 1990. "Lamarckian Definitions of Identity on Kapingamarangi and Pohnpei." In *Cultural Identity and Ethnicity in the Pacific*, edited by Jocelyn Linnekin and Lin Poyer. Honolulu: University of Hawai'i Press.

Lindstrom, Lamont. 1994. "Traditional Cultural Policy in Melanesia (Kastom Polisi Long Kastom)." In *Culture, Kastom, Tradition: Developing Cultural Policy in Melanesia*, edited by Lamont Lindstrom and Geoffrey M. White. Suva, Fiji: Institute of Pacific Studies, University of the South Pacific.

Lindstrom, Lamont, and Geoffrey M. White. 1994a. "Cultural Policy," introduction to *Culture, Kastom, Tradition: Developing Cultural Policy in Melanesia*, edited by Lamont Lindstrom and Geoffrey M. White. Suva, Fiji: Institute of Pacific Studies, University of the South Pacific.

——. 1994b. *Culture, Kastom, Tradition: Developing Cultural Policy in Melanesia*. Suva, Fiji: Institute of Pacific Studies, University of the South Pacific.

Linnekin, Jocelyn. 1983. "Defining Tradition: Variations on the Hawaiian Identity." *American Ethnologist* 10:241–52.

——. 1985. *Children of the Land: Exchange and Status in a Hawaiian Community*. New Brunswick, N.J.: Rutgers University Press.

——. 1990. "The Politics of Culture in the Pacific." In *Cultural Identity and Ethnicity in the Pacific*, edited by Jocelyn Linnekin and Lin Poyer. Honolulu: University of Hawai'i Press.

——. 1991. "Cultural Invention and the Dilemma of Authority." *American Anthropologist* 93:446–49.

——. 1992. "On the Theory and Politics of Cultural Construction in the Pacific." *Oceania* 62:249–63.

Linnekin, Jocelyn, and Lin Poyer. 1990. Introduction to *Cultural Identity and Ethnicity in the Pacific*, edited by Jocelyn Linnekin and Lin Poyer. Honolulu: University of Hawai'i Press.

Lord, Albert B. 1960. *The Singer of Tales*. Cambridge: Harvard University Press.

Lucatt, Edward. 1851. *Rovings in the Pacific, 1837–49 . . . by a Merchant Long Resident in Tahiti*. Vol. 1. London: Longman, Brown, Green and Longman.

Lundsgaarde, Henry P. 1974. "Pacific Land Tenure in a Nutshell." In *Land Tenure in Oceania*, edited by Henry P. Lundsgaarde. ASAO Monograph Series, no. 2. Honolulu: University of Hawai'i Press.

MacClancy, Jeremy. 1996a. "Popularizing Anthropology." In *Popularizing Anthropology*, edited by Jeremy MacClancy and Chris McDonaugh. London: Routledge.

———. 1996b. "Fieldwork Styles." In *Popularizing Anthropology*, edited by Jeremy Mac-Clancy and Chris McDonaugh. London: Routledge.

Macdonald, Judith. 2000. "The Tikopia and 'What Raymond Said.'" In *Ethnographic Artifacts: Challenges to a Reflexive Anthropology*, edited by Sjoerd R. Jaarsma and Marta A. Rohatynskyj. Honolulu: University of Hawai'i Press.

MacDonald, Mary N. 2000. "Writing about Culture and Talking about God: Christian Ethnography in Melanesia." In *Ethnographic Artifacts: Challenges to a Reflexive Anthropology*, edited by Sjoerd R. Jaarsma and Marta A. Rohatynskyj. Honolulu: University of Hawai'i Press.

MacGregor, Gordon. 1932. "Fieldnotes on Culture and Physical Anthropology from Rotuma." ⟨www.hawaii.edu / oceanic / rotuma / os / MacGregor / MacGregor. html⟩, accessed 24 April 2000. Manuscript, storage case 3 (3 boxes). Honolulu: Bernice P. Bishop Museum.

Malinowski, Bronislaw. [1926] 1982. *Crime and Custom in Savage Society*. Totowa, N.J.: Littlefield, Adams and Company.

Malkki, Liisa. 1992. "National Geographic: The Rooting of Peoples and the Territorialization of National Identity Among Scholars and Refugees." *Cultural Anthropology* 7, no. 1:24–44.

Malo, David. 1951. *Hawaiian Antiquities (Moolelo Hawai'i)*. Translated by Nathaniel B. Emerson. 2d. ed. Bernice P. Bishop Museum Special Publication, no. 2. Honolulu: Bishop Museum Press.

———. 1996. *Ka Mo'olelo Hawai'i: Hawaiian Traditions*. Translated by M. N. Chun. N.p.: First People's Productions.

Marks, J. 1995. "Nude Posture Photos and Physical Anthropology." *Anthropology Newsletter* 36, no. 11:15.

McCall, Grant. 2000. "A Question of Audience: The Effects of What We Write." In *Ethnographic Artifacts: Challenges to a Reflexive Anthropology*, edited by Sjoerd R. Jaarsma and Marta A. Rohatynskyj. Honolulu: University of Hawai'i Press.

McNabb, Steven. 1995. "Social Research and Litigation: Good Intentions versus Good Ethics." *Human Organization* 54, no. 3:331–35.

McPhetres, Samuel F. 1992a. *The Practical User's Guide to the Trust Territory Archives*. MARC Educational Series, no. 14. Mangilao, Guam: Micronesian Area Research Center, University of Guam.

———. 1992b. *The Trust Territory Archives: An Introduction*. MARC Working Papers, no. 58. Mangilao, Guam: Micronesian Area Research Center, University of Guam.

Mead, Aroha Te Ao Maohi Pareake. 1998–1999. "Misappropriation of Indigenous Knowledge: The Next Wave of Colonisation." *Tok Blong Pasific* 52, no. 4:8–11, 18.

Mead, Margaret. 1979. *Margaret Mead: Some Personal Views*. Edited by Rhoda Metraux. New York: Norton.

Meyer, M. A. 1998. "Native Hawaiian Epistemology: Contemporary Narratives." Ed.D. diss., Harvard University.

Mills, Sherylle. 1996. "Indigenous Music and the Law: An Analysis of National and International Legislation." *Yearbook for Traditional Music* 28:57–85.

Mitchell, William E. 1996. "Communicating Culture: Margaret Mead and the Practice of Popular Anthropology." In *Popularizing Anthropology*, edited by Jeremy Mac-Clancy and Chris McDonaugh. London: Routledge.

Monroe, Dan L. 1997. "The Politics of Repatriation." In *American Indian Studies: An Interdisciplinary Approach to Contemporary Issues*, edited by Dane Morrison. New York: Peter Lang.

Murphy, Raymond E. 1948. "Land Ownership on a Micronesian Atoll." *Geographical Review* 38, no. 4:598–614.

———. 1949. "High and Low Islands in the Eastern Carolines." *Geographical Review* 39, no. 3:425–39.

———. 1950. "The Economic Geography of a Micronesian Atoll." *Annals of the Association of American Geographers* 40:58–83.

Native American Graves Protection and Repatriation Act. 1990. U.S. Code. Vol. 25, secs. 3001–13.

National Historic Preservation Act. 1966. U.S. Code. Vol. 16, sec. 470a.

Nelson, Paula. 1947. "The Hula Pahu, Ancient Hawaiian Dance." *Paradise of the Pacific* 59, no. 7:19–21.

O'Hanlon, Michael. 1989. *Reading the Skin: Adornment, Display, and Society among the Wahgi.* London: British Museum Publications.

O'Hanlon, Michael, and Robert L. Welsch, eds. 1990. *Hunting the Gatherers: Ethnographic Collectors and Agency in Melanesia, 1870s–1930s.* Oxford: Berghahn Books.

Oosterwal, Gottfried. 1959. "The Position of the Bachelor in the Upper Tor Territory." *American Anthropologist* 61, no. 5:829–38.

———. 1961. *People of the Tor: A Cultural-anthropological Study on the Tribes of the Tor Territory.* Assen, the Netherlands: van Gorcum.

OMB (United States Office of Management and the Budget). 1999a. *Uniform Administrative Requirements for Grants and Agreements with Institutions of Higher Education, Hospitals, and Other Non-profit Organizations* (Circular A-110). Washington, D.C.: GPO.

———. 1999b. *Circular A-110 Revisions.* Washington, D.C.: GPO.

Orlovich, Peter. 1996. "Strategies for Archival Development in Oceania." *PARBICA Panorama* 96, no. 1:7–9.

Otto, Ton, and Robert J. Verloop. 1996. "The Asaro Mudmen: Local Property, Public Culture?" *The Contemporary Pacific: A Journal of Island Affairs* 8, no. 2:349–86.

PARBICA Minutes. 1992. PARBICA Minutes of the Fifth Biennial General Conference. Edited by T. Kaiku, notated by Peter Orlovich. *Pacific Archives Journal* 11:26–70.

Parezo, Nancy J., and Ruth Person. 1995. "Saving the Past: Guidelines for Individuals." In *Preserving the Anthropological Record*, edited by Sydel Silverman and Nancy J. Parezo. 2d ed. New York: Wenner-Gren Foundation for Anthropological Research.

Parry, Milman, ed. 1971. *The Making of Homeric Verse: The Collected Papers of Milman Parry.* Oxford: Clarendon Press.

Peacock, Karen M. 1989. "Across All Micronesia: Records of the US Trust Territory of the Pacific Islands." *The Contemporary Pacific: A Journal of Island Affairs* 1, nos. 1–2:167–72.

———. 1995. "Online Access to the Trust Territory Archives Photograph Collection." *The Contemporary Pacific: A Journal of Island Affairs* 7, no. 1:177–86. Also published in *PARBICA Panorama* 95, no. 2:17–21.

[Peacock, Karen M.]. 1994. *Trust Territory Archives, Pacific Collection, University of Hawai'i Library.* Honolulu: University of Hawai'i Library.

Pels, Peter. 1997. "The Anthropology of Colonialism: Culture, History, and the Emergence of Western Governmentality." *Annual Review of Anthropology* 26:163–83.

———. 1999. "Ethical View from Europe." *Anthropology News* 40, no. 6:30–31.

Pinney, Christopher. 1995. "Moral Topophilia: The Significations of Landscape in Indian Oleographs." In *The Anthropology of Landscape: Perspectives on Place and Space*, edited by E. Hirsch and Michael O'Hanlon. Oxford: Clarendon Press.

Pohnpei State Government. 1996. *1994 FSM Census of Population and Housing: Detailed Social and Economic Characteristics.* Kolonia, Pohnpei: Office of the Governor, Statistics Section.

Posey, Darrell A. 1990. "Intellectual Property Rights and Just Compensation for Indigenous Knowledge." *Anthropology Today* 6, no. 4:13–16.

———. 1995. "Workshop on Indigenous Peoples and Traditional Resource Rights." ⟨users.ox.ac.uk / ~wgtrr / greencol.htm⟩, accessed on 24 May 1999. Oxford: Green College Centre for Environmental Policy and Understanding.

Posey, Darrell A., and Graham Dutfield. 1996. *Beyond Intellectual Property: Toward Traditional Resource Rights for Indigenous Peoples and Local Communities.* Ottawa, Canada: International Development Resource Center.

Poyer, Lin. 1993. *The Ngatik Massacre: History and Identity on a Micronesian Atoll.* Washington, D.C.: Smithsonian Institution Press.

Poyer, Lin, Suzanne Falgout, and Larry Carucci. 2001. *The Typhoon of War: Micronesian Experiences of World War II.* Honolulu: University of Hawai'i Press.

Pratt, Mary Louise. 1986. "Fieldwork in Common Places." In *Writing Culture,* edited by James Clifford and George E. Marcus. Berkeley and Los Angeles: University of California Press.

President. 1996. "Executive Order 13007 of 24 May 1996, Protection and Accommodation of Access to 'Indian Sacred Sites.' " *Federal Register* 61, no. 104 (29 May 1996): 26771–72. Microfiche.

Price, David H. 1997. "Anthropological Research and the Freedom of Information Act." *Cultural Anthropology Methods* 9:12–15.

Privacy Act. 1974. U.S. Code. Vol. 5, sec. 552a.

Pukui, Mary Kawena. 1936. "Ancient Hulas of Kauai." *The Garden Island*, 18, 25 February; 3,10, 17, 24 March. Reprinted in *Hula: Historical Perspectives.* Edited by Dorothy B. Barrere, Mary Kawena Pukui, and Marion Kelly. Pacific Anthropological Records, no. 30. Honolulu: Department of Anthropology, Bernice P. Bishop Museum.

———. 1942. "The Hula, Hawaii's Own Dance." In *Thrum's Hawaiian Annual and . . . All about Hawaii.* Reprinted in *Hula: Historical Perspectives.* Edited by Dorothy B. Barrere, Mary Kawena Pukui, and Marion Kelly. Pacific Anthropological Records, no. 30. Honolulu: Department of Anthropology, Bernice P. Bishop Museum.

——. 1943. "Games of My Hawaiian Childhood." *California Folklore Quarterly* 2:205–20. Reprinted in *Hula: Historical Perspectives*. Edited by Dorothy B. Barrere, Mary Kawena Pukui, and Marion Kelly. Pacific Anthropological Records, no. 30. Honolulu: Department of Anthropology, Bernice P. Bishop Museum.

——. 1983. *Olelo No'eau: Hawaiian Proverbs and Poetical Sayings*. Bernice P. Bishop Museum Special Publication, no. 71. Honolulu: Bishop Museum Press.

Pukui, Mary Kawena, trans. 1995. *Na Mele Welo: Songs of Our Heritage*. Honolulu: Bishop Museum Press.

Pukui, Mary Kawena, E. W. Haertig, and C. A. Lee. 1972. *Nana I Ke Kumu* [Look to the Source]. 2 vols. Honolulu: Hui Hanai, Queen Liliuokalani Children's Center.

Roberts, Helen H. 1926. *Ancient Hawaiian Music*. Bishop Museum Bulletin, no. 29. Honolulu: Bishop Museum Press.

Rodman, Margery. 1984. "Masters of Tradition: Customary Land Tenure and New Forms of Social Inequality in a Vanuatu Peasantry." *American Ethnologist* 11, no. 1:61–80.

Rohatynskyj, Marta A., and Sjoerd R. Jaarsma. 2000. "Ethnographic Artifacts," introduction to *Ethnographic Artifacts: Challenges to a Reflexive Anthropology*, edited by Sjoerd R. Jaarsma and Marta A. Rohatynskyj. Honolulu: University of Hawai'i Press.

Ruwell, Mary E. 1985. Introduction to *Preserving Field Records: Archival Techniques for Archaeologists and Anthropologists*, edited by Mary A. Kenworthy, Eleanor King, Mary E. Ruwell, and Trudy van Houten. Philadelphia: University Museum, University of Pennsylvania.

Said, Edward. 1979. *Orientalism*. New York: Vintage Books.

Sapir, Edward. 1949. "Why Cultural Anthropology Needs the Psychiatrist." In *Selected Writings of Edward Sapir in Language, Culture, and Personality*, edited by D. Mandelbaum. Berkeley and Los Angeles: University of California Press.

Sandburg, Brenda. 1999. "Music to Their Ears." *The Recorder*, 24 June, 1, 11.

Sanjek, Roger. 1990. "A Vocabulary for Fieldnotes." In *Fieldnotes: The Making of Anthropology*, edited by Roger Sanjek. Ithaca, N.Y.: Cornell University Press.

Schieffelin, Edward L. 1995. "Some Factors Behind Village Openness to Logging Interests." *PNG Rainforest Campaign News*, 10 September 1995. ⟨forests.org / archive / png / papappen.txt⟩, accessed 20 April 2000.

Schneider, Gerhard. 1998. "Reinventing Identities: Redefining Cultural Concepts in the Struggle between Villagers in Munda, Roviana Lagoon, New Georgia Island, Solomon Islands, for the Control of Land." In *Pacific Answers to Western Hegemony: Cultural Practices of Identity Construction*, edited by Jürg Wassman. Oxford and New York: Berg.

Schwimmer, Eric G. 1977. "What Did the Eruption Mean?" In *Exiles and Migrants in Oceania*, edited by Michael D. Lieber. ASAO Monograph Series, no. 5. Honolulu: University of Hawai'i Press.

Secretariat of the Pacific Community. 1999a. *Symposium on the Protection of Traditional Knowledge and Expressions of Indigenous Cultures in the Pacific Islands (Noumea, New Caledonia, 15–19 February 1999): Report of the meeting*. Organized by the Secretariat of the Pacific Community and the United Nations Educational, Scientific, and Cultural Organization (UNESCO) at the request of the Pacific Arts Council. Noumea, New Caledonia: Secretariat of the Pacific Community.

——. 1999b. *Symposium on the Protection of Traditional Knowledge and Expressions of Indigenous Cultures in the Pacific Islands (Noumea, New Caledonia, 15–19 February 1999): Technical paper.* Organized by the Secretariat of the Pacific Community and the United Nations Educational, Scientific, and Cultural Organization (UNESCO) at the request of the Pacific Arts Council. Noumea, New Caledonia: Secretariat of the Pacific Community.

Seeger, Anthony. 1992. "Ethnomusicology and Music Law." *Ethnomusicology* 36. no. 3:345–59.

——. 1996. "Ethnomusicologists, Archives, Professional Organizations, and the Shifting Ethics of Intellectual Property." *Yearbook for Traditional Music* 28:87–105.

Sinclair, Karen P. 1990. "Tangi: Funeral Rituals and the Construction of Maori Identity." In *Cultural Identity and Ethnicity in the Pacific*, edited by Jocelyn Linnekin and Lin Poyer. Honolulu: University of Hawai'i Press.

Silverman, Sydel, and Nancy J. Parezo, eds. 1995. *Preserving the Anthropological Record.* 2d ed. New York: Wenner-Gren Foundation for Anthropological Research.

Smith, Linda Tuhiwai. 1999. *Decolonizing Methodologies: Research and Indigenous Peoples.* London: Zed Books; Dunedin: University of Otago Press.

Smithsonian Folkways. 1989. *Hawaiian Drum Dance Chants: Sounds of Power in Time.* Compiled and annotated by Elizabeth Tatar. Compact disc SF 40015. Washington, D.C.: Smithsonian.

Society of American Archivists. 1992. "A Code of Ethics for Archivists with Commentary." In *Council Handbook. Society of American Archivists*, appendix L. ⟨www. archivists.org / governance / handbook / app__ ethics.htm⟩, accessed on 24 May 2000. Chicago: Society of American Archivists.

Stanley, Nick. 1998. *Being Ourselves for You: The Global Display of Cultures.* London: Middlesex University Press.

Stillman, Amy Ku'uleialoha. 1987. "Published Hawaiian Songbooks." *Notes* 44:221–39.

——. 1994. " 'Na Lei o Hawai'i: On Hula Songs, Floral Emblems, Island Princesses, and *Wahi Pana*." *Hawaiian Journal of History* 23:1–30.

——. 1996a. "Hawaiian Hula Competitions: Event, Repertoire, Performance, Tradition." *Journal of American Folklore* 109, no. 434:357–80.

——. 1996b. "Queen Kapi'olani's Lei Chants." *Hawaiian Journal of History* 30:119–52.

——. 1998. *Sacred Hula: The Historical Hula 'Āla'apapa.* Bishop Museum Bulletin in Anthropology, no. 8. Honolulu: Bishop Museum Press.

Tatar, Elizabeth. 1982. *Nineteenth Century Hawaiian Chant.* Pacific Anthropological Records, no. 33. Honolulu: Department of Anthropology, Bernice P. Bishop Museum.

——. 1993. *The Hula Pahu: Hawaiian Drum Dances.* Vol. 2 of The Pahu: Sounds of Power. Bishop Museum Bulletin in Anthropology, no. 3. Honolulu: Bishop Museum Press.

Thomas, Nicholas. 1992. "The Inversion of Tradition." *American Ethnologist* 19: 213–32.

Tonkinson, Myrna E. 1990. "Is It in the Blood? Australian Aboriginal Identity." In *Cultural Identity and Ethnicity in the Pacific*, edited by Jocelyn Linnekin and Lyn Poyer. Honolulu: University of Hawai'i Press.

Trask, Haunani-Kay. 1986. Review of *Children of the Land*, by Jocelyn Linnekin. *Hawaiian Journal of History* 20:232–35.

——. 1991. "Natives and Anthropologists: The Colonial Struggle." *The Contemporary Pacific: A Journal of Island Affairs* 3, no. 1: 159–67.

Trasoff, David. 1999. "The Development of *Sarod* Performance Practice: Innovation and Tradition in North Indian Classical Instrumental Music." Ph.D. diss. University of California, Santa Barbara.

Trust Territory Government. 1968. *TTPI Files System Manual: Files Maintenance and Disposition*. Drafted by the National Archives and Records service, San Francisco, 1968. Saipan: Trust Territory of the Pacific Islands.

Trust Territory of the Pacific Islands. 1970. *Trust Territory Code*. Charlottesville, Va.: Michie Publishing Company and University of Virginia Law School.

Trust Territory of The Pacific Islands Information Retrieval System. 1979. *Microfilm Retrieval System: Index to Microfilmed Materials*. 2 vols. Saipan: Trust Territory of the Pacific Islands.

Tuzin, Donald F. 1995. "The Melanesian Archive." In *Preserving the Anthropological Record*, edited by Sydel Silverman and Nancy J. Parezo. 2d ed. New York: Wenner-Gren Foundation for Anthropological Research.

UNDP (United Nations Development Program). 1995. *Final Statement from the UNDP Consultation on Indigenous Peoples' Knowledge and Intellectual Property Rights*. Suva, Fiji.

UNESCO (United Nations Education, Scientific, and Cultural Organization). 1989. *First Draft of a Recommendation on the Safeguarding of Folklore: Final Report Prepared in Accordance with Article 10(3) of the Rules of Procedure Concerning Recommendations to Member States and International Conventions Covered by the Terms of Article IV, Paragraph 4, of the Constitution*. Paris: Unesco.

Underwood, Robert A. 1985. "Excursions into Inauthenticity: The Chamorros of Guam." *Pacific Viewpoint* 26, no. 1:160–84.

"United States Trust Territory Archives Project." 1989. *Pacific Archives Journal* 7:10–15.

U.S. Public Law 105–277. 105th Cong., 1st sess., 1 June 1998.

USTT (United States Trust Territory) Archives. 1950–1960. Unpublished records of the U.S. Trust Territory. Copy on file in the Hawaiian and Pacific Collection, Hamilton Library, University of Hawai'i, Manoa.

van der Leeden, Alex C. 1956. *Hoofdtrekken der sociale structuur in het westelijk binnenland van Sarmi*. Leiden: IJdo.

van Meijl, Toon. 2000. "The Politics of Ethnography in New Zealand." In *Ethnographic Artifacts: Challenges to a Reflexive Anthropology*, edited by Sjoerd R. Jaarsma and Marta A. Rohatynskyj. Honolulu: University of Hawai'i Press.

Venne, Sharon H. 1998. *Our Elders Understand Our Rights: Evolving International Law Regarding Indigenous Rights*. Penticton, British Columbia, Canada: Theytus.

Vogt-O'Connor, D. 1998. "Legal Issues." In chapter 2, part 3 of *Museum Handbook*. Washington, D.C.: Museum Collections, National Park Service.

Voi, Mali. 1994. "An Overview of Cultural Policy in Papua New Guinea Since 1974." In *Culture, Kastom, Tradition: Developing Cultural Policy in Melanesia,* edited by Lamont Lindstrom and Geoffrey M. White. Suva, Fiji: Institute of Pacific Studies, University of the South Pacific.

Wagner, Roy. 1975. *The Invention of Culture.* Chicago: University of Chicago Press.

Walter, Michael A. H. B. 1978. "The Conflict of the Traditional and the Traditionalized: An Analysis of Fijian Land Tenure." *Journal of the Polynesian Society* 87, no. 2:89–108.

Wenner-Gren Foundation for Anthropological Research. 1998. "Historical Archives Program." ⟨www.wennergren.org/Hap.htm⟩, accessed 18 April 2000. New York: Wenner-Gren Foundation for Anthropological Research.

Weckler, Joseph E. 1949. "Land and Livelihood on Mokil, an Atoll in the Eastern Carolines. Part 1 of 'Coordinated Investigation of Micronesian Anthropology.'" Final Report, no. 25. Unpublished manuscript. Los Angeles: University of Southern California.

———.1953. "Adoption on Mokil." *American Anthropologist* 55, no. 4:555–68.

Wright, John. 1995. "Alele: Museum, Library, Archives and More." *PARBICA Panorama* 95, no. 2:4.

———. 1998. "News." *PARBICA Panorama* 98, no. 2:4.

Zemp, Hugo. 1996. The/An Ethnomusicologist and the Record Business. *Yearbook for Traditional Music* 28:36–56.

Contributors

DAVID AKIN is an independent scholar living in Ann Arbor, Michigan, where he manages the journal *Comparative Studies in Society and History*. He has spent a total of five years living in the Kwaio area of Malaita in the Solomon Islands since 1979, most recently in 1997. His publications about Kwaio include studies of spirits, politics, economics, oral history, suicide, art, and educational development. He is currently writing a book about how Kwaio religious change is transforming gender relations.

ANNE CHAMBERS was born in Hawai'i and spent several years at the University of Hawai'i, Manoa, before completing her undergraduate work at the University of California, Berkeley, where she also received a M.A. and Ph.D. in anthropology. Her Pacific anthropology interests include the interface between indigenous agency and development issues, as well as social change, ritual, and gender. Along with her husband, Keith S. Chambers, her major research work has been in Tuvalu. Anne is an associate professor of anthropology and currently serves as department chair at Southern Oregon University. She is the mother of two daughters and one son, all of whom have been fortunate to have spent time in Tuvalu on family research trips.

KEITH S. CHAMBERS was educated at the University of Hawai'i, Manoa (B.A., 1969), and the University of California, Berkeley (M.A., Ph.D.). He has carried out research in the Pacific since 1967. Along with his wife, Anne Chambers, his major work has been in Tuvalu, initially in Nanumea, but increasingly focusing on how outer-island communities and the growing national constituency interrelate. One of his particular interests is in the esoteric lore and other qualities that play important roles in cultural identity and politics. He is director of the Office of International Programs at Southern Oregon University, where he also teaches anthropology part-time. He and Anne have three children and hope to continue their long-term work in Tuvalu.

DAVID R. COUNTS is professor emeritus, McMaster University, Hamilton in Ontario, Canada. With Dorothy Counts he conducted five periods of anthropological research in Kaliai, West New Britain, Papua New Guinea between 1966 and 1985. Since 1990, he and Dorothy Counts have been doing research with retired North Americans who live on the road in their recreational vehicles. He is author, editor, or coeditor of six books covering topics from RVing in North America to linguistics in New Britain.

DOROTHY A. COUNTS is distinguished professor emeritus, the University of Waterloo in Ontario, Canada. She and David Counts did anthropological field-work in the Kaliai area of West New Britain Province, Papua New Guinea, on five occasions between 1966 and 1985. In 1990 and 1993–1994 they did anthro-pological research with retired North Americans who sold their homes and live full-time in their RVs. She is the author, editor, and coeditor of eight books, which include a collection of Kaliai myths, studies of domestic violence in Oceania, and RV retirement in North America.

KATHRYN CREELY has been the librarian for the Melanesian Archive at the University of California, San Diego, since 1983. From 1979 to 1983 she was the assistant librarian for the South Pacific Commission (now the Secretariat of the Pacific Community) in Noumea, New Caledonia. She has a master's degree (library science, 1979) from the University of Hawai'i and completed her under-graduate studies in history at the University of Massachusetts, Amherst, in 1976.

SUZANNE FALGOUT is a professor of anthropology at the University of Ha-wai'i, West O'ahu. She is a specialist in Micronesia, particularly the island of Pohnpei. Her research and writing topics have included archaeology, ethnohis-tory, self and gender, epistemology, World War II, anthropology and colonial-ism, and cultural tourism. She received her B.A. in anthropology from the University of New Orleans and her M.A. from the University of Oregon.

NANCY GUY is an ethnomusicologist. A specialist in the music of Taiwan, she is particularly interested in music and politics. Her recent research explores issues of copyright and cultural ownership as they relate to the experiences of Taiwan aboriginal musicians. She received her Ph.D. from the University of Pittsburgh in 1996 with a dissertation entitled "Peking Opera and Politics in Post-1949 Taiwan" and is currently an assistant professor of music at the University of California, San Diego.

ALAN HOWARD is professor emeritus in anthropology at the University of Hawai'i, where he created and manages websites for the Department of Anthro-pology, the Cultural Studies Program, and the Association for Social Anthro-pology in Oceania in addition to the Rotuma website. He received his degrees— B.A. (sociology, 1955) and M.A. and Ph.D. (anthropology, 1959, 1962)—from Stanford University. He is author of *Hef Ran Ta: A Biography of Wilson Inia* (1993) and has assisted Wilson's widow, Elizabeth Inia, in publishing books preserving

Rotuma's traditional knowledge, including *Fäeag 'Es Füaga: Rotuman Proverbs* (1998), *A New Rotuman Dictionary* (1998), and *Kato'aga: Rotuman Ceremonies* (forthcoming).

SJOERD R. JAARSMA is a graduate of Utrecht University and obtained his Ph.D. at the University of Nijmegen (1990), both in the Netherlands. An anthropologist by training, he specializes in the history of anthropology and comparative ethnography of the island of New Guinea. He is attached to the Centre for Pacific and Asian Studies, University of Nijmegen. He has recently published *Ethnographic Artifacts: Challenges to a Reflexive Anthropology* (2000, coedited with Marta A. Rohatynskyj, University of Guelph, Canada).

MARY MCCUTCHEON received her Ph.D. in 1981 from the University of Arizona. Her major research pertains to land tenure and resource use in the Palau Islands of the Western Pacific. She has worked at the Smithsonian Institution, where she became interested in archival and collections access, and has taught at the University of Guam. She currently teaches at George Mason University in Fairfax, Virginia.

BRYAN P. OLES is a research associate with LTG Associates, Inc., an anthropological consulting firm specializing in the design, development, and evaluation of health and human service systems. He received his Ph.D. in cultural anthropology from the University of Pittsburgh in 1999. His dissertation is based on fourteen months of fieldwork among Mokilese living in Pohnpei State, Federated States of Micronesia. He has recently published "Family Ties and Corporate Land Ownership in Micronesia" (*Cultural Survival Quarterly* 24, no. 1:46–47). In addition to his work in the field of applied anthropology, he is pursuing research interests in political ecology, the phenomenology of place, and economic development and social change in Micronesia.

KAREN M. PEACOCK is the curator of the Pacific Collection at the University of Hawai'i Library. She was raised in the islands of Micronesia and in 1973 earned a master's degree in library studies at the University of Hawai'i. In 1978 she completed a master's degree in Pacific studies, and in 1990 she received a Ph.D. in Pacific history. Peacock is the editor of the resources section of *The Contemporary Pacific: A Journal of Island Affairs*. She teaches a course on Pacific resources for the University of Hawai'i Library and Information Studies program. Her research focus is the history of the Trust Territory of the Pacific Islands.

AMY KU'ULEIALOHA STILLMAN is associate professor of music and American culture and director of Asian Pacific American studies at the University of Michigan. She has also taught ethnomusicology at the University of California,

Santa Barbara, and the University of Hawai'i, Manoa. Her research focuses on historical study of music and dance in Polynesia. Her first book, *Sacred Hula: The Historical Hula 'Āla'apapa*, was published by Bishop Museum Press in 1998. Born and raised in Hawai'i, she began hula lessons in early childhood. She also serves as facilitator for Kūlia i ka Punawai, the Kumu Hula Association of Southern California.

Index

Aboriginal and Torres Strait Islander Library and Information Resource Network (ATSILIRN), 71

Aboriginals, 10. *See also* indigenous peoples

academic audiences, 20, 47; as exclusive, 21–23

access, 5–12, 56–59, 85–96, 112–16, 123–29, 141–45, 159–60, 165–73; discrepancies in, 37, 216n6; educational threshold, 6, 22–23, 47, 60–62, 182; indigenous control of, 6, 22, 27–28, 40–43, 48–52, 63, 86, 88, 102–6, 145, 154, 212–14, 219n5, 223–24n6; Internet, 7, 11–12, 23–24, 29, 38, 113–14, 116, 123–24, 128, 216n7, 217n11, 219n4, 230n5; media interests, 7; mismanagement, 9, 27, 63–78, 178, 216–17n11, 219n6, 220–21n13. *See also* media; privacy

acculturation. *See* culture change

acts, affecting access to ethnographic materials: Archeological Resources Protection Act, 75; Copyright Act, 9–10, 44, 75–76, 140, 196; Executive Order 13007, 75; Freedom of Information Act (FOIA), 10, 74–78, 216n10, 222n11; National Historic Preservation Act, 75; Native American Graves Protection Act (NAGPRA), 5, 68, 132; Privacy Act, 74; U.S. Public Law 105–277 (Shelby amendment), 77

activism. *See* anthropology, advocacy

advocacy. *See* anthropology, advocacy

agreements on intellectual property rights. *See* intellectual property rights, conferences on

American administration (Micronesia), 96, 105; anthropology conference, 225n13–14; district anthropologist, 8, 95, 97, 99–105, 225n12; research, 97–98, 100, 174–81, 183, 189, 224n8, 225n10, 230n1–2; staff anthropologist, 75, 97, 100, 225n11. *See also* CIMA, Department of the Interior; Naval Administration; SIM, USCC

American Anthropological Association (AAA), 4, 6, 10, 18, 20, 58–59, 65, 77–78, 86, 171, 220n9, 222n1; code of ethics, 6, 58, 65, 171, 222–23n1

Amis, Taiwan, 196–97, 201–2, 204, 206, 208. *See also* indigenous peoples

anthropological jargon. *See* jargon, anthropological

anthropologists: accountability of, 11; archiving arrangements of, 85, 87–88; as caretaker, 51, 82; as copyright holder, 9, 220n13; as expert witness, 10, 95, 197, 205, 216n9; knowledge brokerage by, 144–45, 147, 192; legal and moral obligations of, 154, 209; national associations of, 6, 10, 18, 24, 77–78, 86, 171, 220n9; privileged information of, 74–75, 98, 225n15; as protective of data, 56; as storyteller, 27; tenure system of, 24, 52. *See also* access, indigenous control of; American administration (Micronesia); writing ethnography

anthropology: advocacy in, 43, 46, 54, 57, 59, 71–72, 74, 101, 203–4, 216n9; applied 18, 216n6; as "butterfly collecting," 163, 191, 230n3; changes in, 52; ethical codes of, 2, 5–6, 11, 86, 213, 222–23n1; globalization and, 46; museums and, 216n6; postcolonial, 3, 46, 50, 82, 178, 214; postmodern perspective and, 34; reflexivity and, 47, 49, 151; "serious" vs. "non-serious," 20, 24; traditional, 3, 94. *See also* ethical codes; ethics; media; writing ethnography, popularizing anthropology

fieldwork: abuse of power in, 46, 49–51, 136; accountability in, 11, 13; basic tools of, 99, 215–16n5; changes in, 11, 52, 82; continuity of, 6, 178, 212; distrust, 178; emancipated subjects, 47, 62; erroneous impressions, 41; indigenous appreciation of, 50, 62, 154, 179–80; informant confidentiality, 33, 65, 85–86, 89, 95, 105; long-term, 9, 50, 153, 170; obligations resulting from, 1–2, 209; politically desirable, 11; rapport, 3, 46, 49–50, 101, 175, 178, 181, 193; as reciprocity, 83, 170, 191; and repatriation, 165, 167; traditional, 20, 25, 151, 195. *See also* ethics, informed consent

First International Conference on the Cultural and Intellectual Property Rights of Indigenous Peoples (Mataatua Declaration), 4, 69, 86, 146, 222–23n1

First International Congress of Ethnobiology, 215n1, 215n4

First World, 46, 52, 195–97

Firth, Raymond, 57, 61, 186

Fischer, Ann, 100, 103; informants, 100

Fischer, John L. (Jack), 8, 68, 95–96, 98–106; informants, 100; *soupad* (master historian), 101

FOIA. *See* acts, affecting access to ethnographic materials

Folk Song Collection Movement (*minge caiji yundong*), 200–201

Fortune, Reo, 49, 197

fourth estate, the. *See* media

Fourth World, 4–5, 52

Freedom of Information Act (FOIA), *See* acts, affecting access to ethnographic materials

genealogical data, 9, 67, 131, 162, 164–65, 175, 223n3; access and, 36, 48, 56, 165–68, 192; assessment of, 159–60, 165–66, 171, 179–80, 193, 218n4, 219n4, 223–24n6; as field notes, 81, 88, 92, 98, 102, 106, 154–55; synthesized, 159–60, 171–73, 192, 218n4, 223–24n6. *See also* land rights

George, Jones S., 114, 116, 118–21, 124, 127

Gilbert and Ellice Islands, 153–54. *See* Kiribati; Tuvalu

Guam (USA), 73, 75, 109, 112, 124, 127–28

Hawai'i (USA), 53, 70, 75, 137–38, 220n11, 232n11

Hawaiian Ethnology Notes, 139. *See also* hula collections

Hawai'i State Archives, 137

Hawaiian cultural renaissance, 8, 130, 135, 140. *See also* cultural revival

historical consciousness, 42, 44, 182, 185, 213, 218n8, 221n19, 231n7

historical records, value placed on 42, 44, 181–82

Hocart, A. M., 37

Hsu Tsang-houei, 198, 200–202, 204, 206, 209

Hui Malama I Na Kupuna O Hawai'i Nei, 70–71

hula: archival collections on, 8; categories of, 134; deinstitutionalization, 131; ethnographic studies of, 131, 135; indigenous reinterpretation, 135, 142; institutionalized repertoire, 130, 140–141; modern vs. traditional, 130; ownership rights and, 140; performance of, 130, 132–34, 136, 139–40, 142–47; poetic repertoire, 9, 131, 133–43, 147; revival, 130, 140. *See also* Hawaiian cultural renaissance; hula collections

hula collections: field collections, 137–39, 143–44; Kuluwaimaka collection, 137–38; mele books (index), 133–34, 137–39; personal souvenir books, 137–39, 143; Roberts collection, 137–38; songbooks, 133. *See also* Hawaiian Ethnology Notes; hula

Human Studies Film Archives. *See* Smithsonian Institution

impact analysis, 7, 40, 54–55, 57–58, 93, 171. *See also* repatriation

indigenous audiences, 11, 47; critical, 20–22, 159; excluded, 22; literate, 20; publishing for, 24. *See also* access, audiences, repatriation

Indigenous Cultural and Intellectual Property Task Force, 222–23n1

indigenous peoples: emancipating, 47; expatriate populations, 11, 38. *See* Aboriginals; Amis; Maori; Native Americans; Native Hawaiians

indigenous self-determination, rights to, 3–4, 11